Mornings *with* JESUS 2018

DAILY ENCOURAGEMENT *for your* SOUL

365 DEVOTIONS

SUSANNA FOTH AUGHTMON

GWEN FORD FAULKENBERRY

GRACE FOX

TRICIA GOYER

SHARON HINCK

REBECCA BARLOW JORDAN

ERIN KEELEY MARSHALL

DIANNE NEAL MATTHEWS

GARI MEACHAM

CYNTHIA RUCHTI

SUZANNE DAVENPORT TIETJEN

ISABELLA YOSUICO

Guideposts

New York

Mornings with Jesus 2018

Published by Guideposts & Inspirational Media
110 William Street
New York, New York 10038
Guideposts.org

Acknowledgments

Every attempt has been made to credit the sources of copyrighted material used in this book. If any such acknowledgment has been inadvertently omitted or miscredited, receipt of such information would be appreciated.

Scripture quotations marked (AMP) are taken from *The Amplified Bible* and *The Amplified Bible, Classic Edition.* Copyright © 2015 by The Lockman Foundation, La Habra, CA 90631. All rights reserved. Copyright © 1954, 1958, 1962, 1964, 1965, 1987 by The Lockman Foundation. Used by permission. www.Lockman.org

Scripture quotations marked (ERV) are taken from *Easy-to-Read Version Bible.* Copyright © 2006 by Bible League International.

Scripture quotations marked (ESV) are taken from the *Holy Bible, English Standard Version*, copyright © 2001 by Crossway Bibles, a division of Good News Publishers. Used by permission. All rights reserved.

Scripture quotations marked (GNT) are taken from *Good News Translation.* Copyright © 1992 by American Bible Society.

Scripture quotations marked (GW) are taken from *God's Word Translation.* Copyright © 1995 by God's Word to the Nations. Used by permission of Baker Publishing Group.

Scripture quotations marked (HCS) are taken from the *Holman Christian Standard Bible.* Copyright © 1999, 2000, 2002, 2003 by Holman Bible Publishers, Nashville, Tennessee. All rights reserved.

Scripture quotations marked (ICB) are taken from *The Holy Bible, International Children's Bible.* Copyright© 1986, 1988, 1999, 2015 by Tommy Nelson, a division of Thomas Nelson. Used by permission.

Scripture quotations marked (ISV) are taken from *The International Standard Version of the Bible.* Copyright © 1995-2014 by ISV Foundation. All rights reserved internationally. Used by permission of Davidson Press, LL.

Scripture quotations marked (KJV) are taken from *The King James Version of the Bible.*

Scripture quotations marked (MSG) are taken from *The Message.* Copyright © 1993, 1994, 1995, 1996, 2000, 2001, 2002 by Eugene H. Peterson.

Scripture quotations marked (NAS) are taken from the *New American Standard Bible.* Copyright © 1960, 1962, 1963, 1968, 1971, 1972, 1973, 1975, 1977, 1995 by the Lockman Foundation. Used by permission. www.Lockman.org

Scripture quotations marked (NCV) are taken from the *New Century Version.* Copyright © 2005 by Thomas Nelson, Inc. Used by permission. All rights reserved.

Scripture quotations marked (NIV) are taken from two editions: *The Holy Bible, New International Version, NIV.* Copyright © 1973, 1978, 1984, 2011 by Biblica. All rights reserved worldwide. *The Holy Bible, New International Version.* Copyright © 1973, 1978, 1984 International Bible Society. Used by permission of Zondervan Bible Publishers.

Scripture quotations marked (NKJV) are taken from *The Holy Bible, New King James Version.* Copyright © , 1983, 1985, 1990, 1997 by Thomas Nelson, Inc.

Scripture quotations marked (NLT) are taken from the *Holy Bible, New Living Translation.* Copyright © 1996. Used by permission of Tyndale House Publishers, Inc., Wheaton, Illinois 60189. All rights reserved.

Scripture quotations marked (NRSV) are taken from the *New Revised Standard Version Bible.* Copyright © 1989 by the Division of Christian Education of the National Council of the Churches of Christ in the U.S.A. Used by permission. All rights reserved.

Scripture quotations marked (RSV) are taken from the *Revised Standard Version of the Bible.* Copyright © 1946, 1952, and 1971 the Division of Christian Education of the National Council of the Churches of Christ in the United States of America. Used by permission. All rights reserved.

Scripture quotations marked (TLB) are taken from *The Living Bible.* Copyright © 1971 by Tyndale House Foundation. Used by permission of Tyndale House Publishers Inc., Carol Stream, Illinois 60188. All rights reserved.

Cover and interior design by Müllerhaus
Cover photo by Shutterstock
Indexed by Indexing Research
Typeset by Aptara

Printed and bound in the United States of America
10 9 8 7 6 5 4 3 2 1

Dear Friends,

Welcome to *Mornings with Jesus 2018*! The 365 devotions were written as a reminder of the faithfulness of Jesus and the inspiration of His teachings. Our hope is you are able to breathe new life into your morning and bring special blessings to your day by reading each one. Learn from the wisdom of Scriptures, be comforted by personal narratives, and find encouragement through the daily practice of taking a "Faith Step."

Mornings with Jesus is a devotional written with care by twelve women of faith. They share personal stories about their walk with Jesus. These friendly, sometimes familiar, voices affirm this truth: the peace and promises of Jesus are real. Gari Meacham, a devoted missionary in Uganda, Suzanne Davenport Tietjen, a retired nurse-turned-beekeeper, and Gwen Ford Faulkenberry, a church pianist and college professor, are among the writers who describe how they came to understand their relationship with Jesus as a lifelong process. We know you will relate to their stories of courage after loss, grace in the moment of surrender, and wisdom at embracing the new year with open hearts and minds.

Jesus said, "I am the light of the world. Whoever follows me will never walk in darkness, but will have the light of life" (John 8:12, NIV). *Mornings with Jesus 2018* will light your path as you begin each day knowing you are in His care every step of the way.

This year we've included Ash Wednesday and Easter reflections by Isabella Yosuico and an Advent series by Rebecca Barlow Jordan. *Mornings with Jesus 2018* offers you the reassurance of Jesus's close presence and constant comfort throughout the seasons. Though we face financial difficulties, overwhelming obligations, and even physical suffering, Jesus's boundless love provides the strength we need to live beyond our challenges. He reminds us that His love is greater. And that great love draws us ever closer to Him.

It is our hope that *Mornings with Jesus 2018* will fill you with peace and inspire you to embrace each day with Jesus by your side. We invite you to be encouraged by His promises of hope, forgiveness, mercy, and grace. May you begin your day with the love of Jesus in your heart!

Faithfully yours,
Editors of Guideposts

P.S. We love hearing from you! Let us know what *Mornings with Jesus 2018* means to you by e-mailing BookEditors@guideposts.org or writing to Guideposts Books & Inspirational Media, 110 William Street, New York, New York 10038. You can also keep up with your *Mornings with Jesus* friends on Facebook.com/MorningswithJesus.

Especially for You!

Enjoy the daily encouragement of *Mornings with Jesus 2018* wherever you are! Receive each day's devotion on your computer, tablet, or smartphone. Visit MorningswithJesus.org/MWJ2018 and enter this code: Faith.

Sign up for the online newsletter *Mornings with Jesus* through MorningswithJesus.org. Each week you'll receive an inspiring devotion with personal thoughts from one of the writers about her own devotional time and prayer life, how focusing on Jesus influenced her relationship with Him, and more!

Monday, January 1

Shout to the LORD, all the earth; break out in praise and sing for joy!
Psalm 98:4 (NLT)

New Year's is a big deal for our family. My brother and sisters and I rarely get to see each other as the years have scattered us far and wide. But each year we congregate at my parents' house for the week between Christmas and New Year's Day. There are about twenty of us including in-laws and kids. We look forward to our time together all year long.

On our last night together, we want to do it up right. We want to soak up every minute. Ringing in the New Year involves sparkling cider, delicious appetizers, and the end-of-the-year countdown. If we are lucky, my brother, Chris, will serve up his gourmet pizza with imported olive oil and cheeses. My sister, Jenny, makes her famous meatballs that all the boy cousins fight over. We play games. We laugh hard. And we relish the fact that we are all together. The night's celebration ends with watching the New York City ball drop on TV amidst shouting and lots of hugging.

There are moments in life that need to be heralded with joy. Jesus is so good to us. There are a million reasons to celebrate this New Year—all of the obstacles we have overcome in the last year. The joy and healing that Jesus has brought about in our hearts. His faithfulness and bountiful provision. The cherished relationships He has brought into our lives. The goodness of being alive. The prospect of a new, untarnished year in front of us. The promise that Jesus will be with us in every circumstance, no matter what. So many reasons to bring in the New Year with a shout of praise! —Susanna Foth Aughtmon

Faith Step: *Do a countdown of the top ten things you are thankful to Jesus for as you go into this New Year.*

TUESDAY, JANUARY 2

So all of us who have had that veil removed can see and reflect the glory of the Lord. And the Lord—who is the Spirit—makes us more and more like him as we are changed into his glorious image. 2 Corinthians 3:18 (NLT)

"YOU ARE THE AVERAGE OF the five people you spend the most time with." As I read posts from a favorite blog, this quote from author Jim Rohn jumped out at me. Trying to apply the concept to my life proved to be difficult since we had just relocated to a new city in a new state. I decided that, for now, I must be a combination of my husband, our realtor, and—that's it.

Although we each have our own inborn personality and character traits, we are influenced a great deal by those with whom we spend a lot of time. This is especially true when we're young; our close relatives and friends influence the person we will become. And studies have shown that those around us affect our moods. That's why as believers we want to make sure we spend plenty of time with Jesus. If we hope to love others unconditionally and reflect His character to the world, we need time with Him in prayer and Bible study, along with an intentional awareness of His presence and guidance each day.

Right now I'm eagerly anticipating a trip to visit family. My husband and I will see our moms, siblings, children, grandchildren, and any other relatives or old friends we can squeeze into our schedule. I'll be spending time with some people who have been good influences on me. But since I want to be more like Jesus than anyone else, I'm looking forward to spending as much time as possible with Him every day. —DIANNE NEAL MATTHEWS

FAITH STEP: *Think about specific attitudes, habits, and behaviors that would change if you became more like Jesus. Commit to scheduling more time to hang out with Him.*

WEDNESDAY, JANUARY 3

Therefore do not worry about tomorrow, for tomorrow will worry about itself. Each day has enough trouble of its own. Matthew 6:34 (NIV)

IN THE LAST YEAR MY husband, John, and I have adopted four girls from foster care, ages eleven to fifteen, bringing our total number of kids to ten. Through the adoption process there has been a lot to worry about, financial and emotional worries topping the list. But while it's easy to pay attention to the kids, it's harder to focus on each other. As a couple we used to have dedicated date nights, but the cost of childcare for so many kids has made that a thing of the past. Many times I found myself worrying about our relationship. I didn't want to neglect my role as a wife as my role of a mom grew.

I've learned over the years that instead of worrying, I need to pray. It seemed silly to pray about date nights, especially when there were "bigger issues," like helping children who had past trauma, but I did. Then, my prayer was answered in an unexpected way.

One day I received a text message from a friend at church, "Tricia, I feel called to help foster and adoptive parents in our church. I'm organizing a once-a-month Parents Night Out, with other church members helping. Would you be interested in bringing your kids and enjoying a date night?" I couldn't write back fast enough to say, "Yes!"

I'm thankful that Jesus saw my need, and He used others in His body to help meet it—not because I asked for help, but because Jesus's Spirit put the need on someone else's heart. I'm thankful that as we help and support orphans, Jesus has brought people to help and support us, too. —TRICIA GOYER

FAITH STEP: *Consider gathering other friends to provide a date night. Even a monthly service will greatly encourage weary parents who need time together.*

THURSDAY, JANUARY 4

*"With your unfailing love you lead the people you have redeemed.
In your might, you guide them to your sacred home." Exodus 15:13 (NLT)*

HAVE YOU EVER BEEN so full of relief and joy that a song burst out of you? Exodus 15 is that sort of song. The children of Israel, after 430 years in Egypt, were delivered and led out—only to face destruction as the pharaoh and his chariots chased them down. The Lord parted the sea, and they were saved—a beautiful foretaste of the redemption that would one day be provided by Jesus.

Yes, the Israelites were relieved to be alive. They were relieved they weren't being dragged back to abject slavery. But this verse also shows a new understanding of their Lord. He not only redeemed them, He is leading them. And He is not leading them randomly, but leading them to their home with Him.

We know that Jesus died to save us. We rejoice in being freed from slavery to sin and death. But Jesus also offers to lead us. He is willing to be involved in our lives. What a relief to know that we aren't in the wilderness of life alone! And there is a purpose to His leading. His goal is to bring us to our new home with Him.

A friend from Bible study recently graduated to Heaven, her body finally succumbing to cancer. As much as it hurts to know I won't see her smiling face or feel her warm hug here on earth, I can celebrate that she is home, restored, and joyful. Each person who goes to his or her eternal home is a reminder that Jesus is aiming us in the direction of our ultimate home. Knowing this can spur us to seek His guidance each day. —SHARON HINCK

FAITH STEP: *List the names of friends and family whom Jesus has led home, and thank Him for His faithfulness. Ask Him for guidance and leadership today.*

FRIDAY, JANUARY 5

Then a cloud overshadowed them, and a voice from the cloud said, "This is my dearly loved Son. Listen to him." Mark 9:7 (NLT)

MY SON IS A COMPUTER guru. I do my utmost to listen and understand when he talks about his work, but honestly, he speaks a foreign language to me. I'm not the only one who needs a translation. On one occasion when he and my husband were deep in conversation about his latest software project, his wife looked at me, raised her eyebrows, and smiled. I immediately knew what she was thinking: *I don't have a clue. Do you?*

Without a doubt his knowledge about computers far surpasses mine. And so, I listen to him when he tells me how to handle computer issues. He's the expert; I'm not.

Peter, James, and John understood the benefits of listening to an expert when they ascended a mountain with Jesus. While on the summit, a cloud enveloped them and a voice spoke. The voice—clearly God's—said that Jesus was His Son and they were to listen to Him.

So many voices clamor for our attention today. Some try to lure us into temptation. Others say we're not enough, that we need to work harder to earn Jesus's love and people's admiration. Some tell us to pursue happiness regardless of the price. But those voices can't offer expertise on how to live a godly life. Only one voice speaks absolute truth, and that voice belongs to Jesus.

Jesus speaks words of truth, comfort, and wisdom. He guides His followers so we can have an abundant life, and we would do well to listen. He's the expert; we're not. —GRACE FOX

FAITH STEP: *Play a favorite praise and worship song. Close your eyes and focus on the lyrics. Sing along, or simply be still and listen, allowing the truth to remind you of Jesus's amazing love for you.*

SATURDAY, JANUARY 6

Finally, brothers, whatever is true, whatever is honorable, whatever is just,
whatever is pure, whatever is lovely, whatever is commendable,
if there is any excellence, if there is anything worthy of praise,
think about these things. Philippians 4:8 (ESV)

FOR A LONG TIME, I gave "positive thinking" a bad rap. I thought of it as some kind of godless hocus-pocus aimed at attaining all the wrong stuff for all the wrong reasons. I would roll my eyes at motivational speakers, affirmation-laden therapists, and preachers who "spoke things into being," dismissing them as charlatans or worse. Of course, we do need to seek discernment about the source and content of positive thinking, but let's not toss the baby out with the bathwater. The point is, what is truly positive?

Paul's very practical, hopeful thank-you note to the people of Philippi ends with a rousing inspirational speech and a call to positive thinking. Verse 8 defines the nature of its content: True, honorable, just, pure, lovely, commendable, excellent, and worthy of praise.

I don't know about you, but I know much of my thinking doesn't automatically reflect those terms. Elsewhere, Paul describes taking decisive action to attain the transformed, positive mind of Christ, which is our re-birthright. We are urged to choose to focus on that which is truly positive by God's definition.

That's not as easy to do. In fact, it can seem like a tall order from where I'm sometimes sitting, so then I can recall that Paul wrote this hope-filled book from prison. How about that? —ISABELLA YOSUICO

FAITH STEP: *Read the short book of Philippians three times. The first time, simply read it through. The second time, only read Chapter 4. The third time, use a highlighter to mark positive actions and thoughts in Chapter 4. Finally, write down three verses that speak to you today, and read them daily.*

Sunday, January 7

"But lay up for yourselves treasures in heaven. . . ." Matthew 6:20 (KJV)

"Don't mortgage future generations." I chewed on the concept for days. I resisted the magnetic pull of wanting to know how other people might be setting up future generations to pay a huge price for the heart-purchases the current generation is making—pride, greed, excess, self-absorption.

Instead, I asked Jesus to do what David asked in Psalm 139. I said, "Examine me and see if there is any ungodly way in me."

If I live beyond my means, I'm creating a habit in my children and grandchildren, mortgaging their futures.

If I speak unkindly about others, I'm mortgaging their future relationships. They'll either have to fight off the pattern I established, or they'll repeat it.

If I let disappointment become resentment, or allow an offense to take root in me, I'm mortgaging their souls' health.

If I treat alone time with the Lord as an insignificant or a joyless duty, I'm mortgaging their spiritual futures.

If I say, "The check's in the mail," and it isn't, I'm mortgaging the integrity of future generations.

Jesus told us that the seeds we plant today bear fruit long into the future, that those who invest in the spiritual futures of their children and grandchildren—laying up treasures that count in heaven—leave a legacy, not a mortgage. —Cynthia Ruchti

FAITH STEP: *Consider the spiritual legacy you're leaving for those who follow you. Will the patterns you've established feel like a burden or a blessing?*

MONDAY, JANUARY 8

"If you had known Me, you would have known My Father also; and from now on you know Him and have seen Him." Philip said to Him, "Lord, show us the Father, and it is sufficient for us." Jesus said to him, "Have I been with you so long, and yet you have not known Me, Philip? . . ." John 14:7–9 (NKJV)

I TOOK ONE OF THOSE silly Facebook quizzes the other day. This one had you answer questions in order to find out which disciple of Jesus you are most like. My result was Philip. The explanation said that Philip was a thinker, prone to pay more attention to logic than feelings. I was surprised because I always relate the most to Peter, since he's the one always messing up, or even doubting Thomas. I never heard much about Philip.

I decided to do a little research and ended up reading this exchange in John 14. It's the question Jesus asks, I think, that is so revealing: "Have I been with you so long, and yet you have not known me, Philip?"

Oswald Chambers writes: "The last One with whom we get intimate is Jesus. . . . We receive His blessings and know His word, but do we know Him?" I wonder if I really do. I was raised in a Christian home, and the natural progression for me as a child was to ask Jesus into my heart and then grow up learning about Him. I've repeated that same experience while raising my own kids. But do I know Him? Intimately?

Chambers goes on to say that "the saint who is intimate with Jesus will never leave impressions of himself but only the impression that Jesus is having unhindered way, because the last abyss of his nature has been satisfied by Jesus." I'm pretty sure if this is intimacy with Jesus, I have a long way to go. —GWEN FORD FAULKENBERRY

FAITH STEP: *How long have you known Jesus? Ask Him to fill every nook and cranny of your being, down to the last abyss, that you may know Him intimately.*

TUESDAY, JANUARY 9

Stay with what you heard from the beginning, the original message.
Let it sink into your life. If what you heard from the beginning lives deeply in
you, you will live deeply in both the Son and the Father. 1 John 2:24 (MSG)

I'M A TRANSPLANT TO THE Upper Peninsula of Michigan, and I've come to love the sauna. I learned when I moved here that the Finns invented sauna, and its first syllable rhymes with *Ow!*—so don't say "saw-na." You'll be enthusiastically corrected if you do. More than a traditional way of bathing, sauna can be a solitary or social occasion and its practice confers physical and psychological benefits on those who engage in it.

Some don't like it, and I have to say my initial attempt was difficult. I started out on the highest and thus hottest bench. Within moments, the surface of my skin felt like it was on fire. I moved lower and was able to stay until the sensation passed. I sweated, jumped in the lake, and came back for more. Afterward my skin absorbed copious amounts of lotion and I felt relaxed, loose, and noodle-y all evening.

I learned that the burning sensation can be eased by relaxing and mentally allowing the heat in—letting it go deeper into the skin. No more discomfort and maybe more understanding when someone says she tried a sauna and didn't like it!

This verse reminds me of my early experience of taking a sauna and it gives me a visceral illustration of what it means to let the truth that Jesus loves me sink deep into my life. Trying to keep it outside is uncomfortable, but giving way to His relentless love affects me deeply. Knowing His love changes and softens me.

It's meant to be received. —SUZANNE DAVENPORT TIETJEN

FAITH STEP: *You don't have to take a sauna (although you can, if you like). Instead, notice the ways you take things in today. Eating, applying lotion, warming yourself by the fireside. Now do your Bible reading. Let it sink in.*

WEDNESDAY, JANUARY 10

"Do you wish to get well?" John 5:6 (NASB)

I SAT ON THE EDGE of my bed feeling absolutely hopeless. Over the course of several years I was consumed with one thing: food. I was either compulsively overeating it, or strictly starving myself so I wouldn't touch it. Either way, I wasn't content because the numbers on the scale would never stay perfect.

When I did arrive at the "perfect weight" I felt compelled to lose even more; and when I got sick of extreme dieting and went back to overeating—I was still on the miserable merry-go-round of obsession.

One day, while reading my Bible, I stumbled across Jesus asking a man who'd been paralyzed for thirty-eight years if he wanted to get well. I was struck by how obvious the answer was, but still...Jesus asked. Immediately I thought about my struggle with food. Even though I prayed and acted like I wanted to get well, was I really willing to make the right choices?

I began to filter all my thoughts and actions through that one question, "Do you wish to get well?" Sometimes we cling to the very things that paralyze us. Attitudes, old hurts, habits, and behaviors that keep us stuck rather than set us free. Sometimes Jesus has to ask the obvious question so we will see our own excuses. Once we do, we can finally move past them. —GARI MEACHAM

FAITH STEP: *Are your habits and behaviors making you sick? If Jesus were to ask, "Do you wish to get well?"—what kind of excuses would you respond with?*

THURSDAY, JANUARY 11

But the king said to Araunah, "No, I will not have it as a gift. I will buy it, for I don't want to offer to the Lord my God burnt offerings that have cost me nothing."... 2 Samuel 24:24 (TLB)

ON A FLIGHT SEVERAL YEARS ago, I sat next to a young woman from the Pacific Islands who was coming to spend a year in Salt Lake City. As we neared the valley, she stayed glued to the window, seeing snow for the very first time. I looked at her short-sleeved blouse, thin cotton skirt, and bare legs. The wind chill would be well below freezing in the late afternoon. Just before our descent, I took off my jacket and insisted that she take it.

Two days later I stood in line at a fast food restaurant. A young man with an Indian accent complimented my wool coat. He mentioned that when his family moved to America, his mother tried to find a coat in the same off-white color. I wish I could say that I sent it to his mother as a gift from Jesus. The first choice was easier since I'd grown tired of that jacket—nothing to compare with the joy I felt seeing the woman wrapped in it outside the airport. But the washable wool coat would have been harder to replace. Today I still regret missing that second opportunity.

We may think of giving as dropping a check in the church offering plate or supporting a ministry. But Jesus surrounds us with opportunities to give someone our time, our possessions, or maybe just our attention. He wants us to be willing to give up anything and everything in His name. That may be inconvenient, hard, or downright painful. But it's the costliest sacrifices that bring the most joy. And why wouldn't we be willing to give in honor of the One Who sacrificed His life for us? —DIANNE NEAL MATTHEWS

FAITH STEP: *Ask Jesus to show you a way to give something in His name.*

FRIDAY, JANUARY 12

But the fruit of the Spirit is love, joy, peace, longsuffering, kindness, goodness, faithfulness, . . . Galatians 5:22 (NKJV)

LATELY I ALMOST DREAD HEARING the national news on television. In the last few months, reports of senseless murders and other violent crimes have left me wondering, can it get any worse?

When Adam and Eve sinned, mayhem began. History records brutality through the years. But the other day I was reading in 1 Kings about one of the kings of Israel named Omri, who ruled around 885 BC. According to God's standards, Omri "set new records in evil," living an "empty-headed, empty-hearted life" (1 Kings 16:25–26, MSG). King Ahab followed, setting "an all-time record in making big business of evil" (1 Kings 21:25, MSG).

Then, almost eight centuries later, Jesus entered the picture. He embraced the hurting and taught the multitudes. He healed the sick and raised the dead. To some, Jesus represented heresy. His wisdom confused them; His theology challenged them.

The recipients of Jesus's touch would agree with the apostle Paul in Acts 10:38: "Jesus...went about doing good" (NKJV). In fact, Jesus set new records in goodness, no one could ever match.

After comparing King Omri and Ahab with Jesus, I experienced a new desire. Because I accepted His gift of salvation, His Spirit lives inside me. That means even though I was born with a sin nature, Jesus will produce His goodness in me if I will let Him.

We hear about new records of evil daily. But what if we all work together to overcome evil with good? Will you join me in asking Jesus to do that? —REBECCA BARLOW JORDAN

FAITH STEP: *Make a list of "good" things you can do this week for others. Ask Jesus to produce His goodness through you, wherever you go.*

SATURDAY, JANUARY 13

To you I lift up my eyes, O you who are enthroned in the heavens!
Psalm 123:1 (ESV)

"I NEED TO GET OUT the long duster and get those cobwebs," my husband, Steve, said one morning. "We've got them all over."

I followed his gaze up to the bathroom ceiling, where a dusty gray string hung forlornly.

Later, at my desk I happened to look up at the office ceiling. Sure enough, another cobweb. Obviously, ceiling cleaning catches me unawares. I'm not in the habit of looking up.

Sort of like when I go through my daily routine without looking up at Jesus often enough. When I don't make a point to look up for Him, I'm sidetracked by everything else around me, and I'm stuck looking at only the circumstances happening around me, good or bad.

It's hard to see Jesus's bigger picture for me if my focus is off because I'm discouraged. I get caught off guard with dusty spaces in my outlook, in my heart, too. Pretty soon the environment I'm surrounded by is neither bright nor productive.

Jesus reminds us of Who He is through the simplest encounters —even with forlorn, abandoned cobwebs no one likes.

Steve and I have been trusting Jesus with some next steps for our family. We've got questions about future schooling for our kids, career choices and changes, and financial decisions. Through it all, we're reminded to look up to Him when we don't have the answers for next month, much less next year.

Look up at Jesus, the Great Cobweb Cleaner. —ERIN KEELEY MARSHALL

FAITH STEP: *Clean something outside of your typical routine. Then read these verses: Psalm 34:5 and 121:1; Isaiah 40:26; Daniel 4:34; John 11:41.*

SUNDAY, JANUARY 14

*When Jesus came by, he looked up at Zacchaeus and called him
by name. "Zacchaeus!" he said. "Quick, come down!
I must be a guest in your home today." Luke 19:5 (NLT)*

I ATTENDED SUNDAY SCHOOL EVERY week as a child and singing was
an important part of our services. One of my favorite choruses was
about Zacchaeus. When he heard about Jesus coming to town, he
climbed into a sycamore tree "for he wanted the Lord to see."

Jesus was a busy man. He had things to do. How easy it would
have been to blow past that sycamore tree without giving its occu-
pant a second thought. But Jesus was all about loving people, and
He never missed an opportunity to do so.

Jesus stopped at the tree, called Zacchaeus by name, and gave him
personal time. His actions showed Zacchaeus that he mattered. The
result? Zacchaeus placed his faith in Him that day.

I'll confess that, in the midst of my busyness, I don't always love
people Jesus-style. I've been guilty of regarding them as interruptions, focusing more on my goals than on their souls. I've even
questioned how I'm supposed to serve in ministry if people continue
to request my attention. Thankfully, Jesus is faithful to challenge
and to change my attitude.

Let's follow Christ's example and look for opportunities to show
His love. Perhaps a neighbor needs help weeding her flowerbed.
Maybe a friend would appreciate a dinner invitation. A homeless
man might enjoy a cup of coffee and conversation.

That person could be a decision away from spending eternity in
heaven, and our actions will be the tipping point. —GRACE FOX

FAITH STEP: *Has someone been on your mind recently? Take a few moments to
either write a note, or phone them. Ask how you can pray for her or him.*

MONDAY, JANUARY 15

His divine power has given us everything we need for a godly life through our knowledge of him who called us by his own glory and goodness. 2 Peter 1:3 (NIV)

WINTER IN THE UPPER PENINSULA of Michigan is beautiful but danger hides beneath its splendor. The roads are treacherous and the weather even more so. I keep survival kits in all of our vehicles. They hold water, matches, candles, blankets, food, dry socks, and more. We wear smaller versions for hiking, snowshoeing, or skiing. A lot can go wrong, and cell phones don't work out here.

Second Peter 1:3 is one verse I *say* I believe but, if I'm honest, I don't always live like I have everything I need for life and godliness. Navigating our culture, churches, and neighborhoods can be as spiritually hazardous as the wild tantrums of an UP winter. How do I react to the driver who scoots into the parking place I was waiting for with my blinker on? When I tell someone I'll pray for them, do I? Do I love my enemies?

I live a life of godliness intermittently at best and I don't *feel* well-equipped. I excuse myself saying, "I did my best," as if that was all God could expect.

None of us is able, on our own, to live that life of godliness we're told we've been equipped to live. The Bible says we can live that life by knowing Jesus, not intellectually, but personally. Jesus gave us His precious promises, and as we exercise our faith, the qualities He wants to see will grow and mature, resulting in lives that please Him. —SUZANNE DAVENPORT TIETJEN

FAITH STEP: *Has knowing someone changed your behavior or the choices you've made? Knowing Jesus is the way we're equipped for this life. Ask Him to help you know Him better.*

TUESDAY, JANUARY 16

"Why do you look at the speck in your brother's eye but don't notice the log in your own eye? Or how can you say to your brother, 'Let me take the speck out of your eye,' and look, there's a log in your eye? Hypocrite! First take the log out of your eye, and then you will see clearly to take the speck out of your brother's eye." Matthew 7:3–5 (HCSB)

IN ADDITION TO THE GOLDEN Rule, this passage offers some invaluable advice when it comes to relationships. And when I have the presence of mind to employ it, I'm straightened out by the compact and catchier paraphrase of this verse: "If you can spot it, you got it."

Analyzing other people's motives, citing chapter and verse, looking at their specks has taken up too much of my time. Now, I will also say that I've done more than my fair share of checking out my own logs. But I often miss the parallels between the two and the lessons that may come in those moments. Even more troubling, or what really gets to me, is what seems so obviously wrong in others is usually the very thing that's wrong with me.

Sometimes, this is something I know about, and given a moment's reflection, I see it clearly. More often, I need to deliberately apply this speck-log truth to learn something new about myself.

In the end, I recognize that Jesus's purpose is to prompt the humble recognition of how desperately we need to receive His forgiveness. In turn, seeing our shared condition, maybe I can ease up on spotting specks in others, or, for that matter, my own logs.

—ISABELLA YOSUICO

FAITH STEP: *Next time you catch yourself looking at a speck, acknowledge the log. Then, ask Jesus to help you forgive yourself and your brother for all that firewood.*

WEDNESDAY, JANUARY 17

Those who are wise will find a time and a way to do what is right, for there is a time and a way for everything. . . . Ecclesiastes 8:5–6 (NLT)

MOST OF US ARE BETTER at making excuses than we are at finding solutions: More exercise? *Too tired.* More family time? *So much to do.* More study of God's Word? *Not enough time.* Finding extra moments seems impossible. And no matter what age we are, we still need to manage our time well as good stewards.

Recently, I discovered a hidden block of time while working in the backyard. Underground sprinklers water my flower gardens, but hanging baskets on a fence or tree get a shower only if it rains—or if I hand-water them. And on days with a heat index of over a hundred degrees, mosquitoes still swarming, and no clouds in sight, that means dragging the hose around the yard for an extra forty minutes, armed with insect repellant. I complained about that ritual often and saw no acceptable solutions for changing it.

Not so long ago we went away for a few days, and before we left I moved all those hanging plants into my perennial gardens where the sprinkler would reach them. When I returned, those flowers had prospered. So I decided to leave them there. I love yard art, so why not replace those other hanging spots with creative pieces? Imagine my delight when I ended my old ritual and netted a new opportunity for things I wanted or needed to do. A smile soon replaced my complaints—and my excuses.

Sometimes, letting go of simple things frees us for the best things. Jesus is more than willing to show us what those are if we'll only ask. —REBECCA BARLOW JORDAN

FAITH STEP: *What excuses are you making for neglecting the things you really need or want to do? Ask Jesus to show you some creative solutions.*

THURSDAY, JANUARY 18

---

*So do not be ashamed of the testimony about our Lord or of me
his prisoner. Rather, join with me in suffering for the gospel, by the
power of God. 2 Timothy 1:8 (NIV)*

RECENTLY I HAD THE OPPORTUNITY to speak at a conference in
Johannesburg, South Africa. Women, young and old, came from
a dozen countries all around Africa. As I prepared, I felt that my
approach should be simple. I talked about my longing for love as a
teen, getting pregnant in high school, finding salvation, and how
Jesus has transformed my life. My story revealed all the ways I've
fallen short and all the ways I've been redeemed.

After one of my talks a tall, regal woman approached me. With
fine features, and flawless ebony skin she reminded me of a beautiful African queen from a children's storybook. She approached
gracefully, but when our eyes met the tears came. "The love you
were looking for as a teen is the same love I've been looking for—
for fifty years," she told me. "I know now that I won't find it in
relationships with men, but in a relationship with Jesus. I need to
feel His love first. Only when I know His love will I be prepared
to look for love in other places." We cried and prayed together. As
I watched her walk away, I was impressed by the power of God
displayed through the sharing of testimonies.

When we declare Jesus's marvelous deeds to another person, we make
hard-to-understand concepts personal. When they see the changes in
our lives they dare to hope for the same in themselves, and because
Jesus is faithful, they will not be disappointed. —TRICIA GOYER

FAITH STEP: *Find one person with whom you can share a story about how Jesus
has transformed your life this week.*

FRIDAY, JANUARY 19

Very early in the morning, while it was still dark, Jesus got up, left the house and went off to a solitary place, where he prayed. Mark 1:35 (NIV)

I WANT TO BE LIKE Jesus. I say it. I sing it. I write it in my journal. Yes, Jesus, I'll love the unlovable. I'll forgive when I don't feel like it. I'll reach out to widows and orphans. I'll follow You.

And then I stumble on a verse like Mark 1:35. It reads the same basic way in every version. Will I follow Him if it means getting up while it's still dark to pray? And not just dark, but leave the house to find a place quiet enough and solitary enough to be ultrafocused in prayer?

I'm not moving to Jerusalem or training to overturn tables in temples. It's not that I want to wear sandals here in the Northwoods of Wisconsin all year long. (Well, I do, but it's inadvisable in the season of eight-foot snowdrifts.)

I admire, though, the commitment Jesus had to prayer. And I believe that commitment is high on the list of ways in which He does want me to follow Him, footstep by footstep.

While it is still dark. Will I get up to pray while it's still dark? When it's been too long, way too long waiting for the answer? When the dark is emotional, or spiritual, or relational? Will I get up, get moving, get serious about praying even if I'm completely alone in the prayer, or especially if I am? Will I be as faithful as He was, even in the moonless predawn, and no matter how far I have to go to get away from the noise?

How far would you have to go? And would you? —CYNTHIA RUCHTI

FAITH STEP: *Will you join me in a weeklong discipline to carve out time that feels inconvenient in order to get extraquiet and extrafocused in prayer? Like Jesus did for us? And then make it a month? A year? A lifetime?*

SATURDAY, JANUARY 20

Beloved, never avenge yourselves, but leave it to the wrath of God, for it is written, "Vengeance is mine, I will repay, says the Lord." Romans 12:19 (ESV)

WE LANDED IN A BAD situation after moving into our current house. We contracted with the seller to keep the refrigerator and washing machine in lieu of her fixing the items on the inspection report. She was elderly, my husband could handle the inspection items, and she seemed relieved. She sent us a letter signing over to us the refrigerator warranty she'd purchased since she'd had trouble with the ice maker.

Sure enough the ice maker soon broke, and the warranty company agreed to send us a check to replace the appliance. Long story short, the check was made out to the previous owner's name and forwarded to her new address, and she cashed it.

But when I called the woman, her pleasant manner during negotiations was gone. She insisted that the money was hers and has since refused two certified letters, one in which my husband wrote that we're trying to work this out without suing her because we want to show her Jesus's love. Earthly justice seems lost, but Jesus is still on the case.

Most important, she needs to know that He died to be her Savior—she needs that more than we need the two thousand dollars for the refrigerator. But I still feel we've been treated like dirt.

In the end, we are all accountable to Jesus for our actions, including our responses to others' actions. This wrong over a broken ice maker is Jesus's to handle. Ultimately, the primary need I ought to pray for is hers for salvation, while leaving my well-being to Jesus.
—ERIN KEELEY MARSHALL

FAITH STEP: *When have you been mistreated? Many injustices are far greater than my missing fridge money. Earthly justice may not come, but ask Jesus to help you leave it to His handling while He cares for you.*

SUNDAY, JANUARY 21

Meanwhile, Zacchaeus stood before the Lord and said, "I will give half my wealth to the poor, Lord, and if I have cheated people on their taxes, I will give them back four times as much!" Luke 19:8 (NLT)

ONE OF MY FAVORITE THINGS is hearing stories of personal transformation in the lives of those who have chosen to follow Jesus. My friend, Donna, is a perfect example. She felt miserable in her marriage. In fact, Donna and her husband teetered on the brink of divorce. Then a neighbor invited them to Bible study. They figured they had nothing to lose, so they went. God's Word captured their attention, and Jesus captivated their hearts. Several weeks later, they placed their faith in Him.

Three decades later, Donna is one of the godliest women I know. Jesus has been her strength and joy, and she loves nothing more than telling others about Him.

A genuine encounter with Jesus always spawns change. Most often it's gradual, but sometimes—as with Zacchaeus—it's instantaneous. One evening spent in Jesus's presence opened his eyes to his own sinfulness. He found courage to admit his wrongdoing and motivation to set things right. The notorious tax collector would be notorious no longer.

Every believer's testimony is unique, but all share a common theme: personal transformation. That's because Jesus is about newness of life. He loves us too much to leave us stuck in our old ways, and He loves us so much that He'll continue the good work He's begun until His image is seen in us. —GRACE FOX

FAITH STEP: *Read 2 Corinthians 5:17. How has Jesus changed you? Thank Him for making necessary changes. Give Him permission to continue the good work He's begun in you.*

MONDAY, JANUARY 22

Now, this is what the LORD says: Do not be afraid, because I have reclaimed you. I have called you by name; you are mine. Isaiah 43:1 (GW)

OUR YOUNGEST GRANDDAUGHTER WAITED LATER to start speaking than her two older siblings. Although Lilah obviously understood what people said, she preferred communicating through grunts and body language rather than words. Finally, she began talking. My husband was delighted each time she called him Pawpaw during a Facetime call on our iPhone, but no matter how much I coaxed her, Lilah's name for me sounded like something an alien might say.

I rationalized that the p sound was probably one of the easiest to master. And one of her earliest words had been the name of her favorite cartoon: Peppa Pig. But really, I'd spent much more time with her while Pawpaw had hardly changed a diaper. Then one day my daughter texted me that Lilah had learned the n sound on a road trip. I could hardly wait until our next Facetime call. When she said "Nana," my heart melted just a little (okay, a lot).

There's something about hearing our name spoken by a loved one, isn't there? But let's not forget the wonderful truth that we've been called by name by Our Creator and Redeemer. Every day Jesus speaks to us through the Holy Spirit and the Word. The Bible is not like the form letters I receive in the mail where my name has been inserted in key places to manipulate me into purchasing something. Its pages are filled with thoughts and promises that offer guidance, hope, and encouragement. And Jesus is calling your name and saying those things to you. Doesn't that melt your heart just a little?
—DIANNE NEAL MATTHEWS

FAITH STEP: *Read your favorite verses that affirm God's love. Say them out loud, insert your own name, and envision Him speaking directly to you.*

TUESDAY, JANUARY 23

"Do not work for the food which perishes, but for the food which endures to eternal life, which the Son of Man will give to you, for on Him the Father, God, has set His seal." John 6:27 (NASB)

I GRABBED THE REMOTE AND began flipping channels as I started to relax one evening. I surfed from *The Pioneer Woman,* to *The Rachael Ray Show,* to *The Chew*, finally stopping at *Ramsay's Kitchen Nightmares* on the Food Network. The show was interrupted by commercials showing every type of burger and taco from the east coast to the west. All the focus and attention toward food reminded me of a time when I, too, was obsessed with it.

As a former food junkie I've seen our country morph into a gourmet, food-obsessed frenzy. One minute we're told how to eat clean and healthy—and the next we're taunted with a chocolate salted caramel cupcake. When Jesus instructed His disciples to not "work" for the food that perishes, He wasn't saying it's wrong to enjoy food, and use it to nourish our bodies. He's merely pointing out that there are more important things to set our minds to, things that have eternal value, and won't end up spoiling or being thrown away when their shelf life is through.

I wonder what our world would look like if we put the care and attention toward people that we put toward food. When I first began to experience freedom from my compulsive behaviors with food, it was as if my mind went from a tight closet to a spacious meadow. I had ample time to focus on Jesus and allow Him to inspire "kingdom thoughts" rather than "refrigerator thoughts"—and it was exhilarating. —GARI MEACHAM

FAITH STEP: *Take an honest spiritual inventory of your habits with food. Ask God to give you the right perspective and approach toward food.*

WEDNESDAY, JANUARY 24

You, Lord, are all I have, and you give me all I need;
my future is in your hands. Psalm 16:5 (GNT)

THE E-MAIL IN MY IN-BOX caused my heart to skip a beat. My editor had a request from the marketing team. They wanted to read a few chapters of my latest book to get a sense of it in order to pitch it to bookstores. The only problem was that I was way behind and the chapters I had written needed a lot of work. I was also sidetracked as I was dealing with difficult teenagers at home. Would that be a good enough excuse to ask for more time?

When I'm worried about a book project, I walk to my shelf with the other books I've written, and I take a stroll down memory lane. I remember the people I've interviewed and the research that showed up at just the right time. I remember how Jesus strengthened me and guided me. Remembering His faithfulness gives me faith for my current project. I visualize the finished book on the bookstore shelf, or better yet, in the hands of a reader. And the wonderful thing about gaining trust in Jesus is that this trust extends to other areas of my life.

When I'm dealing with an emotional, irrational teenager I picture my difficult teen faithfully serving Jesus. When the month seems longer than the paycheck, I remember all the ways Jesus has financially provided in unexpected ways, and I thank Him for His continued provision. Jesus has never failed me, and He never will. You'd think I'd understand this now, but sometimes it just takes a little remembering. And the right type of remembering can calm and steady any worried and fearful heart. —TRICIA GOYER

FAITH STEP: *Are there questions and worries assaulting you today? Remember Jesus's faithfulness in the past and visualize His faithfulness now.*

THURSDAY, JANUARY 25

Jesus said to Simon Peter . . . "do you love me more than these?" . . .
John 21:15 (NIV)

COWER: TO CROUCH DOWN IN fear or shame. Dictionaries also list these synonyms: cringe, shrink, recoil, flinch, pull back. . . .

You might wonder what had me looking up behind-the-scenes details about a word like cower. Not what. Who. Peter. In my Bible, a section header within John chapter 18 says simply, "Peter denies Jesus *again*." In my mind, the emphasis on the word again is as heavy as a cruise ship's anchor.

His action and what happens after the fact say more about Jesus than about Peter. The man recoiled from the scene when Jesus was arrested. He pulled back and snuck away to warm himself at the enemy's fire. We would expect him to also cower when he saw Jesus face-to-face after His resurrection.

Jesus had been right about everything. He'd been faithful. And Peter had both cowered and been a coward through it all. But the forgiveness in the heart of Jesus completely overwhelmed the after-resurrection scenes.

If I had been in Peter's shoes, I would have expected Jesus's wrath. I would have cowered in the presence of the One I had betrayed. But Jesus's approach was love, acceptance, and instantaneous for-giveness. And then He went beyond all that.

Jesus walked with Peter along the shore after cooking breakfast for His betrayer (John 21:15–17). He spoke gently to Peter, and gave him three chances to express his love for Jesus. Cowering shame and regret were seared into oblivion in the light of that kind of love. —CYNTHIA RUCHTI

FAITH STEP: *The next time you visit a beach, collect a small vial of sand or take a picture that you keep near as a reminder of the way Jesus walked with Peter.*

FRIDAY, JANUARY 26

Ask, and it will be given to you; seek, and you will find; knock,
and it will be opened to you. Luke 11:9 (ESV)

MY DAUGHTER LIKES TO ASK for things whenever we're at a store. She's a sweetheart who is refreshed by new-new-new, whom I am trying to teach not to nag with her requests. My son, on the other hand, often feels guilty asking for something as minor as a special drink when we're out and seems to think that if he's thirsty he ought to go for the bare minimum, not what his heart truly wants.

I'm more like my son in this way, especially with Jesus, so today's Scripture is meaningful and perplexing to me. I often get stumped about whether I really need what I desire—or if what I truly need is to buck up and grow without it.

But Jesus says ask. Asking in humility shows we realize that everything we need and desire comes from Him. Even if it's a worldly desire, like money to repair a dent on our SUV, I realize it's a need because that SUV is a necessity to live where He's planted us.

If we don't ask, we lose some joy seeing Him answer us personally and specifically. Asking puts us in proper relationship with Him as the Giver of life. It reminds us of our fallibility.

This section of Scripture ends with a reminder of how He most loves to give us His Spirit in abundance (verse 13). When we ask for Him most, He'll fill us with willingness to let Him answer in His way and time, as He knows best.

So ask, and let Him answer. Don't feel guilty, because His presence through our requests is one way we learn to be loved by Him, specially and personally. —ERIN KEELEY MARSHALL

FAITH STEP: *Whether you currently feel guilty for wanting something or you're wondering if Jesus is listening, ask Him for it—after you ask for more of Him.*

SATURDAY, JANUARY 27

A final word: Be strong in the Lord and in his mighty power. Put on all of God's armor so that you will be able to stand firm against all strategies of the devil. Ephesians 6:10–11 (NLT)

I HAVE HAD A FIVE-YEAR journey with back pain. Recently, I went to a physical therapist to get help. In an effort to give me some relief, she had me lie on a table and said, "Try and tighten your core muscles." Her hand on my stomach, she had a pained expression on her face that read, "I know there should be stomach muscles here… but where are they?" She asked me again, "Can you tighten them?" I tried…. I really did. She finally said, "Oh, okay … here we go." Finding my stomach muscles took some searching on her part. After birthing three giant babies, my stomach muscles have all but given up.

After the physical therapist, I went to a back specialist. She took a look at my x-rays and said, "Your back and hips actually look great." I wanted to give her a high five. Then she said, "But from now on, you will need to do back exercises to strengthen your core…. FOR THE REST OF YOUR LIFE." It was the stomach-muscles thing all over again. I felt like a kid who had been given a lifetime assignment of PE class. I thanked her. Kind of. And I took my pamphlet of forever-until-I-die back exercises. Because even though I hate exercising, what I really want is to be strong.

Jesus wants us to be strong, too. He knows all that we face in this life. And He doesn't want us battered and beaten. He wants to strengthen us and our ability to believe in His goodness. He wants us to build up our faith muscles, so we can stand firm in Him… no matter what comes our way. —SUSANNA FOTH AUGHTMON

FAITH STEP: *Read and meditate on Ephesians 6:10–18. Know Jesus is protecting you and building up your spiritual muscles.*

SUNDAY, JANUARY 28

But far be it from me to boast except in the cross of our Lord Jesus Christ,
by which the world has been crucified to me, and I to the world.
Galatians 6:14 (ESV)

PAUL HAD REASONS TO BRAG. His credentials as a devout religious student and leader were impressive. He also suffered more than most. And then we read of the miracles Jesus performed through him—including raising a boy from the dead.

The apostle could focus on his past accomplishments, but following in the light of Jesus made him count his own works as unimportant. Can I also stop basing my self-image on scholarly degrees, best-seller lists, or awards?

Paul also decides not to dwell on his sufferings. He is a follower of the Suffering Servant, and accepts this as a temporary part of his calling. Can I also refrain from telling everyone how my struggles are worse than most—than theirs?

Paul had miraculous experiences in His service to Jesus, but didn't boast. When I glimpse Jesus working through my life, can I humbly rejoice instead of turning the focus to myself?

Christ is the sure and unchanging One worthy of our praise. When we recognize that we've reached a challenging goal, we can thank Him for the strength to overcome and for working through us. When we suffer, we can thank Him for His constant love. When He intervenes, we can rejoice in His faithfulness. As we bounce our thoughts away from ourselves and boast only in Him, we'll move forward with new freedom. —SHARON HINCK

FAITH STEP: *Today, each time you are tempted to boast about achievements, or testify to large amounts of suffering, turn those thoughts into a prayer of thanks that Jesus, and His crucifixion and resurrection, has brought you new life.*

MONDAY, JANUARY 29

Make a clean break with all cutting, backbiting, profane talk. Be gentle with one another, sensitive. Forgive one another as quickly and thoroughly as God in Christ forgave you. Ephesians 4:31–32 (MSG)

I WAS TALKING TO MY boss the other day about how to approach difficult issues with students. In Higher Ed right now there's a debate raging about safe spaces, and micro-aggressions, and how easily people are offended. As a teacher, you're always walking the line between challenging people to think critically and respecting their individual experiences.

"I don't know what you can do, Gwen, to be honest," my boss admitted. "I think you just try to do what Jesus would do."

This led us into a discussion of what Jesus actually did. I mentioned that He turned over tables to prove a point in the temple.

"He picked his battles, though," my boss reminded me. "He was a radical, but He was gentle."

If my long game as a teacher is to help students confront their own biases, to think critically, to become better communicators, and ultimately to contribute to the good of society, I have to have their trust—or they won't listen to a word I say. It's the same, I think, with being a Christian. If the long game is to lead others to Jesus, to bring about the kingdom of heaven on earth by connecting people to God, we need to be gentle with our truth. Sensitive. Kind. We have to practice the quiet strength of His radical love.
—GWEN FORD FAULKENBERRY

FAITH STEP: *What is one tangible way you can show gentleness to others today? Ask Jesus to give you His Spirit as you reach out in love.*

TUESDAY, JANUARY 30

Your attitude should be the kind that was shown us by Jesus Christ,
who, though he was God, did not demand and cling to his rights as God.
Philippians 2:5–6 (TLB)

YEARS AGO I READ A story with a profound lesson, published by the Institute of Basic Youth Conflicts. A missionary who taught on an island planted a pineapple field. He paid a local man to help him and waited three years. But as soon as the pineapples ripened, the natives stole them. The missionary became so angry that he shut down his wife's clinic to punish them. People got sick, and babies died. The missionary relented and reopened the clinic. But the natives stole the fruit again. He tried bribery and grew a new garden. But when all of the pineapples disappeared, his anger exploded. So he closed the store.

The natives soon moved away. No people and no ministry now. He relented again, but the same thing happened. So he bought a German shepherd. But the dog frightened the natives away and bred wild mongrels with the village dogs. Finally, he learned a new principle at a conference: "Give all you own to God." So that's what he did. But the natives still stole his pineapples.

This time the missionary remained calm. The baffled natives asked him if he had become a Christian. Everything changed when the natives realized they were now stealing from God's pineapple garden—and people came to know Jesus.

Practicing what we preach is never easy. But as we follow Jesus's example and submit to Him, others will recognize that we belong to Christ. —REBECCA BARLOW JORDAN

FAITH STEP: *Identify the things or situations that make you angry or test your "rights." Then transfer ownership of all that you have to Jesus.*

WEDNESDAY, JANUARY 31

He will keep you strong to the end so that you will be free from all blame on the day when our Lord Jesus Christ returns. God will do this, for he is faithful to do what he says, and he has invited you into partnership with his Son, Jesus Christ our Lord. 1 Corinthians 1:8–9 (NLT)

I HAVE RECENTLY BECOME OBSESSED with the hymn, "Be Still My Soul." I even researched it online and found out that it was originally penned in German by Katharina A. von Schlegel in the mid-1700s. With over three hundred years separating us, I would think life was very different for Katharina. But it seems that the desires of the heart and the needs of human condition are timeless. It feels so relevant to the place where I am right now.

My favorite lines say: "Leave to thy God to order and provide. In every change, He faithful will remain." It is the truth that I long to hear. That Jesus is ordering and providing for me. That even though life is so very mixed-up, He is and always will be faithful.

We long to connect with the One Who loves us most of all. We have seen Jesus's faithfulness in the greatest joys and deepest despair of our lives. Believers through the ages have experienced the same truths. Life is ever changing, wild, and unpredictable. But Jesus remains the same. Both now and forever. His goodness and mercy are never ending. His protection and peace enfold us. His great love sets us on a firm path of grace, no matter what our situation. And we can know that He will always be with us from now, until that great moment when we see Him face-to-face.
—SUSANNA FOTH AUGHTMON

FAITH STEP: *Recount all of the ways that Jesus has been faithful to you during this past year. Thank Him for showing you His faithfulness.*

THURSDAY, FEBRUARY 1

This is how we know we're living steadily and deeply in him, and he in us: He's given us life from his life, from his very own Spirit. 1 John 4:13 (MSG)

THE SNOW, NO LONGER FRESH and new, lies deep in the Hiawatha Forest. Bits of debris—branches, fallen leaves six months too late—lie scattered on the crusty white floor of the woods. A tiny twig sprawls in the driveway, its bark soaking up sunrays. After an hour or so the dark twig itself radiates heat, melting the snow as it sinks gently into a stick-shaped pool of water.

The temperature is still below freezing, but the sticks and leaves serve as passive solar collectors and begin the thaw. They stay where they are, freezing after dark but drawing in heat the next day and the next, changing the world around them through no power of their own.

I have days when I feel as disconnected and useless as one of those twigs. Small and broken, I stare at a computer screen wishing for words. Forcing them doesn't work. They're marred by the effort; they neither flow nor sing. I wish I could crumble the screen like a sheet of paper and fling it toward the waste basket. Tired of trying, I trade my desk chair for the sunny window seat. Where I notice sticks melting snow.

Jesus said, "I do nothing on my own.... The one who sent me is with me; he has not left me alone, for I always do what pleases him" (John 8:28–29 NIV). Jesus emptied Himself (Philippians 2:6) and laid aside His glory to become human. To do His Father's will.

There by my window, I imagined Jesus with me like His Father was with Him, empowering Him. Soaked in the thought like sunshine. Then I went back to the computer. —SUZANNE DAVENPORT TIETJEN

FAITH STEP: *Find a sunny spot. Close your eyes in prayer and quietly receive the love of Jesus. Then watch for the opportunity to send it on.*

FRIDAY, FEBRUARY 2

We love each other because he loved us first. 1 John 4:19 (NLT)

THE OTHER NIGHT MY YOUNGEST son, Addison, and I were lying on the couch watching TV. This is becoming difficult since he is ten years old and already five feet tall. I am snuggling a small adult. He still lets me kiss him every once in a while, even though he is so big. With his arm wrapped around my neck, I looked at him and said, "Addie, how much do you love me?" He said, "A lot." And I said, "How much is a lot?" He said, "You and Dad are under God. Then comes Flash. Then my brothers. Then my friends." Then he turned back to watch the show.

It is a good thing to be loved more than the dog. That is high praise. But I especially love that Addie knows the One Who loves him most of all. He knows that my husband, Scott, and I love him to death. But Jesus? Jesus's love gives Addison a chance at new life.

Jesus surrounds us on every side, never leaving us for a moment. Even when we can't feel Him. Even when life is difficult or even tragic. Even when we are questioning and doubting. His love is ever present. Tethering us to His goodness and His grace. It is so huge we can't fathom it. There are moments when we catch a small glimpse of the greatness of Jesus's love. The knowledge that He gave everything so that we could have a relationship with Him. The understanding that without His love we have nothing. With it we have all that we'll ever need. It leaves us breathless. All we can do is try to love Him back with everything that is within us. Because He loved us first. —SUSANNA FOTH AUGHTMON

FAITH STEP: *Draw a heart on a piece of paper. Fill the heart with five distinct ways that Jesus shows you His love.*

SATURDAY, FEBRUARY 3

This is eternal life, that they may know You, the only true God, and Jesus Christ whom You have sent. John 17:3 (NASB)

THIS IS MY HUSBAND'S FAVORITE verse. It seems pretty straightforward, especially to the evangelical mind-set. We tend to think of eternal life in terms of heaven, so this is about knowing God by having a relationship with Jesus, and going to heaven as a result. But deeper study reveals a few interesting nuances.

First, eternal life here is not just about heaven. It's about life that starts when we meet Jesus. We cultivate it on earth, experiencing eternal life here and now. His kingdom comes on earth as it is in heaven.

Next, and even more beautiful, I think, is the knowing. In the original language this verse translates as *to know intimately*. So eternal life is to be intimate with God, with Jesus.

Something I've noticed in my own relationships is that intimacy is hard. True intimacy requires me to be vulnerable. To open myself up in complete trust, holding nothing back. It is so much easier to hide behind a screen and type my feelings than to look into someone's eyes. So much easier to cover my stretchmarks and other imperfections in clothes than to be naked and exposed.

But that's what God calls us to do. And most importantly, that's what Jesus offers. The intimacy of eternal life. —GWEN FORD FAULKENBERRY

FAITH STEP: *What does knowing Jesus intimately look like to you? Draw a picture of it.*

Sunday, February 4

Every good and perfect gift is from above, coming down from the Father of the heavenly lights, who does not change like shifting shadows.
James 1:17 (NIV)

My husband earns most of our income. In various seasons I've been a stay-at-home mom, worked in the arts, I've volunteered, and I'm an author. I understood there was value in giving or serving in those ways even if I didn't provide much financial support to my family. I tried to be satisfied with that. Yet each week when my husband wrote a check for the church offering, I felt a bit wistful.

One weekend I shared my feelings. That Sunday in church, as the offering plate was passed, my husband handed me the envelope with our gift so I could place it in the plate. I felt symbolically part of the offering, and it became our new tradition.

This week in church, as I tucked the envelope into the plate and passed it along, it hit me that Jesus does the same thing in our lives. Every gift we have—finances, time, health, relationships, talents—comes from Him. He entrusts each gift to us and allows us to give them back as our offering.

As Jesus views the many needs of the world, He could directly send provision to each person without our involvement. Yet often, He gives us the blessing of being part of His answer. We aren't the source of grace or wisdom, but He puts His resources into our hands so that we can touch them briefly and then pass them along. That idea can give us a new perspective on blessings that come into our lives. We can thank Him and then look for a way to share. —Sharon Hinck

Faith Step: *Next time you receive a gift, a paycheck, or some other blessing, ask Jesus to show you a way to pass that blessing along to someone else.*

MONDAY, FEBRUARY 5

For even when we came into Macedonia our flesh had no rest,
but we were afflicted on every side: conflicts without, fears within.
2 Corinthians 7:5 (NASB)

HAVE YOU EVER FELT LIKE you're taking hits from all sides? Relationship struggles, parenting heartaches, financial woes, tough decisions, bad decisions, conflicts that lead to fear? At times, life can feel like a full-on assault, and we're wise to realize that even a great spiritual leader like Paul struggled with hardship. When I feel overwhelmed, I think about an image I remember from washing dishes.

We used to have a nasty skillet that was so difficult to clean it seemed to attract every ounce of grime and hang on to it—no matter how hard I scrubbed and scoured. One day I got so sick of the skillet I dumped it in the trash and said, "I'm through!" It wasn't until I bought a new skillet, freshly coated with Teflon, that I realized how easy cleaning a skillet could be. The Teflon coating made it impossible for the grime and gunk to stick. I could easily swipe off the residue with a rag and the skillet was back to looking new. I only wish I hadn't wasted years battling that nasty skillet, but I learned something from it.

Useful things are going to get dirty simply by being used, but the grime isn't meant to be permanent—and it doesn't have to be such a battle to overcome. Paul said, "I am overflowing with joy in all our affliction" (2 Corinthians 7:4, NASB). His struggles were difficult, but his love for Jesus and his way of approaching problems wasn't. He chose joy in the midst of conflict and fear—and joy was his Teflon.
—GARI MEACHAM

FAITH STEP: *Today when you wash dishes thank Jesus that, even through conflict and fear, His joy is your strength. You have spiritual Teflon!*

TUESDAY, FEBRUARY 6

So then, take your stand! Fasten truth around your waist like a belt.
Put on God's approval as your breastplate. Ephesians 6:14 (GW)

I REMEMBER THE FIRST TIME one of my adopted daughters called me mom. There was pain and confusion in her gaze, and I knew the endearment brought back painful memories—first because of a neglectful relationship with her birth mom and then because of the previous adoption placement that fell through. By the time our daughters arrived at our home, they were wounded and fearful. When we told these girls that we would be their forever home, they had little reason to trust that. To them there was no place secure in this world and no one they could trust. It has only been through our loving actions that they finally believed. There wasn't a dry eye in the courtroom the day the adoption was finalized. Our daughters at last realized the truth, that we would be their forever parents and our home their forever home.

In the same way, truth girds us as Christians. The truth of Who Jesus is and what He has done must be firm around our waist—at the core of our faith. And above this belt of truth, knowing who we are protects our hearts. We can take our stand, knowing we will not be pushed to the side, overlooked, or passed over.

For many years our daughters were wards of the state, but now they are Goyers. For many years I never truly understood my role as heir with Christ. Everything changed with truth and approval. With Jesus, each of us can look to the future with hope, no matter what we've previously faced. —TRICIA GOYER

FAITH STEP: *Do you have a hard time believing Jesus's truth or accepting His approval? Today pray and ask Him to help you see yourself according to how He sees you and not according to how the world has treated you.*

WEDNESDAY, FEBRUARY 7

And the Word became flesh and dwelt among us, and we have seen his glory, glory as of the only Son from the Father, full of grace and truth. John 1:14 (ESV)

MY COUSIN TERRY RECENTLY TEXTED me photos of his older son, whom I hadn't seen in years. When I commented that Alexander had grown into a handsome young man, Terry responded that he'd always been glad that all five kids favored their mom. "Oh, I think each one of them is a combination of you and Millie," I texted. "A winning combination, I might add."

That same phrase sprang to mind the next week as I read John's description of Jesus: "full of grace and truth." In His dealings with people, Jesus displayed the perfect combination of grace and truth. He always spoke the exact truth that the other person needed to hear, even when it was hard to accept. At the same time, He freely extended grace to anyone willing to respond.

Jesus calls us to follow His example as we interact with others. This means maintaining the right balance in our attitudes and speech. But if we only emphasize the hard truths, we'll sound self-righteous and grow harsh and judgmental. On the other hand, if we solely focus on grace and don't speak the truth that someone needs to hear, we may miss an opportunity for Jesus to use us to change someone's life for the better.

Jesus wants to help each one of us to become more like Him. Imagine what a difference we can make in our world as we allow Him to grow us into that winning combination of grace and truth.
—DIANNE NEAL MATTHEWS

FAITH STEP: *Think about recent conversations you've had with family, friends, acquaintances, and strangers. Did your words and attitudes display grace and truth? If not, ask Jesus to help you do better in the future.*

THURSDAY, FEBRUARY 8

What causes quarrels and what causes fights among you? Is it not this, that your passions are at war within you? You desire and do not have, so you murder. You covet and cannot obtain, so you fight and quarrel. You do not have, because you do not ask. You ask and do not receive, because you ask wrongly, to spend it on your passions. James 4:1–3 (ESV)

IT SEEMS THE GREATEST CAUSE of inner conflict for me is my double-mindedness. As James tells us here, my heart so often desires to satisfy my own warring passions, going against what is sometimes obviously God's will. The battle rages on, and the frequent wars are both costly and destructive.

I won't begin to catalog all my worldly wants, but let's just say I'm a far cry from the kind of self-sacrifice and simplicity that Jesus Himself and many of His subsequent followers to date exemplify. Even now, after a number of years as a Christ follower, my flesh tends to scream, "Me, me, me!"

On my own, I simply cannot escape my sinful nature. It's a battle I struggle daily to overcome. But James explains further in this chapter that the answer to this struggle is humility. True humility cannot be faked. It only comes from the honest realization that we are indeed powerless over our sins, including the sin of double-mindedness.

Still, I know that God doesn't leave me in this wretched state. He extends grace to those in conflict in the form of Jesus, Who in turn extends His peace. —ISABELLA YOSUICO

FAITH STEP: *Are you in a battle with yourself? Ask Jesus to show you what the opposing forces are—and surrender to One who has already won the victory.*

FRIDAY, FEBRUARY 9

When the Father sends the Comforter instead of me—and by the Comforter I mean the Holy Spirit—he will teach you much, as well as remind you of everything I myself have told you. John 14:26 (TLB)

RECENTLY I MADE A SMALL investment in a company that delivers healthful food choices for more efficient supper planning. Flashy, I know. But in a few hours, including shopping, chopping, and measuring some ready-made seasonings, I can put ten meals into my family's deep-freezer. That's one third of the month's suppers—done! That's a gift that gives back.

The idea usually takes a while to catch on. People show great interest at first, but most people ask me about it several times before committing. I try not to push, and I'm open to answering questions and sharing how the process saves time on busy nights.

I understand their hesitation because it took me several years to try it. Now I'm sold. And it's my new normal.

I think it takes many people several times of hearing about Jesus's salvation before they realize just what it can mean for them. Believing in and following Him can be an "I didn't get it till I got it" sort of thing, even when we've shared with others all that He has done for us. Thankfully, Jesus's Spirit speaks to hearts that are ready, in ways we cannot articulate as humans.

Far more than my freezer-meals have transformed our suppers, He changes entire lives, and He knows just how to speak to someone's spirit with His Own. He frees us from the confusion and chaos that sin wreaks on life. —ERIN KEELEY MARSHALL

FAITH STEP: *Do one thing to make one meal easier just one time this week. Spend your extra energy and time enjoying Jesus and the freedom He brings. Ask Him to open other hearts around you to the life-saving truth about Him.*

SATURDAY, FEBRUARY 10

Run to win. All good athletes train hard. They do it for a gold medal that tarnishes and fades. You're after one that's gold eternally.
1 Corinthians 9:24–25 (MSG)

EVERY TIME I WATCH THE Olympics on television, the efforts of those involved always inspire me. Recently I observed the dichotomy of emotions between contestants. During an interview, one Olympian broke into tears after his event: "I didn't win! I lost! I wanted to win!" Actually he did win—silver.

Another athlete fell on her face in tears. But her broad smile reflected joy, even though she finished last. A fellow contestant, seeing her fall, had helped her back on her feet. Both women, arms draped around each other, were ecstatic. Why? The woman who had stumbled said it all: "I finished the race."

In our society, no one offers a medal to a loser. And promotions usually follow the best, the fastest, and the first—not the one who stumbles along the way. Not so in Jesus's scheme of things. In the race of life, it's not who breaks the world record or who crosses the line first. Jesus said many who were considered first will be last, and those counted last will be first (Luke 13:30).

Jesus's example says it all. His last words on the Cross as He hung dying were, "It is finished." He "finished" the "race" appointed Him. And because He finished, so can we. When we reach the end of our lives, it's not how fast or slow we ran; it's that we know the One Who died for us, and we completed our race.

Yes, we do run to win. But in heaven, everyone who finishes the race, looking forward to Jesus's appearing, wins a crown (2 Timothy 4:8).
—REBECCA BARLOW JORDAN

FAITH STEP: *Thank Jesus today for the race He made possible for you to win.*

SUNDAY, FEBRUARY 11

They came up to Jesus and saw the madman sitting there wearing decent clothes and making sense, no longer a walking madhouse of a man.
Mark 5:15 (MSG)

As I READ THE BIBLICAL accounts of Jesus's encounters with different people, I often visualize the "before" and "after" scenes. For example, take the story in Mark 5 of Jesus meeting a man plagued by evil spirits. Picture how wild he must have looked: disheveled hair, ragged, dirty clothing (if any). Perhaps broken chains dragged from his arms or feet, reminders of the villagers' failed attempts to bind him for his own protection. Imagine his screams piercing the air as he wandered among the hillside tombs.

How the scene changed after Jesus spent a few moments with the man! Chaos fled before the Prince of Peace. The people from the surrounding countryside arrived to find the former madman sitting quietly, fully clothed, and speaking calmly and sensibly.

A person's mental state is not always as obvious as this man's. We sometimes look calm and collected on the outside, while inside we may be screaming in terror. As I was during my first MRI, after I discovered how narrow that tube was. We may respond to such situations or disturbances by freezing up.

I try to remember that Jesus always knows what's going on with me at the deepest level, regardless of how well I hide my emotions from those around me. Doubts, fears, hurts, confusion—Jesus knows exactly what I need. He offers to wipe away negative emotions and to replace them with peace and contentment. It's amazing how a few moments in His presence can transform a troubled mind. —DIANNE NEAL MATTHEWS

FAITH STEP: *Prayerfully search your heart for any troubling thoughts that might keep your mind from being fully at peace. Ask Jesus for His soothing touch.*

MONDAY, FEBRUARY 12

Love is patient, love is kind. It does not envy, it does not boast, it is not proud. It does not dishonor others, it is not self-seeking, it is not easily angered, it keeps no record of wrongs. Love does not delight in evil but rejoices with the truth. It always protects, always trusts, always hopes, always perseveres. 1 Corinthians 13:4–7 (NIV)

WE RECENTLY MOVED TO FLORIDA and I was eager to connect with the people around me. After the dust settled, I met a woman through my son's new classmate. Also a recent transplant, she and I hit it off, swapping stories about our boys' difficult adjustments and our shared writing background. She kindly offered to help me with unpacking. We exchanged a few texts and suddenly, it seemed, communication slowed, then stopped. My mind went into overdrive.

Did she not like my house? Did I offend her when we weren't available for a playdate?

Perhaps you know someone who is familiar with this pattern of take-everything-personally, worst-case thinking?

Among other things, this passage cautions me against self-seeking and toward believing the best. How often do I take things personally, thinking the absolute worst? How often does my fear prevent me from reaching out to others or simply enjoying life?

I am grateful that I've grown enough spiritually to not always act on my self-centered interpretation of events, but to pray my way through. I'm thankful I didn't act on my interpretation and give this woman the cold shoulder.

When I ran into her at school, she was happy to see me. She'd been overwhelmed and wanted to get together soon. I smiled at my silly self. Maybe next time I'll assume it's not about me. Better still, I can be more available to others. —ISABELLA YOSUICO

FAITH STEP: *Next time you take offense ask Jesus for help in living the verses.*

TUESDAY, FEBRUARY 13

"And you must love the Lord your God with all your heart, all your soul and all your strength." Deuteronomy 6:5 *(NLT)*

THE TRUTH IS, NO MATTER how hard I try to stay focused on loving Jesus, I am easily distracted. I can start off my day with the thought, *Jesus, I want what You want for me today. I want to love You with everything that is in me.* And this thought is interrupted by my thinking that the waistline of my pants is so snug that I can barely breathe. Suddenly, I am not thinking about Jesus; I am online looking for sales on cute jeans. It is very unspiritual of me, I know. But I am very unspiritual. I am still learning. I am an apprentice in loving.

Jesus is still doing His good, long work in me. It is a lifelong work that won't be complete until I am with Him forever. He is forgiving my sins, renewing my mind, and directing my steps. And in each of these acts, He is loving me relentlessly. He loves you relentlessly. Wave upon wave of His goodness and mercy wash over us daily. Peace and grace hem us in. Loving Jesus back isn't merely an act of will. It is the reaction of our entire person to being loved. It is falling headlong into the immenseness of His affection.

Jesus loves us with every inch of His being. He loves us with all of His power and might. He loves us with a faithfulness that cannot be explained. And our response? It is not a checklist. Do we love Him with our minds? Do we love Him with our hearts? Do we love Him with our souls? It is a flinging of ourselves into His presence and loving Him back. Because He has loved us first.
—SUSANNA FOTH AUGHTMON

FAITH STEP: *Think about what it means to be surrounded by love on all sides. Thank Jesus for His enormous love that surrounds you.*

ASH WEDNESDAY, FEBRUARY 14

*"The time is fulfilled, and the kingdom of God is at hand; repent
and believe in the gospel." Mark 1:15 (ESV)*

JESUS DECLARED THE ABOVE, HERALDING the start of His ministry.

I can be petty.

I tend to be overly critical of myself and others.

I'm inclined to pride.

I sometimes have a short temper.

I am vain.

Unfortunately my list can go on.

Sometimes I am deeply saddened by my defects and promptly
repent. Other times I choose to indulge and contentedly, even self-
righteously, act in a way that is less pleasing to Him, for a little
while at least.

That's when I remind myself: Repent and believe in the Gospel!

On Ash Wednesday, many faith traditions include the speaking of
Jesus's words while ashes are placed on our foreheads. It's a reminder
that we are dust. Fragile, fallible, and in need of saving.

We need to repent and believe in the Gospel every day.

By His stripes, we are healed. Our sin-sick souls are redeemed. I
am free to be who I am, a work in progress, perfectly imperfect and
beloved in Christ. —ISABELLA YOSUICO

FAITH STEP: *This Ash Wednesday, contemplate the wonder of the Gospel.*

THURSDAY, FEBRUARY 15

I determined not to know anything among you, save Jesus Christ, and him crucified. 1 Corinthians 2:2 *(KJV)*

THIS IS A DIFFICULT VERSE for me, a difficult challenge of Paul's. Because if I understand Paul correctly, it's all about Jesus. That seems to be all He cares about.

I love Jesus. I do. Jesus fascinates me. I feel His love all around me and through me. I see His miracles in the world. But while I am a Christian and have pledged my allegiance to Jesus and His teachings, there are other things I want to know. I'm a scholar. An academic. I'm a writer, and something of an activist. There are causes I believe in. Many things I want to address as a teacher trying to make the world a better place.

I'm reminded of a story I once heard Max Lucado tell. He said that his wife sent him to the store to pick up bread. On the way to the bread aisle he saw cookies. So he put them into his basket. And thoughts of cookies led him to the milk, so he picked up milk. When he got home, he showed his wife the cookies and milk and invited her to a sweet little feast. "But, Max, where's the bread?" she asked him.

I'm like this. While my ultimate goal is to know Jesus, I can get sidetracked by other things that seem—and are—important. If I'm not careful, I can become so absorbed in learning information, even supporting good causes, that I forget the most important thing, the only thing that really matters for me or anyone else. Jesus.
—GWEN FORD FAULKENBERRY

FAITH STEP: *As you go through your day today, don't forget the Bread of Life. He's the One essential.*

FRIDAY, FEBRUARY 16

You, God, are my God, earnestly I seek you; I thirst for you,
my whole being longs for you, in a dry and parched land where
there is no water. Psalm 63:1 (NIV)

LAST MONTH, OUR WATER HEATER broke. My husband picked up a new one and called a plumber who installed it for us. That evening, I started running a bath. I looked forward to relaxing in the soothing, warm water, which always helps ease my aches and pains. When I went back in to check the water level, I stopped short. The tub was full of rusty brown water. A bath no longer held any appeal...at least not until we got the new problem fixed.

In the Gospels, Jesus constantly reminded His followers to question whether what they were seeking could really satisfy them. Often I chase after recognition, or popularity, or entertainment and distractions, or control—things that I think will help heal the aches and pains of my soul. Instead, they turn out to be murky water that can't meet my need.

Like the psalmist, our souls do feel deep longing. We don't need to pretend. We live in a troubled world that isn't our true home. But we have a choice about where to turn with our longings: to things that disappoint—like my rusty pipes, or to the Savior Who keeps every promise to refresh us in this parched land. The water that Jesus provides is never disappointing. He offered a Samaritan woman the water of life. He used water to wash His disciples' feet. He even turned humble water into delicious wine.

When we let our hearts long for Jesus, He provides more than a few drops to quench our thirst or wipe a bit of dirt from our feet. He creates a fountain of life within us. —SHARON HINCK

FAITH STEP: *Take a bath or shower and thank Jesus that as water pours out to meet our needs, His love pours out as we seek Him.*

SATURDAY, FEBRUARY 17

"Listen carefully to what I am about to tell you. . . ." Luke 9:44 *(NIV)*

MY HUSBAND THOUGHT HE KNEW what I was going to tell him. I didn't want to dishonor him in any way but found myself using a technique I'd tried when my children were small.

"I love you. Please listen carefully to what I'm saying."

The expression of love—first—set him up for my next words, which set him up for the words after those, my actual message to him.

How many times did Jesus begin an important teaching with, "Listen carefully"? Sometimes He said, "Hear My words" or "Hear these words." Other times He simply said, "Listen to Me" or "Listen."

How well He knows our hearts. How well He understands our tendency to run ahead of Him in conversation, guessing what He's likely to say next. And how many times our preconceived ideas interfere with what He's really saying to us.

"Listen carefully," He says.

A favorite worship song from years ago begins, "I am Your servant. And I am listening. Speak to me, Lord, speak to me."

But so often a more accurate depiction would be, "I want to be Your servant. And I am speaking. Listen to me, Lord, listen to me." Although He lovingly hears when we speak, the larger question is, "Are we listening?"

The next time someone asks me what I'm doing, I hope I can truthfully answer, "Listening carefully." —CYNTHIA RUCHTI

FAITH STEP: *"Two ears, one mouth. Listen twice as much as you speak."* What great advice for our relationship with Jesus. What visual would help you remember that adage?

SUNDAY, FEBRUARY 18

Come, let us worship and bow down, Let us kneel before the Lord our Maker. Psalm 95:6 (NASB)

THERE'S SOMETHING ABOUT THE KNEELING posture that bends us. It makes us more pliable and able to hear. Before every revival and fresh breath of God…there is a bending.

In 1904 a young preacher from Wales named Evan Roberts was anxious to spread the Gospel and bring new life to a sin-laden, worn-out town. The harder he tried, the deeper the people seemed to sink into sin. One night he listened to an old preacher teach a lesson on revival. The preacher said it starts with three powerful words, "Lord, bend me."

Evan and his friends took this message back to his town and began to teach the people to say, "Bend me, Lord." He instructed them in three ways. First, he said if there is any sin or willful defiance of God in your life—get rid of it. Second, if there is any doubt—confess it. And finally, if the Holy Spirit is prompting you to do something— do it! The entire town took on the motto "Lord, bend me," and remarkable things began to happen. The brothels started to shut down, relationships were restored, crime became nonexistent, and a sense of community was profound.

During the next year over 100,000 people came to know Jesus— and that region of Wales was never the same. It seems the best posture to have with God is a bent one. It's in our bending that He straightens and strengthens us in a way we could never do ourselves. —GARI MEACHAM

FAITH STEP: *Write the phrase "Lord, bend me" on several sticky notes and place them around your house. Repeat the phrase throughout this week and watch the ways God works in a bent heart.*

MONDAY, FEBRUARY 19

You shall bow down no more to the work of your hands. Micah 5:13 (ESV)

YOU SEE THEM EVERYWHERE—STREET CORNERS, restaurants, even national parks. Folks with their heads tipped down at a characteristic angle, their gaze locked onto a screen. People are texting, posting social media updates, mapping routes, or engaging in any number of activities that can be done on the spot as long as they have a phone signal or Wi-Fi connection. They're missing out on the beauty around them, their eyes on their smartphones with their heads bowed as if in worship.

Many of us are addicted to the need to connect. I know I check my phone more often than I should. Ironically, all this attention to the phone disconnects us from other people and real life. At its worst, it can lead to devastating, even fatal accidents.

The overuse of technology has led to a new orthopedic disorder known as Text Neck. The weight of the tipped head strains the neck muscles, causes pain, and eventually can result in irreversible, degenerative changes to the spine.

Our habits change us, for better or for worse. Unhealthy self-interest is destructive. Pride is making self our god. Phones and technology are neither good nor bad in themselves, but used carelessly, they turn us inward, leaving us selfish and inconsiderate.

Jesus didn't do whatever He felt like but said, "I seek not my own will but the will of him who sent me" (John 5:30, ESV).

I don't want to go my own way, but His. With His help, I'll deny myself and follow Him. —SUZANNE DAVENPORT TIETJEN

FAITH STEP: *Today disconnect your electronics. If overconnectedness isn't your problem, pull away from something that is. Spend the time quietly, lovingly.*

TUESDAY, FEBRUARY 20

"I give them eternal life, and they shall never perish; no one will snatch them out of my hand." John 10:28 (NIV)

IF PEOPLE AROUND ME THINK I talk about moving a lot, that's probably because over the past several years I've moved a lot. It wasn't always like this. I spent the first thirty years of my life in west Tennessee. Then my husband took a job in central Illinois, a "temporary" situation that stretched into twenty-eight years. But over the next few years, job changes took us to Utah, Texas, and Louisiana. I shudder to suggest it, but who knows? By the time this book is published, perhaps we'll be relocated in another state.

Whenever anyone asks for my zip code, I pause before answering. Including temporary apartments and rental houses, we've had seven different zip codes over the past six years. I'm not sure where I consider home anymore. Some days when I'm tired, for a moment I even forget where I am.

These moves have not been of my own choosing, but they help me to relate to the Old Testament characters called by God to live a transient way of life. They also help me to remember that this earth is not my permanent home; I'm only a sojourner here for a while. My true home is heaven. In the meantime, He knows exactly where I am no matter how many times I move.

Until we relocate to our forever home, Jesus holds each one of us in His hands. Hands that are loving, powerful, and so protective that no one and nothing can ever snatch us out of them. Since I'm living such a transient life, I consider knowing John 10:28 more important than remembering my current zip code. —DIANNE NEAL MATTHEWS

FAITH STEP: *Think about what it means to be at home in Jesus's hands. Thank Him for holding you so securely.*

WEDNESDAY, FEBRUARY 21

*Set a guard over my mouth, LORD; keep watch over the door of
my lips. Psalm 141:3 (NIV)*

EARLY ON IN MY CHRISTIAN life I suffered from the familiar "foot-in-mouth disease"—times when I thoughtlessly fired words like missiles. And like those speedy rockets, unable to be retrieved, the comments reached their targets in record time. Whether it was an impulsive blurt to a relative, or a critical comment under my breath, the result was not pleasant. Sometimes I didn't even realize what I'd just said until someone close set me straight.

Through the years, Jesus has taught me more about speaking the truth in love, or maybe I've just grown tired of being embarrassed by my occasional outbursts. Still, the temptation to speak without thinking is always there.

The other day Jesus reminded me, as He so faithfully does in His Word, that there is a better way to control our words than trying to discipline ourselves. I read and reread Psalm 141:3 until a fresh visual captured my imagination. I began to picture Jesus as a guard or policeman standing nearby to help keep the "door" of my lips sealed. I also remembered a statement by Paul, whose reputation for outspokenness followed him: "we take captive every thought to make it obedient to Christ" (2 Corinthians 10:5, NIV).

We can't keep temptation away, but we can keep it at bay. Before we let words fly, we can join Jesus and submit every thought to Him. Now as I picture those thoughts bowing before Jesus, my personal Guard, I can see the door of my lips opening. But this time, it's a good thing. —REBECCA BARLOW JORDAN

FAITH STEP: *Draw your own visual of Psalm 141:3 and 2 Corinthians 10:5. Place it where you'll see it often, and ask Jesus to be the Guard of your heart.*

THURSDAY, FEBRUARY 22

The godly will flourish . . . in the courts of our God. Even in old age they will still produce fruit; they will remain vital and green. Psalm 92:12–14 (NLT)

MY HUSBAND, STEVE, AND I have had several conversations about retirement lately. Not our own yet. But among our friends, we know a lot of people helping parents navigate these waters.

Steve and I think about our own retirement, hoping someday we'll be able to quit work and travel and spend time with grandkids. It's got me wondering what Jesus thinks of our later years. While we may stop earning a living, is there any end to our work as His Kingdom builders? Nope.

We're never finished living for Him, which brings along a host of blessings to look forward to. We never cease to be useful, and we'll never outgrow the role, nor will we ever earn too much to make an employer seek someone younger.

Jesus wants us to be more useful the older we get. There's a maturity of faith that age brings and that younger Christ-followers need to see. And He puts His Spirit in His follower to continue that person's growth and effectiveness.

It's beautiful. And what a relief! During a career we're easily made to feel as if we need to prove ourselves or make a name for ourselves. Those motivations grow tiresome. But our primary purpose of loving God and loving others is ours beyond retirement, beyond the day we pass away from this earth.

Whether retirement awaits you or is your current season, enjoy having the greatest purpose possible. —ERIN KEELEY MARSHALL

FAITH STEP: *Write a letter to yourself about your hopes for your growth and faith in Jesus. Remind yourself of your ongoing purpose as Jesus's follower.*

FRIDAY, FEBRUARY 23

It is for freedom that Christ has set us free. Stand firm, then, and do not let yourselves be burdened again by a yoke of slavery. Galatians 5:1 (NIV)

WE BELIEVE THAT SLAVERY IS far removed from us, from our country, but historically it's closer than we think. My older friend, Jan, was recently sharing with me about her great-grandfather. He was born into slavery in North Carolina, and she met him on his one hundredth birthday when she was six years old. After obtaining freedom he bought eighty acres of land in Arkansas, and he and his wife survived on all that they grew and cared for on the farm. Jan's eyes sparkled when she spoke. Freedom changed the course of her family's journey in this country.

It made me think of my life. I say I am free in Christ, but I've struggled with always believing that. There was a time, as a young mom, when I was especially busy with ministry activities. I had no time to rest because I was serving in so many capacities. Yet it is a slave who works from sunup to sundown without rest or reward. That is not what Jesus requires. It is so easy to pile on more and more "for God." Looking back, I realize that I worked so hard because I was afraid of disappointing Jesus.

As Romans 8:15 (NLT) says, "So you have not received a spirit that makes you fearful slaves. Instead, you received God's Spirit when he adopted you as his own children. Now we call him, 'Abba, Father.'" Jesus made a way for me to be God's child and not just someone to work hard for Him with no reward. Jesus has already rewarded us with true freedom in Him. —TRICIA GOYER

FAITH STEP: *Make a list of things you're doing to serve Jesus. Are you doing any of those things out of guilt or duty? Ask Jesus to help you step away from anything that doesn't bloom from a heart of love and freedom.*

SATURDAY, FEBRUARY 24

You took off your former way of life, the old self that is corrupted by deceitful desires; you are being renewed in the spirit of your minds; you put on the new self, the one created according to God's likeness in righteousness and purity of the truth. Ephesians 4:22—24 (HCSB)

WHEN I FIRST GAVE MY life to Christ in my early thirties, the Holy Spirit began to change me. Some changes happened almost immediately. I started to reject the club scene I'd been a part of, and dating began to seem more squalid than glamorous. Climbing the corporate ladder, which was never truly satisfying for me personally, lost its appeal. And some friendships that had seemed important suddenly seemed superficial and toxic.

Soon my life changed completely. I married for the first time, abandoned my high-powered career, and moved away from all that was familiar. This process of transformation, or sanctification, is ongoing. The Holy Spirit is continuing His good work in me.

In the early, troubled years of my marriage, I was tempted to flee. My memories of life before Christ looked gratifying and full of fun. I forgot the misery of my ambition, remembering only the paychecks and titles. I recalled the male attention, easy camaraderie, and free-spirited pleasures of my former social life, forgetting the heartbreak and shame.

Exodus tells us that when the newly freed Israelites encountered hard times in the desert, they longed for Egypt, seemingly forgetting the misery of their captivity. Like the Israelites, I sometimes forget the prison of my former life. I need not go back to the old captive way of living. I can remember that I am a new creation in the Promised Land of Christ's freedom. —ISABELLA YOSUICO

FAITH STEP: *When you find yourself fantasizing about your past, remember the Israelites and consider a few scenarios to remind yourself of the truth.*

SUNDAY, FEBRUARY 25

Then Jesus left them again and prayed the same prayer as before. When he returned to them again, he found them sleeping, for they couldn't keep their eyes open. And they didn't know what to say. Mark 14:39–40 (NLT)

TRUE FRIENDS ARE PEOPLE WE trust. We can ask them for prayer or for practical help, and typically they'll do whatever they can to assist. But what happens when they disappoint? How should we respond? The answer is, follow Jesus's example.

Jesus enjoyed heart-to-heart relationships with Peter, James, and John. They accompanied Him at the Transfiguration (Luke 9:28–36). They also went to Gethsemane with Him before His arrest (Mark 14:32–42). We could have assumed they'd be fervent in their prayers for Jesus after He said, "My soul is crushed with grief to the point of death. Stay here and keep watch with me." But we would have been wrong.

As Jesus "became deeply troubled and distressed," His best friends fell asleep. Not just once or twice, but three times. The average person might consider this a total lack of commitment and toss those friends aside, but Jesus was anything but average. After each instance, He encouraged the men to try again. After the third time, He simply said, "Up, let's be going." In other words, it's time to move on.

Jesus's friends disappointed Him. He saw their foibles and failures firsthand, but He extended grace and loved them anyway. Can we do the same for our friends when they fall short of our expectations?
—GRACE FOX

FAITH STEP: *Think of a friend with whom you haven't connected for a long while. Give that person a phone call and express gratitude for your relationship.*

MONDAY, FEBRUARY 26

But the Lord stood at my side and gave me strength. 2 Timothy 4:17 (NIV)

A RECENT SPEAKING EVENT TOOK me back through one of my favorite stretches of scenery—the Driftless Region of Southwest Wisconsin. Untouched by glaciers, the area is marked by beautifully sculpted topography, deep valleys, bluffs, thickly forested hillsides, and hardscrabble farms that make hayfields and cornfields out of the rich black topsoil in snatches of low places between hillsides.

Driftless. The word "drift" was once used to describe till, or unsorted glacial sediment. The area wasn't covered by ice, so it was undisturbed by advancing and retreating glacial activity. No glacial debris covered it. No icy blades leveled it.

I wonder how hard it would be to explain to a headstone carver that I'd like to have the word "driftless" included under my name, date of birth, and date of death. To have lived wide-open, not covered by artificial ice that leaves its debris strewn across the landscape of my life. And then to have Jesus say, "Thank you. You didn't drift from what I asked of you."

It would be one of those moments when the only fitting response would be to fall at His feet and pour all the gratitude back onto Him. Staying driftless isn't possible without His faithful oversight, His stability, His Word in which to plant my roots.

For a few minutes, I drifted away from writing these words! The temptation to succumb to the pressure of busyness and distractions from life's glaciers is forceful. But when we stand our ground, the keeping power of Jesus is greater still. —CYNTHIA RUCHTI

FAITH STEP: *Take a minute to research images of the beauty of the Driftless Region. Use the images as a reminder of how life's topography grows more beautiful when we remain driftless in Jesus Christ.*

TUESDAY, FEBRUARY 27

All people will know that you are my followers if you love each other.
John 13:35 (NCV)

THERE'S THIS AUTHOR AND MEDIA personality I really like. She and her husband use their public platform to share their Christian faith. She is particularly accessible, I think. She comes across as authentic, sharing her imperfect parenting skills, struggles as a woman, and desire to follow Jesus in a very human way. I especially like her focus on social justice and how following Jesus means—in part—that we love who He loves, which is everyone. And we find tangible ways to engage culture on behalf of the oppressed.

I've watched her evolve in some of her beliefs. Most recently she gave an interview in which she brought up a topic about which she has completely changed her mind.

Some Christian writers applauded her. Some respectfully disagreed or simply remained quiet. But others, in their pulpits and blogs and magazines, aggressively condemned her interpretation of Scripture.

After hearing this, I wondered if what Jesus declared in the above verse had been lost. And what about the many, many other verses throughout the Bible that command us to be kind, to love mercy, to walk humbly? Jesus never said we have to agree about everything. What He cared about most was love. —GWEN FORD FAULKENBERRY

FAITH STEP: *Resist the temptation of a critical spirit. Use your voice to speak truth in love and kindness today.*

WEDNESDAY, FEBRUARY 28

The Lord directs the steps of the godly. He delights in every detail of their lives. Psalm 37:23 (NLT)

THE OTHER DAY MY FRIEND, Angela, and I were discussing our teenage sons. They are completely unwilling to share the state of their hearts with us. Which girls do they like? Who do they think is cute? Which girls do they think are great friends? Jack is a vault. But this is nothing new. The last time I remember hearing who Jack liked was in second grade.

It is no easier getting information out of my other boys, Will and Addison. I ask them questions about their day at school. Did you learn anything exciting? Did you play fun games with your friends? I ask these questions because I am interested. And I miss them when they are not at home. When they were little, I knew everything about the ins and outs of their days. Now they pick and choose what they want to tell me. I am sure they could do without the daily interrogations. But I am not giving up that easily. I love them too much. I want them to know that whatever is important to them is important to me. The state of their hearts most of all.

Jesus is even more concerned about the state of your heart and mine. He loves us so much. Whatever is important to us is important to Him. He longs to be let in on our fondest dreams, to see us through our greatest fears, and to champion our greatest hopes. He wants us to tell Him the ins and outs of our days. Jesus delights in every single detail of our lives. The biggest and smallest ones. His great desire is for you to share your life with Him and let Him guide your steps. —SUSANNA FOTH AUGHTMON

FAITH STEP: *Take a moment to share your heart with Jesus. Let Him in on the details of your life today and ask Him for His guidance.*

THURSDAY, MARCH 1

When they were discouraged, I smiled and that encouraged them and lightened their spirits. Job 29:24 (TLB)

A FEW WEEKS AGO, DORTHY, a friend from one of our earlier churches, sent me a letter about an experience she remembered involving our ministry. I read it with amusement—especially her confession: she always thought of me as "Miss Smiley Face," until we attended a retreat together years before. Admitting to me that she was not in the best place in her life at the time, Dorthy had started attending the church where my husband was the associate pastor. She remembered that I always had a smile on my face—which she assumed was due to my "easy life" as a pastor's wife.

Dorthy reminded me that at the retreat we were paired together and encouraged to share safely and confidentially any personal issues or concerns. Thinking my life was perfect, she felt discouraged until I told her about trying to keep afloat with our family's time crunches and difficult church schedules. To deal with it, I told her about how I would sometimes draw a hot bath and "just sit in that water and stew." She wrote how encouraged she felt that I could actually smile genuinely through my struggles.

I had forgotten about that experience, but Dorthy had no idea how much those struggles had increased through the years as life challenges tested us. I do remember often "letting a smile be my umbrella"—as an old song once said, even though I also shed many tears. Yet nothing can ever wipe out the joy—or the smile—in my heart from knowing Jesus, the One Who put it there.

Now a strong believer herself, Dorthy said she learned from that experience to be careful about judging. And her story taught me to keep smiling. —REBECCA BARLOW JORDAN

FAITH STEP: *Ask Jesus to let your smile be someone else's umbrella this week.*

FRIDAY, MARCH 2

Now as they observed the confidence of Peter and John and understood that they were uneducated and untrained men, they were amazed, and began to recognize them as having been with Jesus. Acts 4:13 (NASB)

ONE DAY WHILE PREPARING FOR our board meeting, with budget reports and project proposals strewn all over the floor in front of me, I suddenly felt the rush of anxiety. "I don't know if I can do this, Lord... I'm just not qualified," I whispered.

In school I had failed eighth-grade math because my best friend and I hung in the back of the room, flirting with boys rather than paying attention to the concepts taught. I was surprised when I got to ninth grade and my teacher began talking about positive and negative numbers. I thought he was talking about numbers that were gloomy or having consistent bad days! I had no understanding of negative numbers, which becomes really important when you run a ministry and an international donor organization. But instead of going down that familiar path of defeat, I remembered something the Lord had spoken to me months before: "I'm not looking for the *brightest* people; I'm looking for the *bravest* people."

The apostles, Peter and John, were confident because they knew Jesus—not because they were skilled leaders. As a matter of fact, they were uneducated and untrained—not the typical pedigree for outstanding world-changers—and yet, their faith flipped humanity upside down. No matter how unprepared we feel, God sees us as vital and victorious. The more we believe this, the more people will say, "That woman knows Jesus." —GARI MEACHAM

FAITH STEP: *Take a sheet of paper and list all the ways in which you feel inadequate for the challenges or dreams you have for your life. In large letters write, "I know Jesus" over them.*

SATURDAY, MARCH 3

Let your conversation be gracious and attractive so that you will have the right response for everyone. Colossians 4:6 (NLT)

I DON'T KNOW ABOUT YOU, but it's hard for me to accept a compliment. If a stranger compliments my kids, I want to explain that they are not always angels. If a coworker says I did a great job on my project, I feel the urge to share how much I've struggled on the job. If a friend tells me I look nice, I want to mention that I haven't been exercising and eating as I should. The thing is, I've been taught to be gracious to others, yet I have a tough time being gracious to myself.

The Bible talks a lot about our words. Ephesians 4:29 says, "Do not let any unwholesome talk come out of your mouths, but only what is helpful for building others up according to their needs, that it may benefit those who listen" (NIV). Most people are good about building up others, while at the same time tearing down themselves. And no one benefits from it. Jesus came to earth to save our souls and to guide us to righteous living, but we often get hung up on all the ways we don't act right. We forget that kind words—more than negative ones—encourage us to do better.

We will never have perfect kids, do a perfect job, or live a perfect life, but I've found I do better when I understand Jesus's grace, and when I'm gracious to myself. When we speak gracious and attractive words, people notice. After all, they hear plenty of words that are harsh and unkind in everyday life. Right responses bring grace, for everyone. —TRICIA GOYER

FAITH STEP: *What is a compliment that you've had a hard time accepting? Write it down on a sticky note; then underneath write a short prayer asking Jesus to help you to be gracious to yourself in this area.*

SUNDAY, MARCH 4

"Woe to you, scribes and Pharisees, hypocrites! You are like whitewashed tombs, which appear beautiful on the outside, but inside are full of dead men's bones and every impurity." Matthew 23:27 (HCSB)

I LIKE TO CITE THE Pharisees as the real bad guys in the Gospel, even worse than the Romans who nailed Jesus to the cross. "Stinking hypocrites," I say. "Acting holier-than-thou, when all along they were full of pride and rotten inside."

I've been known to use the term *hypocrite* with some modern-day Christians, too. I call foul when people wag their fingers at sinners, selectively quoting Scripture to make their point while conveniently overlooking the Scripture that would surely call out their own sin.

When I hear or see this, it really gets me going. Can't they see that their sin is no better than someone else's? Don't they get that God doesn't grade on a curve? Sin is sin is sin! We all need saving grace every day! Cough, ahem...

I also recognize that I am a whitewashed tomb. I am a hypocrite. Isn't it prideful for me to condemn other people's convictions, presuming to know their hearts? What sin do I overlook in myself? Do my insides always match my outsides? Am I so righteous that I can condemn another's sin, whatever it is? Oh my.

Coming to this truth isn't meant to condemn myself either. We are all in this state, but we are all forgiven and made equal by Jesus, the only nonhypocrite who ever walked the earth. —ISABELLA YOSUICO

FAITH STEP: *What would happen if you extended the same gracious love to the nearest hypocrite that Jesus extends to you? How about to yourself?*

MONDAY, MARCH 5

Give all your worries and cares to God, for he cares about you.
1 Peter 5:7 (NLT)

YESTERDAY WHILE THE BOYS WERE doing their homework, my husband, Scott, told me that our former college was going be ninety-seven years old this year. My son, Addison, said, "That is old." I said, "That is old. Speaking of old, who is going to take care of me when I am ninety-seven?" Addie yelled, "Not it!" Will said, "Not me," and gently patted my shoulder. Jack looked sad and said, "I guess it's me." Were those some small tears gathering in the corners of his eyes? This was disheartening.

You would think that at least one of my boys would want to look after me. There are apparently no takers for hanging out with me in my golden years. I am thinking of starting a weekly prayer and fasting time for kind daughters-in-law with a heart for blind, forgetful old ladies who like to laugh and eat chocolate. My great hope is that someone will take care of me when I am old. There are so many unknowns and concerns in this life. It is easy to worry about things over which we have no control.

We often get anxious about the future —even when we are not ninety-seven years old. Jesus wants us to remember that we can come to Him with every care and every worry. He has not forgotten me. Or you. He holds us in the center of His palm. The One Who pinned the stars in place and breathes planets into being cares about you. You are His child. He will never leave you nor forsake you. You are not alone. You are held within the bounty of His grace and His provision from now until eternity. —SUSANNA FOTH AUGHTMON

FAITH STEP: *Call out your worries to Jesus. Remind yourself that the One Who holds the stars in place, with all the power in the universe, is caring for you right now.*

TUESDAY, MARCH 6

*Indeed, I count everything as loss because of the surpassing worth
of knowing Christ Jesus my Lord. For his sake I have suffered the
loss of all things and count them as rubbish, in order that
I may gain Christ. Philippians 3:8 (NIV)*

I HAVE A GERMAN FRIEND who learned the Queen's English in school.
We Southerners here in the US don't use the word "rubbish" unless
we're mocking the British. But she uses it whenever she's gossiping.

The way I understand the above verse makes it immensely challenging—so challenging I can hardly imagine that Paul meant what
he wrote. But based on his life I have to believe he did. He says he
lost everything for the sake of Jesus, and furthermore, it's great. Not
just great, but surpassing greatness. All of those things he's lost are
trash to him—rubbish—compared to what he's gained by knowing
Jesus. Rubbish. Nothing precious, not anything he misses, not anything he wishes he could have kept. Stuff to toss out and be rid of.

Let's consider what Paul has lost at this point. He'd long since
lost his status as the best Jew and Pharisee of his generation. He'd
been flogged, hungry, naked, and cold. He wrote the letter to the
Philippians from prison, where he faced trial before Caesar and the
possibility of death. He'd throw it all away again for Jesus?

I want to have this kind of faith. But I'll be honest: I like my
stuff. I love being safe, and free, and having a good reputation. I
like my comfortable house, and having people I love all around
me, and never being hungry.

I think the key is in the comparison. We don't give up everything
for just anyone. But everything, compared to knowing Jesus, is
rubbish. —GWEN FORD FAULKENBERRY

FAITH STEP: *Consider what you need to give up in order to know Jesus more.*

WEDNESDAY, MARCH 7

But God demonstrates his own love for us in this: While we were still sinners, Christ died for us. Romans 5:8 (NIV)

MY HUSBAND AND I MARRIED nearly thirty-six years ago. It didn't take long to realize that saying "I love you" was nice and necessary, but not enough. We had to back up our words with actions.

For us, this means simple things like giving each other foot rubs, going for walks together, and helping with household chores. We listen without interrupting, and we strive to put the other's needs ahead of our own. Our actions lend credibility to our words.

The Bible is filled with God's declarations of love for us. But He went a step further to demonstrate the depth of His love.

Jesus Christ is the proof of God's extreme love for humankind. He left heaven and came to earth where He became a man, for our sake. He suffered criticism and rejection, endured beatings, and died a criminal's death on the Cross to pay our sins' penalty.

In return, telling Jesus that we love Him is good, but that's not enough. Following His example, we need to prove our love through our actions. This means obeying His commands to love and to forgive and to pray for our enemies, to live blamelessly, to always give thanks, and more. Perhaps the old hymn, "When I Survey the Wondrous Cross," summarizes it best:

"Were the whole realm of nature mine,

That were a present far too small;

Love so amazing, so divine,

Demands my soul, my life, my all." —GRACE FOX

FAITH STEP: *Think of one person to whom you can demonstrate love today. Come up with your own action plan.*

THURSDAY, MARCH 8

*The Day is coming when you'll have it all—life healed and whole.
I know how great this makes you feel, even though you have to put up
with every kind of aggravation in the meantime. 1 Peter 1:5–6 (MSG)*

I LIVE IN AN AREA that's growing a lot. All around us buildings are popping up, schools are being built and district boundaries adjusted, and roads and bridges have been constructed or rerouted.

One bridge connects several neighborhoods with a main shopping area. For the past year, crews have been widening the road from two lanes to four. Even though we've looked forward to the extra space and freedom it'll offer when it's done, we've felt the pinch of lane changes and delayed traffic, even days of closure.

Delays of all kinds make us feel pinched, even when we know Jesus is broadening our lives for His purposes. He uses seasons of delay for fortifying our foundations and reworking our paths to make our lives more accessible to guide others to Him.

Jesus's followers are bridges to lead people to Him, but we need to accept His timing and the way He works. Truthfully, I'd rather not deal with some of His recent moves in my life, but His Spirit whispers to me that He has a good plan for us. We're feeling the pinch in different ways, but until He's ready to launch us on the next new path, He wants us to stay the course.

If we rush the bridge workers, we risk driving on an incomplete and unsafe place. It's for our good that we wait. Our decisions to trust affect others, too.

Let's praise Him by waiting expectantly for the next open road and practice staying the course in faith. —ERIN KEELEY MARSHALL

FAITH STEP: *If you're not experiencing a delay, you might know someone who is. Ask Jesus to finish His good rerouting, and trust that He is working all the time.*

FRIDAY, MARCH 9

---

*"Father, if you are willing, please take this cup of suffering away from me.
Yet I want your will to be done, not mine." Luke 22:42 (NLT)*

I KNOW THE DRILL. I'VE been here before. That's exactly why I'm hesitant to walk through the door opened to me.

I remember my first knee replacement with too much clarity. Although each year brings with it advances in medical techniques and treatments, the path ahead of me causes something in my soul to shrink back. "If this cup could pass from me...?"

By the time you read this, it will be over. It will have gone either well or poorly. Those are the options. The likelihood is that the surgery turned out well and I am now grateful for a knee that will support me without knife-stabbing pain.

When my third baby came into this world, the early stages of labor had me thinking, "I've got this." As labor intensified, my pinched words turned to, "Oh, I remember this now!"

We know the drill. We've waited for an oncologist's call or have kept the lights on until an almost-grown child comes home from the ill-advised party or sent our son or daughter off for another deployment. Anxiety is born of past experience.

And yet, Jesus urges us not to let anxiety win. His "fear not" encouragement bears no caveat—unless you've faced it before.

So we come—as He did—to the Father, asking for the cup to pass, if possible. And if not? We take deep draughts of the courage Jesus bought for us and follow the pattern that won His victory. "Not My will be done, but Thine." —CYNTHIA RUCHTI

FAITH STEP: *Pinpoint what you are most anxious about. Ask yourself if that problem is exempt from the instruction not to worry about anything, but to pray about everything (Philippians 4:6).*

SATURDAY, MARCH 10

Train me, God, to walk straight; then I'll follow your true path.
Put me together, one heart and mind; then, undivided, I'll worship
in joyful fear. Psalm 86:11 (MSG)

WHEN MY CHILDREN WERE TEENAGERS, there was one phrase they said that rubbed me the wrong way: "I know." I'd explain something, often in response to a question, and they'd reply, "I know." The fact that they'd asked in the first place told me they didn't. The actions they took confirmed that they didn't. Still, they looked at me as if I were the one with the problem and told me, "I know!" Maybe they needed to bolster their self-confidence during that difficult time of maturing into the people they are today. I don't know.

But now that my children are grown and gone off, I recognize an echo of that attitude in my own spirit. I'm struggling in my Christian walk, so I pray, "What is it, Lord?" He graciously answers, in a sermon, His Word, or the advice of a friend. Instead of being grateful and following His leading, something within me seems to rise up, resisting the solution in front of me.

"But I know that," my heart cries. "That's nothing new!" I wonder if Jesus looks at me, like I looked at my children back then—none of us ready to take counsel from the One who knows the answers.

We make a mistake when we think we know something because we've heard it before. We imagine we're competent and capable, but He won't use us with that attitude. His ways and abilities are infinitely beyond our humanness, and we need to walk in them long enough to form habits that become second nature.

By latching on to Jesus, we can follow and learn. —SUZANNE DAVENPORT TIETJEN

FAITH STEP: *Have you, like me, been saying, "I know!" to Jesus? Though we don't know much, He invites us to know Him. Rest in that thought today.*

SUNDAY, MARCH 11

And he said, "All these I have kept from my youth." When Jesus heard this,
he said to him, "One thing you still lack. Sell all that you have and distribute
to the poor, and you will have treasure in heaven; and come, follow me."
Luke 18:21–22 (ESV)

I SAT AT THE PIANO, opened my book to a Bach prelude, and prepared to enjoy making music. The piano hadn't been tuned for a few years and one of the keys was a fraction of a tone flat. Each time I hit that note, it jarred against the others, marring the beauty of the music. Even though most of the notes were perfect, when only one was off, the whole harmony suffered.

In Luke, the rich ruler came to ask Jesus how to have eternal life. As he spoke with Jesus, he boasted that he'd kept the commandments all of his life. Yet Jesus heard the jarring sounds of pride and self-reliance, which always clash with repentance and love. Jesus pointed out the alarming truth that none of us is capable of earning eternal life. As soon as we fix one sin, another part of our life falls out of tune.

When we acknowledge this, it leads us quickly to the good news. Jesus alone is holy—in actions, in thoughts, in motives. He lived the perfect life for us. Then He laid down that life for our sake.

On this side of heaven, we'll keep hitting sour notes. We may be tempted to justify our worth by pointing out our few good ones. We might nervously hope that Jesus won't hear the places where we're out of pitch. Instead of concerning ourselves with notes that are not music to His ears, we can invite Jesus to play His symphony of grace over our souls. —SHARON HINCK

FAITH STEP: *Lay down the burden of fine-tuning your own soul. Acknowledge that we can't keep any of the commandments by our own strength. Thank Jesus for bringing us the music of eternal life.*

MONDAY, MARCH 12

All my inmost being, praise his holy name. Psalm 103:1 (NIV)

CONFESSION TIME: I LIKE CLASSIC TV shows. My husband commented recently that I've been watching a lot of *Magnum P.I.*, so on my next library trip I checked out a season of *Murder, She Wrote.*

I could feel silly about this recent obsession, but it's clear to me that mulling over a plotline for the book I'm writing or cleaning the kitchen sink is more fun when either Thomas Magnum or Jessica Fletcher is there to entertain!

The other day I even talked about it with an old friend. She totally got it. When I asked if she ever watched *Murder, She Wrote*, she didn't miss a beat.

"Every day. Have you seen *Diagnosis Murder?*"

"Never."

"Ooh, good stuff." Four days later a package arrived on my doorstep. Season one of *Diagnosis Murder.* Good friend.

Sometimes it's nice to have something for ourselves, personal time in the midst of daily life. Good stuff.

When my kids were little and underfoot, I remember craving a corner of my mind that was just mine, a few moments to think my own thoughts. Years later, time is still short and precious.

Many days it seems tough to carve out time with Jesus, too. Fortunately, if a corner of your mind is the only personal place you can be alone with Jesus, that's still enough. And time with Him never will be relegated to rerun status. He'll reveal new peace and joy and love. Timelessly refreshing. —ERIN KEELEY MARSHALL

FAITH STEP: *Take a few moments with Jesus today, just for the two of you.*

TUESDAY, MARCH 13

Peter asked Jesus, "What about him, Lord?"
Jesus replied, "If I want him to remain alive until I return,
what is that to you? As for you, follow me." John 21:21–22 (NLT)

IT SEEMS THAT BEFORE AN author's manuscript is even mailed, another company publishes a similar book that becomes a best seller. Or the executive is passed over as president of a corporation for one with less experience. And an administrative assistant is replaced by someone younger. No matter where it happens, we've all experienced unfair situations. But how should we respond?

Jesus answered that question with a parable about a landowner who hired workers for his vineyard. He started early, hiring until an hour before closing—yet he paid everyone the same. Cries of "Unfair!" erupted. But the landowner replied, "I'm not being unfair. Are you envious because I'm generous?" (see Matthew 20:13–15).

Just before Jesus's ascension, Peter pointed to John, the disciple often labeled "the one whom Jesus loved," and asked, "What about him?" Apparently Peter was concerned about another kind of fairness. Would John, too, die a martyr's death like Peter?

And Jesus's reply to Peter, I believe, is the same as what He would say to us: "What is that to you? As for you, follow me." We won't understand all the "why's" now. In reality, Jesus is exceedingly generous, giving us more than we deserve. And in the kingdom of God, character and motive matter more than our idea of earthly success. Like most, my initial response to unfair situations is not ideal. But my deep desire is to replace every negative response with trust: "Thank You, Jesus. I love You, and I will follow You, no matter what." —REBECCA BARLOW JORDAN

FAITH STEP: *Write down a time when you felt you were treated unfairly. How did you respond? Reaffirm your commitment to "follow Him, no matter what."*

WEDNESDAY, MARCH 14

If we are unfaithful, he remains faithful because he cannot be untrue to himself. 2 Timothy 2:13 (GW)

I BACKED OUT OF THE driveway, mentally rehearsing my list of errands and the best order in which to complete them. As I merged onto the freeway, a feeling struck me that something bad was about to happen. Guilt quickly followed as I remembered that I'd skipped my prayer and Bible reading time that morning. I breathed out a prayer: *Please keep me safe today.* Suddenly a bird grazed the windshield and bounced off. Startled, I jumped in my seat.

As I kept driving, I thought about how much worse the scene could have been. I've always been easy to startle; when my children were young, they learned the hard way not to hide and jump out at me. If the bird had hit the windshield harder, or obstructed my line of vision, I most likely would have swerved or automatically hit the brakes. In the middle of heavy traffic going 75 miles per hour, that would have been quite a disaster. Peace and gratitude filled me as I thanked Jesus for His protection.

I'm sure we can all think of times when Jesus has been faithful, even when we were less than faithful to Him. Our human nature can be fickle. Regardless of our good intentions, there will be times when we doubt Him or act in disloyal ways. We may break promises, or neglect our relationship with Him. Thankfully our failures and shortcomings do not change Who Jesus is or how He feels about us. Jesus will always be there to guide, comfort, protect, and provide. As human beings we may falter, but we can always depend on the Faithful One. —DIANNE NEAL MATTHEWS

FAITH STEP: *Think of a time when you were not as faithful to Jesus as you could have been. How did He show His faithfulness to you during that time?*

THURSDAY, MARCH 15

The wine supply ran out during the festivities, so Jesus' mother told him, "They have no more wine." "Dear woman, that's not our problem," Jesus replied. "My time has not yet come." John 2:3—4 (NLT)

"THERE IS A TIME FOR everything, a season for every activity under the heavens" (Ecclesiastes 3:1, NIV). Wise words, these are. So wise, in fact, that even Jesus applied them to His life. On several occasions when people urged Him to do things that would risk revealing His identity as the Messiah, He replied, "My time has not yet come." He knew His Father's redemptive plan and refused to rush ahead of it.

Hours before His death, Jesus spoke about time again. He said, "The time has come for the Son of Man to enter into his glory" (John 12:23). The wait was over, and He knew that His life's purpose was about to be fulfilled.

My husband worked as a civil engineer for eleven years, but his heart's desire was to work in career Christian camping. For several months we prayed about the possibility of making the switch, but we felt the answer was "Wait." His time had not yet come to leave his job.

Nine more years passed. Nearly every day we prayed for wisdom to recognize when to take action. And then one day we knew.

Jesus knew the importance of timing in fulfilling His Father's purposes. As always, He's our example and our teacher. We can trust Him to show us whether to wait or move forward in whatever situation we face. When we're intent on following His lead, He'll be faithful to show us what to do. —GRACE FOX

FAITH STEP: *Read Ecclesiastes 3:1—8. The first stanza says, "There is a time for everything." Replace the word everything with a personal application. Then thank Jesus for promising to show you when the time is right for those circumstances to be fulfilled.*

FRIDAY, MARCH 16

Greater love has no one than this: to lay down one's life for one's friends.
John 15:13 (NIV)

MY DAUGHTER SHARED A SONG with me the other day that I really like. It's by Vance Joy and he sings, "Your mess is mine." The idea is that when we love someone, we take on whatever messiness we find in their lives, and it becomes our mess, too. We sort it out, clean it up together, because we believe the beauty of the person is worth the mess. It's a song of hope. A song of commitment.

I've seen that play out in my own life, most poignantly in my marriage. My husband suffered wounds as a child that led to some bad choices and behavior as an adult. He brought a lot of messy baggage with him into our home. But he was and is also the love of my life. A wonderful father. A beautiful person. And ultimately worth the mess that became mine, though it caused a lot of pain. We sorted it out together.

How much more does Jesus do that for us? Even though we really have no beauty to offer, He thinks we're worthy. He took on the mess of our sin, our brokenness, our fallen world, and made it His. He died on a cross because of it. Laid down His life, in order to call us friends. And He didn't stop there. He's still taking on the things that challenge us. He gets down in our messes with us here, daily, helping us sort out and clean up if we let Him.
—GWEN FORD FAULKENBERRY

FAITH STEP: *Have you made a mess of things? Ask Jesus to help you start sorting it out today. Commit to one right thing you can do to start the cleanup.*

SATURDAY, MARCH 17

In return for my love they act as my accusers; but I am in prayer.
Psalm 109:4 (NASB)

NOTHING HURTS LIKE THE WOUNDS from a friend—or the betrayal of someone you thought was an ally. Years ago, when I was a new writer and speaker, a woman in a leadership position broke my heart by spreading malicious comments about me. I endured the pain and continued to serve under her—often praying that God would teach me everything I needed to learn from the situation, and then get me out of there! I sat with her on several occasions with tears rolling down my cheeks as I wept. I kept hoping that perhaps she would understand my heart and love me like I hoped she would...but that day never came.

What are we to do when we're misunderstood, or treated in ways that break our hearts? We pray. It may sound like a futile thing to do—like throwing in the towel and giving up. But in these situations prayer isn't giving up; it's surrendering up. It's giving the hurt and misunderstanding to God so that He can fix it, heal it, change it, or rearrange it as He sees fit. Sometimes He will change the heart of your accuser...and sometimes He'll change *your* heart toward the accuser.

Several years after my accuser quit her job and left, I felt compelled to pray for her, and apologize one last time for any wounds I might have imposed. I wrote a beautiful letter that was hand-delivered by a mutual friend. I never heard back from her, but I know I am free. Loving well doesn't promise a tidy resolve of all pain and conflict. It simply assures us that love never fails—even if we don't see the immediate outcome. —GARI MEACHAM

FAITH STEP: *Write a letter of grace to someone who has wronged you. You don't have to send it, just be mindful of God's healing touch as you do.*

SUNDAY, MARCH 18

And He said to them, "Come aside by yourselves to a deserted place and rest a while." For there were many coming and going, and they did not even have time to eat. Mark 6:31 (NKJV)

IT HAS TAKEN ME OVER a year since my retirement from the neonatal intensive care unit to get over wolfing down my meals. NICUs are noisy, busy, stressful places where the urgent needs of others rightly come before my own simpler needs. When I did get to eat, I refueled so fast the meal sat like a lump in my belly for hours. The only time we had to flee the chaos was on long ambulance rides to other emergencies. The team took advantage of this time by napping (or closing our eyes, earbuds in place, substituting our playlists for road noise).

My manners are better now. I've also recognized how important it still is to pull away from the busyness of life, quiet down, and rest. Jesus knew this all along. His Father rested on the seventh day and instituted Sabbath rest as Law. Jesus began His ministry with a forty-day fast in the wilderness and made a habit of drawing away regularly to rest and pray. He invited His disciples as well.

Their attempt to get away was delayed. People found out where Jesus was headed and they arrived before Him, full of needs. Instead of peace, He saw people milling about "like sheep without a shepherd." His heart broke for them. He offered them wisdom, involved His disciples and a little boy in a miraculous meal, then sent His friends ahead so He could finally climb a mountain to pray. He made rest a priority. So should we. —SUZANNE DAVENPORT TIETJEN

FAITH STEP: *There's always something more to be done. Rest requires intention. Continual frazzled giving in to chaos eliminates rest—to our harm. Prioritize rest today. Jesus knows your situation. Do your best to answer His call.*

MONDAY, MARCH 19

*"Father, if you are willing, remove this cup from me.
Nevertheless, not my will, but yours, be done."* Luke 22:42 (ESV)

MY PRAYER LIST USED TO read a lot like my to-do list of what I wanted done for me and for others. A lot of these items seemed really good by my notion of what was best. I prayed that a friend's husband would get a job to provide for his family. I prayed that my lovely and deeply lonely girlfriend would finally meet Mr. Right. I prayed that another friend's daughter would be cured of her chronic illness. I prayed that my unborn son would not have Down syndrome. But my thoughts on prayer have evolved.

God does indeed encourage us to pray specifically and repeatedly, but in a few words Jesus captures what that means perfectly. In the Garden of Gethsemane, Jesus knew His fate. His desire was to be spared from the pain of death, but He knew that His agonizing earthly end would result in ultimate victory, glory, and fulfillment of an eternal purpose for all humankind. So He prayed for God's will, no matter the cost.

To me, this says that I can be brutally honest with God about what I want or don't want for myself and others, but then I have to entrust that desire to Him Whose will shall be done.

Sometimes, my ideas about what's needed seem really good to me; other times I know what I'm asking isn't all that holy or wise. Either way, I want to trust that God knows better and simply seek Him and His will. —ISABELLA YOSUICO

FAITH STEP: *For the next few days, try praying for each person on your list without making any specific requests. Be still to hear what He has to say, listening with an open mind and heart.*

TUESDAY, MARCH 20

*Now may the God of peace—who brought up from the dead
our Lord Jesus, the great Shepherd of the sheep, and ratified
an eternal covenant with his blood—may he equip you with all
you need for doing his will. Hebrews 13:20–21 (NLT)*

MY DAUGHTER, LESLIE, IS A missionary in the Czech Republic,
and while we read many missionary stories during her growing-up
years, I was preparing her for her role from birth in a way I didn't
realize. Yes, her dad and I taught her about Jesus, which has been
vital, of course. But we also raised her to speak English. The ability
to speak English clearly and effectively opens up wonderful doors
for outreach in ways we never imagined.

In 2008 our family first went to the Czech Republic to volunteer at
an English camp. English classes drew the attendees, and we shared the
truth about Jesus to our captive crowd, speaking in our native tongue.
English is taught in schools in many countries around the world. It's
also the language of commerce and travel. When Czech citizens cross
their border to Austria or take a road trip to Italy, English is commonly
the language spoken. So Leslie was well equipped to minister there.

Every day Jesus may be equipping us to do His will in ways we
don't realize. Jesus can use any skill, complex or common, to reach
others with His Good News. As Philippians 2:13 says, "For God
is working in you, giving you the desire and the power to do what
pleases him" (NLT). When you turn your life to Jesus, He can use
your most basic elements as a megaphone. Jesus equips you with all
you need; the goal is simply to be willing to follow His will, even
if it's as basic as speaking in your native tongue. —TRICIA GOYER

FAITH STEP: *Ask Jesus to open your eyes to abilities you have to reach out to
others with the Good News. Pray that Jesus will open doors so you can use them.*

WEDNESDAY, MARCH 21

First clean the inside of the cup and the plate, that the outside also may be clean. —Matthew 23:26 (ESV)

WITH ITS EVERYDAY IMAGE OF a cup, this verse jump-started a lot of thoughts today—and two special prayers.

Picture the cup . . . All you have to do is look inside it to see what it holds. Nothing can really hide in there. Pretty clear.

But what about when life isn't so obvious?

Consider another image. A while back I stumbled on an article about—brace yourself—maggots growing under drain trays.

If rinse water and missed food particles collect under the drain tray, it can create a prime breeding ground for the gross critters. Unlike a cup that's easy to see into, underneath those drain trays is only visible if you purposely check.

Knowing how to live for Jesus isn't always clear either. Sometimes our sin hides from us. Sometimes circumstances make us forget to ask Him for help. Sometimes we don't know whether to wait on Jesus or act in faith. Our spiritual "eyes" can't see everything. Jesus helps us look deeper.

Years ago a friend prayed for me, and I still repeat her words: "Let nothing remain hidden that needs to come out."

What a powerful way to put ourselves into Jesus's care and cleansing. We can't see everything. But He can.

I've made a habit to ask a similar prayer: Over every work project, my loved ones, areas where He wants to clean me up, and ways Jesus wants to use me, I ask Him to help me see what I wouldn't normally see on my own. —ERIN KEELEY MARSHALL

FAITH STEP: *Two prayers for today: "Jesus, let nothing remain hidden that needs to come out, and help me to see as You do, noticing things I couldn't normally notice on my own."*

THURSDAY, MARCH 22

Weeping may endure for a night, but joy comes in the morning.
Psalm 30:5 *(NKJV)*

THROUGH YEARS OF CHURCH MINISTRY, my husband and I have shared tears and hugs with scores of grieving friends and church members. I remember those phone calls in the middle of the night, and sometimes accompanying my husband to the hospital, where we prayed with those whose loved ones teetered on the edge of life.

At times, I've added an encouraging phrase to my usual hugs: "It's going to be all right." But was that really what they needed to hear? *No, things are not all right. Will they ever be?* I remember losing my parents and my own nights of weeping. No, I didn't cry as those without Jesus might. Still, *joy* was not my primary emotion the next morning.

But *morning* represents a season in the same way, perhaps, that grief is a season. Heaven doesn't count time as we do (Psalm 90:4). Grief takes time to process. Obviously we don't bury someone we love one day and wake up the next with a light, joyful heart—no matter how sure we are that our precious ones now live in the presence of Jesus. We still feel the pain. But there is life after loss.

Maybe that's what Jesus was trying to tell His disciples before His death, burial, and Resurrection. He promised them peace and the Comforter's presence in their lives after He returned to heaven (John 14). Nothing would ever be the same again after their loss. But renewed joy—and *morning*—would come after *mourning*.

It's the same for us. Because of Jesus's comforting promise, it will be all right again. Morning—and joy—will return in heaven one day.
—REBECCA BARLOW JORDAN

FAITH STEP: *Pray today for those you know who have lost loved ones recently. Ask Jesus to bring them joy in their mourning.*

FRIDAY, MARCH 23

"Therefore repent and return, so that your sins may be wiped away, in order that times of refreshing may come from the presence of the Lord." Acts 3:19 (NASB)

WHENEVER I HEAR THE WORD "repent" I want to run. Maybe it's the fear I felt when walking by a screaming street preacher when I was young. He shouted so loudly that the only word I could periodically make out was *R—E—P—E—N—T*! I didn't even know what it meant, but I knew it sounded scary. It wasn't until years later that I grew to understand the word, and eventually even like it. *Repent* means two things: to turn or to return. It's that simple. And Jesus never shouted this word; He gently offered it to men and women going down the wrong path, or to those who need to come back to Him.

As I grow in maturity I see the need to repent on a regular basis. I'm not ashamed to say it, and it doesn't scare me one bit. I know that the words I speak, attitudes I harbor, habits I feed, agendas I try to push, situations I attempt to take charge of—all start with good intent but can become things that need to "turn or return" if left unchecked by Him.

It's funny that when the apostle Peter taught people to repent, he finished his sentence with "so that... times of refreshing may come from the presence of the Lord." I love that he put *repent* and *refresh* in the same sentence. Perhaps the way to fresh adventure and renewed faith isn't so much in the *pressing forward* as it is in the *turning and returning*. It's refreshing to know that Jesus welcomes both. —GARI MEACHAM

FAITH STEP: *Is there an area of your life that doesn't seem right, but you've tried to ignore? Repent today, and experience God's spiritual refreshment.*

SATURDAY, MARCH 24

When Simon Peter heard that it was the Lord, he put on his outer garment, for he was stripped for work, and threw himself into the sea. The other disciples came in the boat, dragging the net full of fish, for they were not far from the land, but about a hundred yards off. John 21:7–8 (ESV)

I HAVE TWO FRIENDS WHO use opposite approaches in their decision-making. One takes forever to make up her mind, considering all the pros and cons. She procrastinates even after the choice seems obvious. The other friend acts on impulse, choosing without weighing her options. She regrets not thinking things through after she finds herself in an undesirable situation.

Peter is a perfect example of someone who acted impulsively. His quick decisions didn't always work out for the best. During his early years of following Jesus, Peter often acted recklessly. He tended to blurt out his thoughts and act without thinking, which sometimes got him into trouble. He vowed that he would die before denying Jesus, then did that very thing three times within hours. When the soldiers came to arrest Jesus, Peter cut off a man's ear; Jesus reprimanded him and healed the man.

There is one example of Peter's impulsiveness that I do want to imitate. Early one morning after His Resurrection, Jesus called out to His disciples, who had been fishing. Once Peter recognized His risen Savior, he dove into the water and swam to shore. His friends, the boat, the net full of fish—all were forgotten. I want to have that same longing to be with Jesus that Peter had. The kind that makes me dive into His presence every day without thinking twice about it. —DIANNE NEAL MATTHEWS

FAITH STEP: *Consider how you would react if you saw Jesus waiting for you on the beach. Now visualize Him waiting for you to spend time with Him in prayer and Bible reading. Will you hold back or rush toward Him?*

PALM SUNDAY, MARCH 25

Rejoice greatly, Daughter Zion! Shout, Daughter Jerusalem! See,
your king comes to you, righteous and victorious, lowly and riding on
a donkey, on a colt, the foal of a donkey. Zechariah 9:9 (NIV)

DIPLOMATS FACE COMPLEX NEGOTIATIONS WHEN meeting with world leaders. Protocol ensures that each person receives the honor he or she is due. Pageantry and pomp are expected. Rulers may take great offense when their relative status isn't respected.

Yet when the King of kings entered Jerusalem, He rode on a humble donkey. He didn't arrive as a conquering warrior, ready to defeat sinful humanity by force. Instead He came as a suffering servant, ready to bear the cost to rescue us. As the prophet Zechariah foretold, Jesus is righteous and victorious. He is sinless and has defeated the wages of sin: death. Yet He is not a king who has ever demanded the trappings of kingship. As Philippians chapter 2 says, He "did not count equality with God a thing to be grasped, but emptied himself, by taking the form of a servant" (ESV).

Since I want to follow Jesus, I find His example here both inspiring and challenging. It's so tempting to look for deference from others. Perhaps an academic degree or an award deceives me into thinking I'm better than others. Or maybe I feel I've endured more suffering than most, so instead of serving others, I expect them to focus on my problems. If I waste energy on protecting my status, I'll miss out on the wonderful procession of my King.

Instead I can take off the heavy coat of pride. I can wave the palm branches of accomplishments and drop them at His feet. All that I am can join the hopeful cry of "Hosanna," acknowledging the true King Who is mighty to save. —SHARON HINCK

FAITH STEP: *Find a palm branch or another type of branch. Wave it and sing glad hosannas to our true King. Ask Him to create a servant heart in you.*

MONDAY, MARCH 26

For forty days and forty nights he fasted and became very hungry.
During that time the devil came and said to him, "If you are the Son of God,
tell these stones to become loaves of bread." But Jesus told him, "No! The
Scriptures say, 'People do not live by bread alone, but by every word that
comes from the mouth of God.'" Matthew 4:2–4 (NLT)

AS CAREER MISSIONARIES, MY HUSBAND and I rely on financial donations to cover our living expenses. As with any faith-based nonprofit, donations fluctuate for various reasons. When giving is down, then paying bills presents a challenge.

On one such occasion, a friend urged us to join a home-based business in which he was involved. He promised we'd earn a good income that would help support our family.

We asked a few questions and realized that the job would interfere with our ministry. Having enough money was a legitimate need, but satisfying it in that way was not okay.

Jesus experienced a legitimate need, too. He felt ravenous after fasting for more than a month, and yet He refused to turn stones into bread. As author Jill Briscoe says, "Jesus had the power but not the permission." God had not given Him the go-ahead to satisfy His needs in that way at that time, and so He said no.

Every one of us encounters legitimate needs—for a spouse, a bigger house, or a different job. Before we rush to satisfy them, we ought to consider Jesus's example. We might have the desire and the power to take action, but do we have divine permission? Perhaps the Lord has a better plan. —GRACE FOX

FAITH STEP: *What legitimate need do you have today? Talk to Jesus about it. Ask Him for wisdom to know whether you should take action, wait for His permission, or trust Him to provide.*

TUESDAY, MARCH 27

Then he said, "This sorrow is crushing my life out. Stay here
and keep vigil with me." Matthew 26:38 (MSG)

OVER THE YEARS, I'VE OBSERVED many hospital visitors in waiting rooms and at bedsides. Some tire their loved ones with chatter and questions, disturbing their rest and draining their limited energy reserves. Others lend them strength by just being there. They may speak words of comfort, of course, but they are okay with silence. The friends' actions speak volumes, but it's their presence and focus that makes the difference. Even when a person is too tiny or too ill or too near death to know that someone is there with them and loves them, keeping watch is still a good thing.

Jesus dreaded being alone that night in Gethsemane. He struggled in prayer so He brought three friends and asked them to keep watch. They failed Him. Far from watchful and supportive, they repeatedly fell asleep, close only in proximity to the Master.

Like His Father, who walked in the garden with Adam and Eve, He met face-to-face with Moses, was friends with Job, and delighted David with His presence. Jesus loved and enjoyed people. His name, after all, is Emmanuel—God with us. Jesus loves us and wants to be with us.

Sometimes I forget that Jesus truly wants my company and my attention. He sometimes seems more like a concept than someone real. Even when I feel alone, I'm really not. I never am.

You see, Jesus said, "I am with you always, even unto the end of the world" (Matthew 28:20 ASV).

And He is. —SUZANNE DAVENPORT TIETJEN

FAITH STEP: *Use your imagination to see Jesus as you pray. Ask Him to give you an opportunity to lend His strength to someone. Now, be vigilant.*

WEDNESDAY, MARCH 28

For God is pleased when, conscious of his will, you patiently endure unjust treatment. . . . Christ suffered for you. He is your example, and you must follow in his steps. . . . He left his case in the hands of God, who always judges fairly. 1 Peter 2:19, 21, 23 (NLT)

HAVE YOU EVER BEEN TREATED unfairly? I had a relationship in which I thought I'd done everything right. I sincerely sought her best interests, but I believe that she viewed my actions through the lens of her insecurities and misinterpreted my motives. As a result, she falsely accused me of wrongdoing and cut me out of her life.

How could this happen? Everything inside me screamed to defend myself, and to recite her own wrongdoings. I shed many tears as I prayed for God to open her eyes, change her heart, and maybe teach her a lesson in the process.

In the end, I was the one who learned a lesson. As weeks passed, I reflected on Jesus and the suffering He experienced. He certainly did nothing to deserve false accusations, beatings, and, ultimately, crucifixion. He had every right to defend Himself and point out humankind's flagrant sin against Him. But He remained silent. "He did not retaliate when he was insulted. *He left his case in the hands of God, who always judges fairly*" (1 Peter 2:23). What enabled Him to respond in such a way? Knowing that God was His defender.

This truth gave me hope and helped me cope. I chose to follow Jesus's example by trusting God to judge fairly. This meant allowing Him to judge my heart, too, and surrendering this situation's outcome to Him. A huge weight was lifted, and I experienced peace.

Jesus left His case in God's hands. Let's follow in His steps and do the same. —GRACE FOX

FAITH STEP: *We're to follow Jesus's example when we suffer unjustly. Are you doing that? If so, great! If not, what changes do you need to make?*

MAUNDY THURSDAY, MARCH 29

He then began to teach them that the Son of Man must suffer many things and be rejected by the elders, the chief priests and the teachers of the law, and that he must be killed and after three days rise again. Mark 8:31 (NIV)

A FRIEND OF MINE RECEIVED life-altering news the other day. Her disease is not curable, as we all once assumed. It's terminal. Doctors have projected how much time she has left. Not much.

She's ready to be freed from the body that housed her spirit all these years, but is now sabotaging her. I know I'm not the only one who wishes that the news was different. But we, too, are at peace because her peace is so contagious.

I'm moved by her "knowingness." She knows the general time and method by which she will leave this life and enter eternity.

So did Jesus. Mark 8:31 records a sobering moment when Jesus revealed that He knew He had little time remaining on earth. He knew that He would have to suffer "many things." He knew He would be rejected. Killed.

From the way He lived and the devotion He gave to His Heavenly Father and to us, if it had all come as a surprise to Him, He would have still suffered with grace. But He knew. He knew.

"Indescribable suffering is ahead for ME. I'll be rejected by everyone with earthly authority to stop the process. And I will die." Those weren't His exact words, but they describe what He was communicating. The wonder is that He accepted what lay ahead for Him because of us. To save us.

I'm praying for my friend today, and thanking Jesus that despite knowing what was about to happen, He considered our need and kept moving forward. —CYNTHIA RUCHTI

FAITH STEP: *Today, reserve some time to tell Jesus how much it means that He knew the enormity of what He was facing and kept walking forward.*

GOOD FRIDAY, MARCH 30

"For God so loved the world, that he gave his only Son, that whoever believes in him should not perish but have eternal life. For God did not send his Son into the world to condemn the world, but in order that the world might be saved through him. Whoever believes in him is not condemned, but whoever does not believe is condemned already, because he has not believed in the name of the only Son of God." John 3:16–18 (ESV)

I DON'T KNOW IF IT'S a rite of passage, a spiritual milestone, or just my emotional baggage, but some of my Christian journey has been marked by an oppressive feeling of condemnation.

I'm not talking about the point at which I recognized my sinfulness and need for a Savior. When I cried out to Jesus, and He answered with an unmistakable tone of loving acceptance.

No, I'm referring to the sense of shame that sideswipes me when I feel, think, or do something even mildly wrong.

Conviction and condemnation are different things. Conviction is the humbling barometer of my spiritual condition. A useful, gentle, Spirit-inspired sense that I need to confess or correct.

On the other hand, condemnation means disapproval and punishment.

What helps me to overcome these feelings is the comfort of God's Word. John 3:16 is a powerful and often-quoted verse that alone is a complete expression of God's love. Verses 17 and 18 remind us, in a very practical way, that on the Cross, Christ endured the punishment that came with God's disapproval. We justly deserve God's punishment, but I'm thankful for Romans 8:1 (ESV): "There is therefore now no condemnation for those who are in Christ Jesus."
—ISABELLA YOSUICO

FAITH STEP: *When you feel shame-filled rejection, remind yourself that Jesus bore your punishment. In Him, you are lovingly forgiven and accepted.*

SATURDAY, MARCH 31

*But one of his disciples, Judas Iscariot, who was later to betray him,
objected, "Why wasn't this perfume sold and the money given to the poor?
It was worth a year's wages." He did not say this because he cared about
the poor but because he was a thief; as keeper of the money bag, he used to
help himself to what was put into it. John 12:4–6 (NIV)*

HAVE YOU EVER WONDERED HOW Judas—who lived and walked
alongside Jesus for years—could betray His Lord and Savior? I
found some clues in this account in the Gospel of John. On the
surface, Judas might have appeared compassionate and concerned
for the poor, but his underlying motive was selfish.

When I read this, I shook my head. My first thought was that if I
had heard Jesus's words daily and walked in His presence, I would
have resisted temptation. Then the Holy Spirit reminded me that I
do walk in Jesus's presence, and Scripture gives me His words, yet I
also cave in to selfish motives.

Last week, I saw a glowing tribute posted for a project in which
I'd been involved. The names of others who had participated were
listed. My name was not. It stung. Recognition wasn't my conscious
goal. I'd worked on the project to serve Jesus and to help others. Yet
my reaction showed me how muddled my motives truly were.

Like Judas, it can be easy for us to present a face of best intentions, perhaps not even realizing how much our human desires are
entangled in the choices we make.

I thanked Jesus for the painful glimpse into my own heart. I asked
Him to forgive me and to live through me. He emptied Himself
and took the form of a servant, and that's the sort of motivation I
want to have. —SHARON HINCK

FAITH STEP: *Ask Jesus to shine a light on any selfish motives lurking within your
choices. Ask Him to give you His heart of genuine love.*

EASTER SUNDAY, APRIL 1

Praise be to the God and Father of our Lord Jesus Christ! In his great mercy he has given us new birth into a living hope through the resurrection of Jesus Christ from the dead. . . . 1 Peter 1:3 (NIV)

EASTER MARKS CHRISTIANITY'S DEFINING MOMENT: Christ's resurrection and the promise of eternal life alongside the Father in Heaven, free from sin, suffering, and death. This amazing grace is the cornerstone of the Christian faith and distinguishes it from other faith traditions. Whoever believes in Jesus shall not perish (John 3:16) and is a new creation (2 Corinthians 5:17) who can enjoy freedom (John 8:36) and an abundant life (John 10:10). Here and now.

I confess that the transforming wonder of Easter dims in the face of the mundane and massive challenges of daily life. My wary, intellectual skepticism rears its head. Most days I don't feel newly born, spiritually or otherwise. And, at fifty, death from a terminal illness doesn't seem as remote as it once did. Yet, like so many aspects of our faith, the truth trumps my feelings. The wonder of Easter is renewed by seeking Him in quiet reflection.

Peter captures the wonder so beautifully in just a few words. Indeed, how gracious the mercy of our God to have given us new life this side of Heaven and life eternal with Him through Christ even while we were still sinners (Romans 5:8). That is a hope that transforms us and our experience of this world.

The Gospel of Christ on the Cross proclaims, "I love you enough to give my life so you can have new life, full and free." Resurrection Sunday declares, we shall live together in glory forever.
—ISABELLA YOSUICO

FAITH STEP: *This Easter, rejoice in the loving, gracious promise of the resurrected Christ. New life and eternal hope. He is risen indeed!*

MONDAY, APRIL 2

Just say the word, and my servant will be healed. Luke 7:7 (NASB)

I LEARNED A NEW SONG the other day, which I consequently taught, along with the rest of the Praise Team, to our church congregation. It's called "Jesus" and it's by Chris Tomlin. The lyrics are basically qualities of Jesus, things we experience in a relationship with Him. One of my favorite lines says, "You stand in the fire beside me," a nod to the story of Shadrach, Meshach, and Abednego in the fiery furnace. The other best line addresses Jesus directly. It says, "You carry my healing in Your hands."

As so often happens, I got lost in that line when I was playing the piano and singing it. An image came to me of Jesus's hands, calloused from carpentry, scarred from the nails that held Him to the cross. Those hands carry my healing. Specifically, those scars. God on a cross paid for my healing. He went there to purchase it. It is finished. *Finished.* He said the word.

Luke tells the story of a centurion who comes to Jesus and requests healing for his servant. He explains, "I know what it's like to be in command. I have an army at my disposal. All I have to do is say so and it's done—I'm in charge. And I recognize that You're in charge here, Jesus. You don't have to lift a finger. "Just say the word, and my servant will be healed" (Luke 7:7).

Such faith pleased Jesus, and it pleases Him still when we recognize He's in charge and we trust His Word to heal us.
—GWEN FORD FAULKENBERRY

FAITH STEP: *What wound needs healing in your life today? Jesus already paid the price for your wholeness. Walk in the newness of life today.*

TUESDAY, APRIL 3

Can't you see that his kindness is intended to turn you from your sin?
Romans 2:4 (NLT)

MY HEART WAS HEAVY FOR a friend who couldn't get over her feelings of shame for what she'd done in her youth. She'd heard about Jesus, loved Him, but resisted fully embracing what He offered her. She clung to the bars of her personal prison, not knowing the iron door had already been unlocked and opened.

One day, she and I sat across from each other with our teacups resting on a table in a downtown coffee shop. She confessed that she still felt distanced from Jesus because of what she perceived as His disappointment and anger toward her well-aged mistakes.

"When we apply the grace of Jesus to the person we once were, our past becomes memories, cautionary tales, but with no relation to the new person we are in Christ."

Her eyes pooled with familiar tears.

"When Jesus looks at you, His face isn't wearing an expression of disgust, disappointment, or anger," I said. "It's His kindness that leads us to repentance. His kindness."

The words echoed in the space between us. I looked up the verse to make sure I remembered it correctly. "Or do you show contempt for the riches of his kindness, forbearance and patience, not realizing that God's kindness is intended to lead you to repentance?" Romans 2:4, (NIV).

"Is that what you want to do? Belittle the riches of His kindness? Or live in the freedom of repentance?" I waited while my friend swiped at a tear, and I wiped away mine, both of us taking a firmer grasp of this newfound freedom. —CYNTHIA RUCHTI

FAITH STEP: *Kindness leads to repentance. If Jesus's kindness is easy for you to ignore or it hasn't led you to repent, linger over that thought.*

WEDNESDAY, APRIL 4

. . . Everything—and I do mean everything—connected with that old way of life has to go . . . Get rid of it! And then take on an entirely new way of life—a God-fashioned life, a life renewed from the inside and working itself into your conduct as God accurately reproduces his character in you. Ephesians 4:22–24 (MSG)

WHEN I SAW THE FILM, *The Passion of the Christ,* I was deeply touched by the moment when Jesus, stumbling toward Golgotha, said, "I make all things new." I went home and looked up the phrase in my concordance. As far as we know, Jesus didn't utter that phrase on the way to the Cross or, indeed, at any time on earth.

The Greek word, *kainos,* doesn't mean *new* in the context of time but of quality. The Good News brings a new covenant, a new commandment, and a changed character that result in a new person, different in essence. More new things are in our future: a new name for the believer and for the Lord, a New Heaven, New Earth, and a New Jerusalem. It was at this time that Jesus said, "Behold, I make all things new" (Revelation 21:5, NKJV).

And He has. He loved us extravagantly, becoming sin for us and paying the price for those sins with His life. Because of this, we are made new and can walk in the newness of life (Romans 6:4). The old way is dead and gone. As willing participants, we can allow ourselves to be changed from the inside out. New characteristics will surface: gentleness, kindness, purity. We can show the world these qualities through our actions.

"Awake, O sleeper, and arise from the dead, and Christ shall shine (make day dawn) upon you *and* give you light" (Ephesians 5:14, AMPC). Walk in that light! —SUZANNE DAVENPORT TIETJEN

FAITH STEP: *Pay attention to your impulses today. Ask Jesus to help you discern their source—your old or new nature. Act on one from your new nature.*

THURSDAY, APRIL 5

The way God designed our bodies is a model for understanding our lives together as a church: every part dependent on every other part... You are Christ's body—that's who you are! You must never forget this. Only as you accept your part of that body does your "part" mean anything.
1 Corinthians 12:25, 27 (MSG)

WHEN MY HUSBAND AND I recently relocated to Louisiana, our car insurance almost doubled and we paid exorbitant rates to register our vehicles in the state. We also discovered that this area has the nation's highest tax rate. At least we learned that our city taxes included membership in the local recreation center. One evening we registered and toured the pool, track, and fitness equipment. Weeks later, I told Richard that we hadn't lost a single pound. I observed, "Hmmm, I guess you have to do more than join; you have to actually exert effort and participate."

Following Jesus is something else that requires active participation. During the years in our previous location, Richard and I attended the early morning worship service at a large church. We never joined the Bible study classes or served in a ministry. As a result, we never got to know any members and failed to live out what it truly means to be a part of Christ's body.

The Christian life is not like connecting with people on social media. When Jesus says, "Follow me," He's not talking about scrolling through tweets or posts online. He wants us to take our place in His body, filling the unique role He's assigned us, using our special gifts, blessing others and receiving blessings. We can't grow in our faith by signing up and then not showing up, or by simply sitting in a back pew. —DIANNE NEAL MATTHEWS

FAITH STEP: *Consider how you fit into Christ's body. How are you using your gifts? What role do you fill? Ask Jesus where He wants you to get involved.*

FRIDAY, APRIL 6

Then the King will desire your beauty. Because He is your Lord, bow down to Him. Psalm 45:11 *(NASB)*

I TRAVEL SO MUCH THAT sometimes I try to adjust my schedule around getting my hair colored. Once, when I got the message that my stylist was booked, I hunkered down and did what I often do when things don't go my way—I took matters into my own hands. Even though I knew this would have a regrettable ending, I searched the aisle of the grocery store looking for just the right shade of blonde. I don't know what went wrong, but somewhere between my left ear and the crown of my head was a patch of fluorescent yellow that looked like part tennis ball—part manila envelope. It was so bad that it forced me to sit down on my bathroom tile and cry. *Why am I so impatient? Why do I try to fix things I'm not qualified to fix?*

Here's what I learned from a box of Clairol: Jesus wants to "highlight" our lives. He longs to bring color when gray takes over. When we're depressed, anxious, bored, or restless—Jesus specializes in "life" highlights. Only Jesus can cover our ugly roots. Try as we may, we can't cover our own sin and ugliness. These days I'd rather trust Jesus with those stubborn, hard-to-reach areas that I used to hide, rationalize, or ignore. Jesus never has trouble fitting us in. Unlike a stylist, Jesus has unlimited time for us. Our spiritual transformation is critical to Him; that's why we never have to wait for an appointment! —GARI MEACHAM

FAITH STEP: *When you brush your hair today, thank Jesus for the way He highlights your life. Thank Him for covering the ugly roots with beautiful grace.*

SATURDAY, APRIL 7

Anyone who doesn't receive the Kingdom of God like a child will never enter it. Luke 18:17 (NLT)

IN MY FIRST DECADE OUT of college, when I was an editor, I edited a lot of devotions for kids and even wrote some. One thing I appreciate about that demographic is the constant reminder to hold on to childlike faith in Jesus.

Life's challenges make us cynical. It's only through Jesus's hand on us that we're able to trust Him, but even then it can be hard to get past experiences that seem to threaten our beliefs.

Editing books about the Bible's promises that Jesus will be with us, that He is good and loving, that He gives eternal life, raised the simple question of whether I still believed it all. More times than I can count, when I'd go into work with something weighing on my heart or when I needed direction from Jesus, I'd reach for the next set of children's book galleys and read again about Jesus's faithfulness.

Hard for doubts to stick when I spent five days a week encouraging little children to fully believe what the Bible says about Jesus. These were truths I fully believe myself but that can sometimes feel distant and clouded over by life's troubles.

I don't often work on children's books anymore, but I am raising two kids, and I still write devotions. I can't get away from reminders of Who Jesus says He is and reminders that I have a long history with Him.

As children, most of us took at face value whatever our parents or other adults said. Those of us who were taught about Jesus early on likely believed every word about His love and care for us.

Those same promises are good for a lifetime. —ERIN KEELEY MARSHALL

FAITH STEP: *Believe Jesus today. That's it.*

SUNDAY, APRIL 8

Jesus said to them, "Have you never read in the Scriptures: 'The stone the builders rejected has become the cornerstone; the Lord has done this, and it is marvelous in our eyes'?" Matthew 21:42 (NIV)

A FRIEND'S FATHER IS A pastor, and his congregation built a new church. The architectural design is unique. The building stands on a hill—like a light to the surrounding area. But it was constructed using rough and flawed bricks, symbolic of the imperfect community of believers. In spite of our weaknesses, Christ puts us together to form His Church and to work through us.

What a beautiful reminder that Jesus utilizes us even when the world rejects us. I wish I could be a sturdy, gleaming brick, but I have plenty of cracks and a tendency to crumble under pressure. The strength of Jesus's Church is not in the perfection of each individual, but in the mortar of His grace that holds us together, and in the Cornerstone Who is perfect and true and trustworthy.

Jesus understands rejection. He is the foundation of all truth, the corner against which everything else can be measured. Yet He was also rejected. He endured suffering and ridicule, walked the road of death, let His body be broken—all because of His great love for us. Now He invites each of us to be part of His ongoing work on this earth, to fit into His design, to join with other disciples who may also have some rough edges. Together our lives can serve as a temple of worship, a dwelling of shelter for the hurting, and even a home for the lost.

We don't need to be ashamed of our flaws. We can point to the Cornerstone, and trust that Jesus can do His work through the bricks He chooses. —SHARON HINCK

FAITH STEP: *Look at some bricks today. Do you spot any cracks or chips? Offer Jesus your life as a brick, trusting that He can build something beautiful.*

MONDAY, APRIL 9

Share each other's burdens, and in this way obey the law of Christ.
Galatians 6:2 (NLT)

THE OTHER DAY, MY HUSBAND, Scott, asked me if I was going to be a part of the parenting challenge at our church and I burst into tears. Scott looked at me like, "Oh, dear Lord, not again." I tried to explain my imminent nervous breakdown. "It's not that I don't want to be a part of it. I just don't think I can track one more thing." That unleashed the floodgate of my to-do list. "I haven't paid the bills yet. I still have to finish the taxes. The house looks like a tornado ripped through it. I'm behind on my writing. We need to take the car in. Do you think it's leaking oil? I need to get my website up before Mother's Day. You know I am terrible at marketing. I haven't gone to the grocery store for a full run in about three weeks. We are down to eating chocolate chips and spaghetti noodles. And…the kids have early pickup from school today." Scott looked at me and said, "How about I pick up the kids today? Would that help?" That made me cry more. "You would do that for me?" "I would do that for you."

There is nothing so loving and kind as lifting someone else's burden. Especially for someone who is clearly overwhelmed. Jesus loves when we take care of each other. Because in that moment, the person struggling is being loved and the person sharing the burden is being love. We are following Jesus's law of loving Him and loving each other. In those moments both hearts are shaped by the giving and the receiving of love. Goodness abounds. Healing takes place. And we are forever linked with the One Who loves us most of all.
—SUSANNA FOTH AUGHTMON

FAITH STEP: *Is there someone you know who is weighed down by the burdens of life today? Reach out to him or her today in love.*

TUESDAY, APRIL 10

Then Jesus placed his hands on the man's eyes again, and his eyes were opened. His sight was completely restored, and he could see everything clearly. Mark 8:25 (NLT)

SOMETIMES I JUST DON'T UNDERSTAND God's ways. Not a day goes by without my wondering why He allows my only sister to suffer with a chronic illness that's left her housebound for more than two years while He's called me to an international ministry. What in the world is He doing? What is the purpose that for me is yet unseen?

I've watched my sister experience one loss after another and I've not been able to fix her situation. I've cried. I've prayed. I've fasted on her behalf with no results. I just don't get it. I'm like the person described in 1 Corinthians 13:12—"For now we see through a glass, darkly; but then face to face: now I know in part; but then shall I know even as also I am known" (KJV).

I'm staring into a glass such as the ancients used—a mirror made from roughly polished metal. The image I see is blurred. I can't distinguish the features. Nothing's clear. Nothing makes sense.

The word darkly means "a riddle, an enigma." One commentator says a riddle is when "a puzzling question is proposed and the solution is left to conjecture." We can surmise what the answer might be, but our thoughts are mere speculations until He reveals the answer.

And so, I continue to pray and wait and hope. Jesus touched the blind man's eyes and he saw clearly. Someday Jesus will touch my eyes, too. On that day I'll see. The riddle will be solved. The enigma will end. Jesus will bring clarity, and then I'll understand.
—GRACE FOX

FAITH STEP: *Look in a mirror. Thank Jesus aloud for the promise that someday He'll bring clarity to every riddle in your life.*

WEDNESDAY, APRIL 11

And so, when Jesus' name is called, the knees of everyone should fall,
wherever they're residing. Then every tongue in one accord,
will say that Jesus the Messiah is Lord, while God the Father praising.
Philippians 2:10–11 (ISV)

ACCORDING TO THE ALZHEIMER'S ASSOCIATION, millions of Americans are living with Alzheimer's disease. Several of my friends' parents have it, and hearing about their struggles breaks my heart.

The brain is an amazing thing capable of so much—including capturing our memories. Imagine, if when the brain was laid open, every word spoken, and every experience we've had could be observed, like a lifelong video. A few people actually have the uncanny ability to remember everything in their lives. Yet, when Alzheimer's seeps in memories are lost in a mysterious maze.

Not long ago our friend, Vanessa, visited a woman with Alzheimer's. During the visit, Vanessa played the piano. Her fingers flew across the keys while she sang an old hymn, "'Tis So Sweet to Trust in Jesus." Then something amazing happened. The woman, whose memory had faded, joined Vanessa in singing.

The Booth Brothers, a Southern gospel singing team, recorded a song called, "She Still Remembers Jesus' Name." As I listened to their song about a woman with Alzheimer's, I couldn't hold back the tears. Caretakers agree: No matter how many memories or names of loved ones elude the patient, one name always remains for those who are Christ followers. Just as the Psalmist said in Psalm 103:2, TLB: "Yes, I will bless the Lord and not forget the glorious things he does for me." —REBECCA BARLOW JORDAN

FAITH STEP: *Pray for the families of those who are walking through this journey.*
And pray for a cure for Alzheimer's.

THURSDAY, APRIL 12

Holy Father . . . As long as I was with them, I guarded them in the pursuit of the life you gave through me; I even posted a night watch. And not one of them got away . . . John 17:11–12 (MSG)

LAST YEAR I THOUGHT I was ready to become a beekeeper. I'd read my books, had a hive in place, and joined a group of beekeepers who was willing to mentor me. There was only one problem. We have more bears than people in the Upper Peninsula of Michigan and the fence I ordered, which needed to deliver a powerful shock to the first hungry bruin who followed her nose to my hive, was defective. Summer here is short and by the time the replacement part arrived, the bees couldn't have stored enough honey for winter. I was tempted to ignore my mentors and start without the fence, but sanity prevailed.

This year, my protected hives survived while two nearby beekeepers lost their unprotected ones and put their apiaries on the bears' mental menus for years to come. The goal of beekeeping is to *keep* your bees. And keeping them means much more than having them; it also involves watching over them.

When His time on earth was ending, Jesus asked His Father to keep His followers, present and future. He prayed, "Make them holy—consecrated—with the truth; your word is consecrating truth" and "I have made your very being known to them—who you are and what you do—and continue to make it known, so that your love for me might be in them exactly as I am in them" (John 17:17, 26, MSG).

Our safety depends on the nature of our Keeper. We are so safe.
—SUZANNE DAVENPORT TIETJEN

FAITH STEP: *List some people who (or things that) depend on you. Like Jesus, we can remember them in our prayers. Tuck your list where you'll see it daily.*

FRIDAY, APRIL 13

*Come to me, all you who are weary and burdened,
and I will give you rest. Matthew 11:28 (NIV)*

WE'D BEEN RUNNING NINETY TO nothing. The three big kids going all of their separate directions to schools; Stella to Granny and Pa's; Stone and I to work; and then all of the other activities—church, ballgames, friends' houses, etc. It was finally Friday, which is my day off from teaching, and the day of the week that belongs to Stella and me. This particular Friday we had dental appointments scheduled, and my daughter Adelaide was coming, too. The plan was to take her to school (third grade) when we were done.

But when we left the dentist, the sun was shining, and it was time for lunch. We decided to take Adelaide with us and pick up a burger. Then we'd take her back to school. But since it was such a nice day, we picked up a picnic and headed to the park.

By the time we had finished playing, it was too late for Adelaide to go back to school. So we went for ice cream. When Stella finished hers, she exclaimed, "I am so reflated!"

"Do you mean inflated?" Adelaide asked.

"No. Reflated."

"What does reflated mean?"

"You know, fulled up."

I think what Stella meant is the same thing we find when we go to Jesus for rest—He fills us up. We get so busy it makes us weary. We may not even realize how heavy the burden is we're carrying until we set it down at the feet of Jesus. Like a flat tire, Jesus fixes us—reflates us—by giving us rest. —GWEN FORD FAULKENBERRY

FAITH STEP: *Let Jesus reflate you today, through a nap, a good book, a walk, or even coffee with a friend.*

SATURDAY, APRIL 14

He will cover you with his feathers, and under his wings you will find refuge;
his faithfulness will be your shield and rampart. You will not fear the terror
of night, nor the arrow that flies by day . . . . Psalm 91:4–5 (NIV)

MY HUSBAND AND I WERE enjoying a walk at a local park. The trail wound along a river and through deep woods. Although the skies had been blue when we started, we soon felt a few raindrops.

"Do we go back?" I asked.

"It's not too bad," my husband answered.

Soon we heard heavier rain hitting the leaves far overhead. The thick trees protected us so only a light mist reached us. The sensation reminded me of the many times that pain clouded my life, yet Jesus filtered each problem so it didn't drown me. In fact, He probably protected me in ways I never recognized.

We are not untouched by sorrow, loss, and disappointment. But Jesus's love provides shelter and protection. He told Jerusalem that He longed to gather its people under His wing. I wonder if that statement brought this psalm to the minds of the disciples.

The love of Jesus protects our hearts from extra damage that trials could bring. We may face loneliness, but it doesn't need to lead to alienation. We may have financial challenges, but they don't have to cause us to slip into greed or anxiety. We might be wounded by thoughtless actions of others, but with His help, we don't have to give in to bitterness and anger.

Until we reach heaven, there will be stormy days in our lives, but we can walk forward boldly trusting that Jesus will be our shield and give us refuge by His grace. —SHARON HINCK

FAITH STEP: *Think about difficult times in your life. Thank Jesus for sheltering you from additional harm and for walking the painful road with you.*

SUNDAY, APRIL 15

"The prayer offered in faith will restore the one who is sick, and the Lord will raise him up, and if he has committed sins, they will be forgiven him." James 5:15 (NASB)

WHEN I WAS NINE MY family suffered a debilitating blow. My father, after a night of drinking, was in a devastating car accident that left him paralyzed from the neck down. My mom tried her best to handle it all. His six-month stint in ICU, the long list of inherited nursing duties when he came home, and the financial and emotional burden, all of which led her to drinking, too, to soothe the pain. My childhood years were riddled with tears and questions. As I grew up, I blamed my father for most of our pain.

When I gave my life to Jesus in college, ironically, the first thing He dealt with me on was my dad. I knew I needed to forgive him, and more importantly, love him. Dad eventually moved out of our home and lived in the town he'd grown up in. The small hospital in a cozy mountain community housed a room for him, so for two summers I spent every weekend visiting him.

One day I told my dad that I believed he could be healed if we prayed. He didn't know Jesus, but wanted to be free of his physical burdens, so he agreed. I showed him the Scripture where friends of a paralyzed man lowered him before Jesus to be healed, but instead of immediately healing him, Jesus says, "Your sins are forgiven." Dad started to weep, and we prayed as he asked Jesus to heal his heart. He never walked again, but that day his life was restored. Some healings are internal, some are external, and some are eternal. Our role is to pray, and let God do the healing. —GARI MEACHAM

FAITH STEP: *Pray a bold prayer of healing for someone you know. Pray consistently for two weeks without fail and see how the Lord works in you, and in them.*

MONDAY, APRIL 16

Jesus looked at them and said, "With man it is impossible, but not with God. For all things are possible with God." Mark 10:27 (ESV)

I HAVE INVOKED THIS VERSE for inspiration when faced with daunting challenges. I've employed it more like a motivational maxim, turning to Jesus to help me achieve an ambitious goal. I don't know that this is wrong, but I've come to appreciate the power of this verse as eminently practical for handling difficulties.

I have faced a variety of challenges in my life, of both the common and glamorous varieties. My mom was mentally ill, her ability to function fluctuated wildly most of my life. In my thirties, I moved from a major metropolitan area to a very small, isolated town, a difficult adjustment. I also have a child with special needs, switched careers, and started businesses that floundered. My marriage as well has weathered rough patches and dry spells.

While going through each trial, there were times I could see no way out, no hope for a tolerable, let alone happy outcome. Although I'm usually resourceful, energetic, and smart, I could not imagine how a situation could play out in any remotely acceptable way. I have tried hard to figure out or fix a problem without any success. Then, once I concede defeat, I cry out to Jesus.

Jesus has proven Himself able to help me overcome, over and over. With His inimitable timing and perfect way, He finds solutions I could never have imagined. He changes my perspective, sometimes instantly.

Jesus spoke this verse in answer to a question about salvation. I need to be saved from myself and my circumstances every day. I am routinely faced with impossibilities! —ISABELLA YOSUICO

FAITH STEP: *Write down your concerns and put them in a God Box for Jesus to handle. Revisit the box every so often to see how He's done the impossible.*

Tuesday, April 17

I appeal to you, brothers and sisters, in the name of our Lord Jesus Christ . . . that you be perfectly united in mind and thought.
1 Corinthians 1:10 (NIV)

Do you love a rainy day? When clouds shade the sun and the house grows dim, I feel like curling up on the couch and falling asleep as I read.

My hubby, Steve, doesn't like rainy days at all. To him an overcast day is dreary, draining his energy and motivation.

We have different makeups and experiences and tastes. And that's good. We're still on the same team.

The New Testament Church in Corinth faced differences, too, sometimes big ones. Some ate meat, which others thought was wrong. Some favored one leader's teachings over another's style. But they shared a common truth: Jesus was God's Son Who came to die for sinners, a group we're all born into.

I love that Jesus is our center no matter how varied our backgrounds, cultures, perspectives, or life experiences. Honestly, huge differences can arise in any relationship.

But Steve always reminds me of something. If we meet at the Cross, there's nothing we can't work out. He even has drawn pictures, with stick-figure Steve and stick-figure Erin kneeling beneath the cross on top of a hill. Our climb to reach the cross from opposite sides of the hill symbolizes laying aside our selfishness to draw closer to Jesus. As we reach the top, we draw closer to Him and inevitably to each other. —Erin Keeley Marshall

Faith Step: *Consider meeting at the cross over a differing view with someone. How can you bless each other through your differences?*

WEDNESDAY, APRIL 18

And I am certain that God, who began the good work within you, will continue his work until it is finally finished on the day when Christ Jesus returns. Philippians 1:6 (NLT)

FOR YEARS WE HAVE BEEN making affordable updates to our home—painting kitchen cabinets and walls and installing new carpet and tile. But the house still needed a major makeover. So in January, we drew up plans and enlisted a contractor friend to do the work.

First came the patio, a project completed within a week. Then, a few months later, the workers shoved furniture aside and began stripping off wood paneling, scraping popcorn ceilings, and demolishing a bathroom cabinet. They worked with us, so we could remain in the house. For weeks we spread cushions on the empty living room floor, tiptoed over paint tarps, and cooked in our small kitchen, which was further reduced in size by a piano and desk.

We *oohed* and *aahed* over each stage of the transformation. But as the days passed, I began to scrutinize the work more closely: a paint chip here, an unfinished corner there. At one point, my husband reminded me, "Honey, they're not finished yet. They'll take care of all those areas."

He was right. When the work was completed, the house sparkled. Jesus reminded me of a similar spiritual truth. In my impatient moments, I've often wondered, *Will this ever pass?* Jesus, in His gentle but firm way, encourages me with the words in Scripture: "I'm not finished yet. Be patient. I started the work, and I'll finish it. And you'll love the completed product!" —REBECCA BARLOW JORDAN

FAITH STEP: *Identify any areas in which you struggle with impatience. Then remind yourself daily that you are still a work in progress.*

THURSDAY, APRIL 19

"This is my beloved Son, with whom I am well pleased." Matthew 3:17 (ESV)

IN 1961, A SPORTS PROGRAM debuted, which introduced a line in its opening moments that has become a household phrase—"The thrill of victory and the agony of defeat."

Jim McKay of *Wide World of Sports* voiced the phrase with which we all identify. We finally get a fresh-from-the-showroom car (thrill of victory) and have a fender bender three weeks later (agony of defeat). Your daughter gets accepted to the college of her choice (thrill of victory) and then the first bill arrives (agony of defeat). I've lost some weight (thrill) but my cholesterol numbers haven't changed (defeat).

Those words came to mind when I was rereading the chronological progression of one of the thrill moments in Jesus's life. Baptized by John in the waters of the Jordan River, He came up out of the water and saw the heavens opened to Him, the Spirit of God like a dove resting on Him, and heard the Father's voice saying, "This is my beloved Son, with whom I am well pleased."

What a moment! And immediately afterward, He was led into the wilderness to be tempted by the devil.

For forty days it must have felt like agony. No food. Little if any water. The constant nagging of the enemy trying to divert Him from His God assignment. But Jesus did not fail His Father, and He did not fail us. He used the Word of God to claim victory and pave the way so we could, too.

Thrills of victory in our lives that are followed—and aren't they so often?—by agonies of defeat don't have to stay that way. The Bible reminds us to claim victory. —CYNTHIA RUCHTI

FAITH STEP: *If there's an area of your life where you feel defeated, check your arsenal. Your most effective weapon is the one Jesus used—Scripture.*

FRIDAY, APRIL 20

If people say they have faith, but do nothing, their faith is worth nothing.
James 2:14 (NCV)

I FINISHED MY FORTIETH NOVEL just last week. You would think it gets easier. But during the writing process there were times when I thought, *I have no idea where this story is going or who these characters are.* Yes, professionals get confused sometimes. The thing that has helped me through the years when I've gotten overwhelmed and uncertain is just to take the next step. I don't have to think about the next chapter when focusing on the next sentence will do.

Israelites had faith to take a step to cross the Jordan. Abraham had to do the same venturing into an unknown land. David had to take the step toward conquering Goliath, and the prophet Samuel had to take a step toward Jesus's tent, knowing he was about to anoint a new king without any ideas who it was. Noah had to pick up his hammer and turn the pile of gopherwood into an ark. The widow had to take the first step and use the last of her flour and oil to prepare a meal for Elijah. In each of these cases a faith step was needed. And only after they trusted to believe Jesus did things change.

Sometimes we believe that faith steps have to be big and monumental, and sometimes—when we look back on them—they are. But many times in my life they have been simply deciding to obey Jesus in the smallest ways. It's amazing what can get done when we take faith-filled steps. One sentence at a time has led to many books. Where could your faith steps lead you? —TRICIA GOYER

FAITH STEP: *Have you got a faith step that you're afraid to take? Close your eyes and visualize the first thing you need to do to take that step. Then turn to Jesus standing right there with you. He's holding out His hand to step together.*

SATURDAY, APRIL 21

But he gives more grace. Therefore it says, "God opposes the proud but gives grace to the humble." Submit yourselves therefore to God.
James 4:6–7 (ESV)

THIS VERSE USED TO BE confusing to me. Is it really bad to be proud? After struggling with crippling insecurity much of my youth, being a little proud of my abilities or accomplishments seemed like a good thing. But even as I grew into adulthood, humility felt too much like humiliation, and I didn't want any of that.

My understanding of this verse is quite different today. It's deeper and, honestly, even harder to accept. The heart of humility is grateful dependence. Life-giving, empowering, and liberating dependence on God. I now know that my abilities and the fruit they can produce are inextricably tied to Jesus the True Vine. Apart from Him, I can do nothing at all (John 15:5). The moment I try to reclaim my own power and boast even in my heart of my gifts, I meet opposition. And I'm forced to admit that I have a drive to go it alone.

When I come to the end of my own resources and self-will, either by God-given wisdom, obedience, or simple failure, God's grace rushes in. In fact, the more empty, willing, surrendered, and even broken I am, the more He pours out His grace, enabling me to live life, day by day. The more I come to this realization, the easier it gets to submit myself to Him. —ISABELLA YOSUICO

FAITH STEP: *When you feel opposition, like forces are working against you, don't automatically push through or assume it's spiritual warfare. Ask Jesus if the issue is pride. If it is, ask for and receive His forgiveness, and renew your dependence on Him.*

SUNDAY, APRIL 22

So the next generation would know them, even the children yet to be born, and they in turn would tell their children. Then they would put their trust in God and would not forget his deeds but would keep his commands.
Psalm 78:6–7 (NIV)

WHEN I CAMP IN THE rain there seems to be only one advantage—the sound of raindrops on the roof of the tent. It's a soothing melody that has rocked me to sleep on several wilderness canoe trips.

The disadvantages are many—wet or damp boots, socks, clothes, sleeping bag, firewood, and tinder.

Finding a way to get a fire started when the rain has soaked beyond the bark into the core of twigs and branches makes the task a herculean challenge. Once a fire—for cooking or warmth—has been started, woe to the camper who lets the fire go out.

I admire the adventurers who have figured out a way to carry a glowing ember from their campfire to another place on their wilderness travels, so they always have a starter for a new fire available to them. They tuck an ember in a small covered tin where it remains alive on the journey and doesn't burn out.

Jesus—the Faithful One—made it clear that He expects us to watch carefully over the embers of faith in our generation so future generations will have something to work with, an advantage in faith fire-starting.

I'm pondering that thought today as it relates to the daily choices I make in the way I talk about Jesus, church, the Bible…Am I helping or hindering those who come behind me to fan an ember into flame? —CYNTHIA RUCHTI

FAITH STEP: *Fire needs three things—heat, fuel, and oxygen. Consider the ways you are stockpiling and tending those elements for others to use to start faith fires of their own.*

MONDAY, APRIL 23

Then a man named Jairus, a synagogue leader, came and fell at Jesus' feet,
pleading with him to come to his house because his only daughter,
a girl of about twelve, was dying. As Jesus was on his way, the crowds
almost crushed him. Luke 8:41–42 (NIV)

MY DAUGHTER HAS A DEMANDING job with a major newspaper. When I spoke with her after a week of long days, she told me she was looking forward to a weekend of doing nothing. We all enjoy those times to catch our breath, pull away from a full schedule, and reconnect with Jesus. I've learned from Jesus's example of going away to quiet places to pray.

But this morning as I paged through the Gospels, I noticed something new. Over and over, the Bible speaks of the crowds that pressed around Jesus as He taught, and healed, and traveled. For most of us, life clamors around us, so I find it reassuring to see that Jesus kept sharing His love with people in the midst of the noise and chaos.

Yes, Jesus meets with us when we spend time in quiet prayer, or linger in the pew after a worship service. I love those peaceful moments of communion with Him. But those aren't our only times of connection with Him. When work fills our schedule, when people's needs bump against us from all directions, when our day is so jam-packed we feel it might crush us, Jesus reminds us that He is there, too. In the crush. In the crowd. In our need.

Jesus is our ever-present Savior. With Him in our heart, we can go on with our business of being His hands and feet to the world even when life presses against us. —SHARON HINCK

FAITH STEP: *Let Jesus live through you during the busy moments of your day. Sing a praise song while stuck in traffic. Comfort a coworker with a word of encouragement. Or add a message of thanks to an e-mail.*

TUESDAY, APRIL 24

"Go borrow vessels at large for yourself from all your neighbors. . . . Go in and shut the door behind you and your sons, and pour out into all these vessels, and you shall set aside what is full." 2 Kings 4:3–4 (NASB)

HAVE YOU EVER FELT HOPELESS? Swept away by the demands and pressures of life? The woman in this Scripture was at the end of her rope. Her husband had died, and left her with a heap of debt and no income. Creditors were threatening to take her sons as payment for her bills, and in a moment of utter helplessness, she cries out to the prophet Elisha. He tells her to go bang on her neighbors' doors, borrowing any kind of container they may have. She probably felt embarrassed going door-to-door looking for containers, but desperate people are willing to do desperate things...and she was desperate!

This month has been stressful as we've been trying to raise funds for our ministry in Uganda. I would rather scrub toilets than ask people for money. On top of that, fund-raising events cost a lot to put on—and we need to fill the room just to break even. With three weeks to go we're only half full...and I'm feeling desperate. Every day I try to get the word out about the event any way I can. I even started calling it our "oil offering" as I remember this dear woman and the state of her heart. The more we bang on doors and collect containers, the more Jesus promises to fill them. The only hindrance to His filling is when we sit tight and don't move toward faithfully trusting Him to fill our containers—regardless of how scared we feel or empty we come. —GARI MEACHAM

FAITH STEP: *Set a small jar on your desk, counter, or bedside table with a little note that says: "As much as I faithfully collect—God will fill."*

WEDNESDAY, APRIL 25

There is therefore now no condemnation for those who are in Christ Jesus.
Romans 8:1 (ESV)

A FEW MONTHS AGO I was asked to speak to a group of about five hundred teenagers at a Future Business Leaders of America competition. I was in FBLA back in the day, and my daughter is now, and one of her friends mentioned that fact at a planning meeting and that's how I ended up on the stage.

As I prepared for the event I remembered why I would much rather write what I want to say than speak it. Because writing your truth is lonely and hard work but speaking it in front of people is downright scary.

I decided that the only way I might reach them was to be honest. I talked to them about when I was a teenager who cared too much about what others thought of how I looked and how popular I was and how I developed an eating disorder. I told them I was forty-four years old and still learning how to be connected to my own body and how I believe you have to be good to yourself before you can be much good to others.

Later I was telling my friend about it and she said, "I cannot believe you told a group of kids all of that. You are shameless!" I'm not sure she meant it as a compliment, but I took it as one. For a person who never wants people to see her warts, being shameless is a badge of honor. It means I'm becoming more real.

Shame makes us want to hide. Shame says people will never love you if they know your truth. But Jesus says the truth sets us free. The truth is that He knows us and loves us just the same and there's no shame in that. —GWEN FORD FAULKENBERRY

FAITH STEP: *Is there something in your past or present that makes you want to hide? Bring it out into the light of Jesus through prayer.*

THURSDAY, APRIL 26

But despite Jesus' instructions, the report of his power spread even faster, and vast crowds came to hear him preach and to be healed of their diseases. But Jesus often withdrew to the wilderness for prayer. Luke 5:15–16 (NLT)

WE LIVE IN A SOCIETY that encourages us to pursue success: build one's platform, climb the corporate ladder, basically do whatever it takes to make our name and brand and ministry recognizable and effective. While success in itself is fine, we need to be careful not to sacrifice what matters most in the pursuit of it. We don't want to end up feeling like hamsters, exhausted and wondering what went wrong.

For the first decade of my professional writing career and speaking ministry, I said yes to every assignment and invitation for the sake of establishing my platform. My calendar was full but my heart eventually felt empty because I'd expended too much energy on the wrong thing—superficial success in ministry.

It didn't take long to realize that I'd become "an expert at serving God but a novice at being His friend." This quote by author and motivational speaker Bruce Wilkinson changed my perspective. I committed to keeping first things first, trusting that by doing so, everything else would fall into place.

Years later I still strive to align my life with Jesus's example. His calendar was packed with preaching and teaching and healing, but busyness never kept Him from spending time alone with His Father. He pursued prayer over platform, and God's purposes for His life fell into place.

Jesus knew the importance of keeping priorities straight. It worked for Him, and it'll work for us, too. —GRACE FOX

FAITH STEP: *Ask a close friend or family member to share some insights about your priorities. Perhaps he or she sees a danger to which you've been blind.*

FRIDAY, APRIL 27

Precious in the sight of the Lord is the death of his saints.
Psalm 116:15 (ESV)

THE CALL FROM THE REHABILITATION center came around five o'clock that spring morning. My mother-in-law had declined, and the nurse said to come. My husband slipped out of bed, dressed, and left. I laid awake in the darkness and prayed.

Less than an hour later, my phone pinged with Steve's text. His mom had passed peacefully.

My breath got caught in my throat and heaven felt close. I imagined the scene of joy as Jesus held her and heaven's residents cheered. My thoughts lingered there as I got out of bed to let out the dog. The house was quiet, the kids slept, unaware what happened.

And then I opened the back door and raised my head to look outside. I gasped at the fiery sunrise spread across the sky as Jesus led the heavenly host in welcoming a precious believer into everlasting life. I let the tears fall then. I was looking at a reality beyond this earth, and I felt Jesus's Spirit assuring me, "She's finally here, and she's so good!"

She faced difficulties in life. We all do. But I can't stop picturing her standing on the shore of a heavenly sea and running into its depths and swimming without fear of being overcome or growing weary. She's strong and whole, and she'll never suffer again.

As sad as it was, that day of her passing was absolutely beautiful, a picture of what awaits all who know Jesus. Losses will come, but Jesus's presence brings beauty and comfort and joy. —ERIN KEELEY MARSHALL

FAITH STEP: *During which moment(s) of your life have you sensed Jesus's closeness? Reflect on those times and thank Him that He holds your days and your life.*

SATURDAY, APRIL 28

After the vision of these things I looked, and there was a great number of people, so many that no one could count them. They were from every nation, tribe, people, and language of the earth. They were all standing before the throne and before the Lamb, wearing white robes and holding palm branches in their hands. Revelation 7:9 (NCV)

WHEN I HAVE THE CHANCE to visit my hometown, I don't usually get to see all three of my brothers and their wives. Job responsibilities or other commitments often cause one or more of them to miss coming to my mom's house while I'm there, which is often only for a day or less. During those rare occasions when we do manage to all gather for a few hours to eat and visit, my mom says afterward that she felt as though she enjoyed a taste of heaven.

I've heard friends say that stunning scenery in nature represents a glimpse of heaven to them. Personally, I think the best sample of heaven is being in a group of diverse people praising and worshiping Jesus together. People from different backgrounds and cultures, displaying different shades of skin color and distinctive accents, yet united in a single purpose. That's why I love the scene in heaven during the end times of a crowd representing every nation, tribe, people, and language group, joining their voices to praise their Savior.

The Revelation verse reminds me of the truth in Galatians 3:28: "We are no longer Jews or Greeks or slaves or free men or even merely men or women, but we are all the same—we are Christians; we are one in Christ Jesus." (TLB) Imagine the pleasure we bring Jesus when we overcome our differences and focus on worshiping the Savior we have in common. —DIANNE NEAL MATTHEWS

FAITH STEP: *How are you showing the world the unity found in Christ's diverse body? Ask Him to show you specific ways you can more fully live out Galatians 3:28.*

SUNDAY, APRIL 29

David, ceremonially dressed in priest's linen, danced with great abandon before God. 2 Samuel 6:14 (MSG)

RECENTLY DURING THE SUNDAY MORNING praise time at our church, I caught a glimpse of some movement closer to the front. What I saw put a wide grin on my face.

A young boy about five years old was dancing in the aisle, pumping a turquoise toy guitar. With fingers flying and body swaying, he was keeping perfect time with the music while singing the words with all of his heart. As I watched him, unconsciously my hands rose higher and my voice grew louder.

I thought later about King David's exuberant spirit as he accompanied the Ark of the Covenant back to Jerusalem. Filled with enthusiasm that this powerful symbol of God's presence would return to its temporary tent home, David danced unashamedly with great abandon. Others joined in the celebration—but not David's wife, Michal.

When David returned home, his wife greeted him with criticism. Maybe his behavior challenged her proper idea of a king's behavior. Perhaps it indicated her personal insecurities, embarrassment, or jealousy. She missed the true purpose of David's dancing—and the object of his worship. God saw David's behavior as characteristic of a "man after God's own heart," a declaration He often made. Michal's refusal of worship, however, cost her dearly. She remained childless until her death (2 Samuel 6:23).

We, too, can miss the true purpose of worship. Jesus wants us to worship Him. Like the young boy in our church or King David among his peers, we can offer Jesus hearts, minds, and spirits that are totally abandoned to Him. —REBECCA BARLOW JORDAN

FAITH STEP: *Listen to a song of praise. Abandon yourself to Jesus.*

MONDAY, APRIL 30

Just go ahead with what you've been given. You received Christ Jesus, the Master; now live him. You're deeply rooted in him. You're well constructed upon him. You know your way around the faith. Now do what you've been taught. School's out; quit studying the subject and start living it! And let your living spill over into thanksgiving. Colossians 2:6–7 (MSG)

EARLY IN MY CHRISTIAN WALK, I dreamed of doing something great for Christ. I wondered if I would have a ministry, and prayed about what it might be. I'd fallen in love with Jesus, which was so amazing I thought my ordinary life had to become extraordinary.

It stayed pretty ordinary. The best thing that resulted from my well-meaning but self-centered delusions of grandeur was that I spent a lot of time studying the Bible and praying. Our family attended churches that were grounded in the Word and benefited from the friendship and wisdom of the believers we found there.

Somewhere along the way, I went from wanting to do some great thing for Jesus to wanting to respond to whomever and whatever He placed in my life in a manner that might please Him. I started looking for chances to do some little thing that might reflect well on Him even (maybe especially) if no one else ever knew my part in it. I sometimes imagine Jesus as the one I was blessing or picture Him smiling, even winking, when I succeeded in remaining anonymous. And for me, it does spill over into thanksgiving.

Opportunities to live out our faith are all around us. Sometimes the opportunities are big and sometimes they are small.

We probably can't know the difference. But I'm grateful they are there. —SUZANNE DAVENPORT TIETJEN

FAITH STEP: *Today, ask Jesus to help you notice people and situations that call for a loving response. Step up as you can to be Jesus for someone today.*

TUESDAY, MAY 1

How sweet are your words to my taste, sweeter than honey to my mouth!
I gain understanding from your precepts; therefore I hate every
wrong path. Your word is a lamp for my feet, a light on my path.
Psalm 119:103–105 (NIV)

MY MOM, RUTH, IS A letter writer. Each month she writes a letter to all of her grandkids. She writes about what is going on in her life and what she and Dad are up to. She includes trivia questions about each of the grandkids and invites them to text her or call her with the answers. She also sends them five dollars of fun money.

Mom wants to know what is going in her grandkids' lives and she wants them to know that she loves them. She prays for them every day and cheers them on, one letter at a time. My kids rip open their letters like they contain winning lottery tickets. Words are powerful. Love is even more so.

Jesus has written us a love letter, too. His words are powerful and full of light and life. Our lives and hearts change every time we read His words, His thoughts, and His stories because we are engaging with the living Word of God. Jesus enjoys communicating with us. He wants us to throw open His book with great excitement because in His Word, Jesus has given us everything that we need for this life. For the joy and pain and struggle of daily living.

When we connect with Him through His Word, He reminds us of Who He is in all of His marvelous glory. He guides our steps and He reminds us of who we are in Him. The more we know Him, the more we become like Him. And that is way better than a lottery ticket. —SUSANNA FOTH AUGHTMON

FAITH STEP: *Read 2 Peter 1–10. Dive in knowing that Jesus meant it as a love letter to you— letting you in on Who He is and how much He loves you!*

WEDNESDAY, MAY 2

"Therefore do not worry about tomorrow, for tomorrow will worry about itself. Each day has enough trouble of its own." Matthew 6:34 (NIV)

WHEN MY KIDS WERE YOUNG, I insisted on using my grandma's white wicker rocking chair in each of their rooms. Every time I had a baby I moved that rocker into a new nursery, changing the material on the cushion to match the colors that best represented that child.

One night after my son was born I was rocking with extreme throttle as I seemed worried about so many things. Our country had just gone to war, three friends and relatives were diagnosed with cancer, my husband and I were out of work, and my mother-in-law passed away with little warning. Every night I wore out that rocker as I worried myself into a tizzy. The "what-ifs" of life seemed to crowd in on every side—choking out my faith and deadening my ability to pray. Suddenly a thought struck me that stopped my rocking. *"Worry is like a rocking chair. You expend lots of energy on it, but travel nowhere."* I wondered what might happen if instead of "worry rock" I decided to "pray rock." I vowed to take every moment I formerly spent worrying and put it toward prayer. At first it seemed awkward, as if I was forcing myself to say things that weren't reality. But isn't that what prayer does? Change our reality? If you find yourself on a rocker of worry, why not trust the words of Jesus and move toward a "rocking" of faith? —GARI MEACHAM

FAITH STEP: *It takes more energy to worry than to pray, and worry is wasted energy! Pay attention to where you are investing your energy today: worry or prayer?*

THURSDAY, MAY 3

But the LORD said to Samuel, "Do not look on his appearance or on the height of his stature, because I have rejected him. For the LORD sees not as man sees: man looks on the outward appearance, but the LORD looks on the heart. 1 Samuel 16:7 (ESV)

THIS MORNING I GLANCED DOWN at my hands and had to blink. How had my grandmother's hands appeared at the ends of my arms? Wrinkles, crepe-like skin, uneven splotches—surely these couldn't be my hands?

Our bodies undergo changes throughout our lives. Some are positive. As a mother, I've marveled at how much my silhouette could change in pregnancy. However, it's been more difficult for me to adjust to the changes caused by aging. Gray hairs have appeared, eyelids sag, parts of me have shifted. In my mind, I'm still young, but my body reminds me that I'm not.

We all have elements of our appearance that we don't love, and it's challenging when we live in a culture that focuses so much on outward appearance. It comforts me to remember that when Jesus walked the dusty hills of Palestine, He chose rough-hewn fishermen as disciples who probably never made a "best-dressed" list. He reached out to touch lepers, whose disfigurements frightened everyone else away. He visited Zacchaeus who was small in stature.

Jesus our Lord doesn't see as we humans see. He looks into our hearts with eyes of love. He sees the persons we are meant to be and offers to live in us and transform us daily. No matter how our appearance may change, we are accepted and embraced by the One Who redeemed us. —SHARON HINCK

FAITH STEP: *However you feel about your outward appearance, thank Jesus for loving you the way you are, and for caring about your heart.*

FRIDAY, MAY 4

"Look! I stand at the door and knock. If you hear my voice and open the door, I will come in, and we will share a meal together as friends."
Revelation 3:20 (NLT)

MY HUSBAND AND I MEET regularly with another couple to pray for our families and ministries. Most often our get-togethers include coffee and dessert, but sometimes we extend our time by eating dinner together as well.

Time flies when we sit around the kitchen table, swapping stories about how our lives have changed since we last met. We listen, we laugh, and sometimes we cry. Our friendship is one that's built on honesty and trust, and we look forward to its growing even deeper.

The local friendships I enjoy have all blossomed around my kitchen table. It seems that's a safe place, a comfortable space where people relax, remove their masks, and share from their hearts. They feel no judgment, no criticism. They're free to be themselves, to receive love and to give love in return.

Jesus—our most faithful friend—desires kitchen-table intimacy with us. He longs for us to remove the masks we wear in a futile effort to impress Him. He desires that we relax in His presence, to receive His love and to love Him in return. He wants us to share our frustrations and fears, assured that He'll not condemn us. He desires that we express our joys with Him, too.

Kitchen-table friendship with us is what Jesus desires. How much do we desire the same thing with Him? —GRACE FOX

FAITH STEP: *Set an extra plate at your kitchen table today. Let it serve as a reminder that Jesus is present and longs for friendship with you.*

SATURDAY, MAY 5

He cuts off every branch of mine that doesn't produce fruit, and he prunes the branches that do bear fruit so they will produce even more.
John 15:2 (NLT)

CERTAIN SEASONS IRRITATE THE BUDGET-CONSCIOUS part of me more deeply than others. Christmas gift-buying and planting season rank highest. After long winters, my enthusiasm for flowering plants often exceeds the dollars in my pocket.

This year, time and money guided my decision to purchase, on clearance, hanging baskets of ordinary red geraniums. My heart preferred a riot of colors—fuchsia and purple and yellow with trailing vinca vines. But I resigned myself to the geraniums.

Against the variety of green in our yard, the clearance-rack geraniums looked stunning. When my eighty-six-year-old mother-in-law visited from Texas, she was captivated by the show they made.

One morning, the hanging baskets needed deadheading. A few leaves had turned crispy brown, and skeletal flower heads needed to make room for new buds. As I clipped the dead leaves and flowers, my heart swelled with the joy the freshened flowers gave me, and with a reminder of why Jesus would think it important to trim a few things from my life. Dead things. Unhealthy. No longer vital.

The complete picture of who I am is inaccurate unless the dead and useless words or attitudes or regrets are snipped. He is Life. Dead things block His view.

If Jesus is faithfully pinching off or pruning what is no longer vital in my life, mustn't I welcome it as removing that which keeps me from being my best? —CYNTHIA RUCHTI

FAITH STEP: *Check your plants for dead leaves that, when removed, reveal a more healthy-looking plant. Ask Jesus to reveal any dryness in your faith.*

SUNDAY, MAY 6

I have learned to be content whatever the circumstances. Philippians 4:11 (NIV)

"IF ONLY I WAS TALLER." "I wish I was shorter." "I wish I had a bigger house." "I need a smaller place." "The weather is too hot." "I hate cold weather." "I don't like change." "It's too dull around here."

Maybe you've said or heard similar complaints in your life. Unfortunately, complaining is a universal language. But not for the apostle Paul. In the past, I elevated Paul's faith because of his ability "to be content whatever the circumstances." How did he come to that conclusion (Philippians 4:12)?

And then I thought about Paul's life. He went from being a formally educated Jew and persecutor of Christians to a helpless, blind disciple. A dramatic encounter with Jesus on the road to Damascus (Acts 9) eventually turned him into a traveling missionary who experienced imprisonment, danger, and too many near-death experiences to count. But he also made disciples and friends in every city who helped support his ministry. He definitely knew about extreme "circumstances"—both good and bad. Yet Paul remained content.

I read and reread Philippians 4:11 recently until I saw the key word, "learned." In another passage Paul admitted that he struggled, like we all do, with an old sinful nature (Romans 7:18–24). However, here Paul admitted that the same secret of victory, that enabled him to be content in every situation was Jesus.

Jesus is our secret, too. Learning usually involves a teacher. But Jesus is more than that. He's our Friend, our Encourager, our Savior, and our Strength. And Jesus is the best reason I know to turn our complaints into celebrations. —REBECCA BARLOW JORDAN

FAITH STEP: *List your complaints—or the situations in which you complain the most. Then thank Jesus for the ability to overcome each circumstance.*

MONDAY, MAY 7

So we, who are many, are [nevertheless just] one body in Christ, and individually [we are] parts one of another [mutually dependent on each other]. Romans 12:5 (AMP)

SINCE I STARTED KEEPING BEES, I've found that they are more like one organism than seventy thousand separate insects. There are lots of bees in my hives, doing any number of tasks. Nurse bees, scouts, warriors, housekeepers, builders, providers—worker bees fill all these roles in the six short weeks they live, but the queen is the heart of the hive. She is attuned to the well-being of the hive and communicates that state of "queen-rightness."

Even I, the inexperienced beekeeper, notice the tenor of their buzzing and sense their mood. When I first open the observation window, I see a gray and yellow mass. Then I look closer and can see individual bees doing unique work. They work together, share information and food, always paying attention to the queen's scented signals. Every bee is part of the whole.

What seems like chaos isn't. Thousands of bees doing different things could be chaotic if they weren't connected to each other and, more importantly, to their queen—who holds all that wild busyness together. Then it's possible to see each bee and its work as essential to the life of the hive.

My beekeeping has changed my perception of the people around me. I slow down and wonder what part they play, rather than making assumptions and assigning value. I'm also paying closer attention to Jesus, Who "in him all things hold together" (Colossians 1:17, NIV). —SUZANNE DAVENPORT TIETJEN

FAITH STEP: Outside, look for creatures working or playing together. Who guides them? Who guides you? Listen for the voice of Jesus as you watch.

TUESDAY, MAY 8

"For everyone who practices wicked things hates the light and avoids it, so that his deeds may not be exposed. But anyone who lives by the truth comes to the light, so that his works may be shown to be accomplished by God."
John 3:20—21 (HCSB)

MY FORMER HOME WAS NESTLED in dense shrubbery and trees. There were lots of windows, but the light only entered in slivers at certain times of the day, when the sun was just so. During those times, dust and grime in some areas of the house, particularly the kitchen, would suddenly be clearly visible.

If I happened to be standing at my kitchen counter at that time of day, I'd be compelled to clean the newly discovered mess. Sometime later, though, the bright light would subside, as would the conspicuousness of the dirt, and I could return to a false sense of my home's tidiness. This scene would repeat itself, revealing that some dirt and dust remained, even after I'd cleaned up in the bright light.

Since moving to my new home, with its several light-filled rooms, I've been startled to see how very dirty some things are, even things I thought I'd cleaned carefully. Jesus, Himself the Light, graciously documents this phenomenon of my hidden spiritual mess in this verse. In the darkness of my denial, I don't see my defects. But when His light reveals them, I am confronted with my mess yet again.

My loving Savior doesn't uncover my persistent mess to shame me, crush me, or condemn me. He reveals it to underscore anew my dependence on His grace, each and every day. In turn, this humble recognition can motivate me to ask for help with "cleaning" and to thank Him for the saving grace. —ISABELLA YOSUICO

FAITH STEP: *When God reveals a new or old defect, don't wallow. Ask Jesus for a good cleansing and thank Him for His salvation and grace for the day.*

WEDNESDAY, MAY 9

How much more will the blood of Christ, who through the eternal Spirit offered himself without blemish to God, purify our conscience from dead works to serve the living God. Hebrews 9:14 (ESV)

I LOOKED AT OUR COUCH and my jaw dropped. When did that cushion get so stained? We have a rule about no shoes, no pets, no food or drinks, and no jumping on it. But, little by little, occasional mishaps had taken a toll.

I remembered the first smudge I'd seen months ago. It was faint, so I put off cleaning it. But more smudges followed, and now the dirty upholstery was all I saw in the room.

I tried to remember what the warranty covered and the process for getting it cleaned through the furniture store. Ugh. I didn't have time for that. If only we'd all been more careful and hadn't gotten lazy. And if only we'd been diligent to clean it as the dirt was collecting, it wouldn't look so bad now.

Unfortunately, housecleaning isn't the only aspect of life that needs daily maintenance. Far more often, I've discovered a negative attitude has grown to form an ugly spirit inside me.

One unchecked thought can seem harmless. But if we're not diligent, it can open the door and leave another negative thought overlooked. Pretty soon, our spirit can be filthy with ungratefulness, hypocrisy, and more. We can dull the brightness of Jesus in us.

But that tendency was no surprise to Him. He paid with His own blood to wash us and to keep us clean.

As I'm cleaning my couch, I need to remember to talk with Him daily to keep my spirit shipshape. —ERIN KEELEY MARSHALL

FAITH STEP: *Clean something that isn't on your weekly list. Talk with Jesus while you work, and ask Him to clean up areas of your spirit that need it.*

THURSDAY, MAY 10

"Oh, that we might know the Lord! Let us press on to know him, and he will respond to us as surely as the coming of dawn or the rain of early spring."
Hosea 6:3 *(TLB)*

To LISTEN TO MY FRIEND talk about Tom Cruise, you would think she knew him personally. She can name every film project of his career, plus rattle off dates and key events in his lifetime. She will tell you about his personality, character, and future plans. But the fact is, she has never met the man; she gets all her information from magazines and television programs that focus on the entertainment industry.

There's a world of difference between knowing about someone and knowing them for real, isn't there? And knowing *about* Jesus is not the same thing as having a personal relationship with Him. We can study the Bible from an academic standpoint, simply adding to our knowledge and ready facts. Or we can read the Bible with a desire to grow closer to the One Who is at the heart of the Scriptures so we can become like Him. We can follow a prayer routine that seems like submitting a wish list, or spend quiet time reaching out to know Jesus and hear His voice.

How can we get to know Jesus on a deeper, more personal level? By letting go of our self-sufficiency and depending on Him—for everything. Letting obedience to Him and His purposes take precedence over our personal desires and plans. Trusting Him even when He doesn't seem to be answering our prayers. In other words, we come to know Him through the hard stuff.

Our relationship with Christ never stays the same; if we haven't moved closer to Him, we've moved farther away. Even if we know all *about* Him. —DIANNE NEAL MATTHEWS

FAITH STEP: *Prayerfully evaluate your faith-centered activities. Do they lead you to know more about Jesus, or to know Him more personally?*

FRIDAY, MAY 11

The Spirit itself beareth witness with our spirit, that we are the children of God: And if children, then heirs; heirs of God, and joint-heirs with Christ; if so be that we suffer with him, that we may be also glorified together. Romans 8:16–17 (KJV)

MY BROTHER AND I ARE tight. It's just the two of us, and from a young age, we've been best friends. That is not to say we always agree. I'm the oldest and bossiest, and one of the most famous scenes of our childhood was when I cocked my head to one side, placed my hand on my hip, and started giving him instructions. Rather than obeying me, his typical response was, "You can just stop standing big."

It's really hard to characterize our relationship. I love all of my family, and I think I have uniquely close relationships with each of them. But Jim is almost not someone *other* to me. He kind of *is* me. I was thinking morbid thoughts the other day about when we are old and one of us dies. I usually take comfort in the fact that I am three years older and if we are just going by age, I should pass on first. But what if I don't? Women usually live longer than men. The thought sent me into a full-blown panic attack. You see, I don't really know how to be without Jim. His existence validates my own.

That may sound weird, and I don't think it is really, but that's the best I can do to explain it. Anyway, apply it to the above verse. It seems to be exactly the same as God's plan for our relationship with Jesus. We are joint-heirs with Him. All He experiences, we experience, too. And all that is His in the kingdom of God is our inheritance as well. He validates our experience—and without Him we are lost. —GWEN FORD FAULKENBERRY

FAITH STEP: *Perhaps you have a sibling like I do. Or perhaps not, but you do have Jesus. Meditate on what it means to have the perfect brother in Jesus.*

SATURDAY, MAY 12

This certain hope of being saved is a strong and trustworthy anchor for our souls, connecting us with God himself behind the sacred curtains of heaven. Hebrews 6:19 (TLB)

BECAUSE THE LAPTOP THAT MY husband, Larry, uses and the desktop that I work from are in two different locations, our Internet connection is not always the best. Larry will move the laptop to various rooms trying to get better reception. Sometimes it works. Most of the time it doesn't. And occasionally even the wireless printer in my office will disconnect as well. We usually end up disconnecting the modem for a short time, which temporarily solves the problem. But while we wait, we often lose time and patience.

In today's world, we're nearly all connected to each other through the Internet by social media, cell phone texts, or e-mails. Businesses depend on computers for their operations; students need them for research; and even preschoolers love computer games. But losing those links can cause frustration in all of us.

The writer of Hebrews talked about a more important connection in our lives than the Internet. From the beginning, God planned to send His Son as the bond our souls desperately needed. Jesus would be our forever connection to God. We may disconnect fellowship temporarily through sin, but once we have received Jesus as our Savior, that relationship and eternal union cannot be severed (John 10:29). Furthermore, our fellowship is restored the moment we confess our sins to Jesus (1 John 1:9).

Jesus, the One Who has given us new life, is our "strong and trustworthy anchor" and guarantees to keep our God-connection secure. —REBECCA BARLOW JORDAN

FAITH STEP: *Each time you work on your computer or portable device, stop and give thanks that Jesus is your secure, divine connection for eternity.*

MOTHER'S DAY SUNDAY, MAY 13

"In my Father's house are many rooms. If it were not so, would I have told you that I go to prepare a place for you? And if I go and prepare a place for you, I will come again and will take you to myself, that where I am you may be also." John 14:2–3 (ESV)

I STILL HAVE VIVID MEMORIES of the excitement of preparing for each of my baby's arrivals. Even though I rarely sew, during each pregnancy I spent hours making curtains and quilts, and coordinating wall hangings for the nursery.

Preparation included more than stocking up on booties and onesies. My husband and I took classes, read books on the latest childcare advice, and arranged our schedules. Most important, we prepared our hearts, filling them with love, eagerness, and prayers for our baby-on-the-way.

That experience gives me a glimpse into the way Jesus is preparing to welcome us to our new and eternal home. He is designing a place especially for us, His heart full of love and expectation.

In the book of Isaiah, we read another depiction of Christ's love for us. "Can a woman forget her nursing child, that she should have no compassion on the son of her womb? Even these may forget, yet I will not forget you" (Isaiah 49:15, ESV).

When pain, injustice, or loss hits our lives, it's easy to feel forgotten. I return to John chapter 14 for reassurance often. If I, as a flawed, sinful woman, could prepare a place for my child with so much love, then I know that Jesus—the flawless and sinless Lamb of God—will never forget me and is preparing my perfect new home. —SHARON HINCK

FAITH STEP: *Think about the last time you eagerly prepared for a new arrival— a baby, a pet, a friend's visit. Thank Jesus for preparing a home for you with that same eagerness.*

MONDAY, MAY 14

See how very much our Father loves us, for he calls us his children, and that is what we are! But the people who belong to this world don't recognize that we are God's children because they don't know him. 1 John 3:1 (NLT)

THIS MORNING WHEN MY BOYS ran out to the car for school, Addie yelled back, "I love you, Mom." I yelled back, "I love you, too, Addie." It is a good thing to be loved. Those words never get old. Those words fill me up. I can't really describe how much I love those boys. It is beyond words. I would do anything for them. I want them to know that, no matter what, I love them. Even when they disappoint me. Even when we clash over how many video games they should play. Even when they punch each other. Even when they call each other names. At their worst, I love them. Because my love for them isn't based on their actions. It is based on who they are. And they are mine. They know they are mine.

It changes us when we know we are loved. It is foundational, shaping everything from how we feel about ourselves to how we view the world. Jesus, at His very core, is love. That good, strong love encompasses us and tethers us to Him in every moment of every day. Everything about Jesus shouts out, "I know you! And I love you! Not because of what you have or haven't done!" Arms flung wide, He calls out, "I love you because you are Mine!" He is shouting for you. He is shouting for me. He is claiming us as His own. He would do anything for us. He gave His life so that we could be called out, known, and loved. And that changes everything. —SUSANNA FOTH AUGHTMON

FAITH STEP: *Find a wide-open space and shout out to Jesus, "I love You!" Let Him know how His love has changed you from the inside out.*

TUESDAY, MAY 15

An open rebuke is better than hidden love! Wounds from a sincere friend are better than many kisses from an enemy. Proverbs 27:5–6 (NLT)

I APPRECIATE FRIENDS WHO ARE bold and loving enough to point out my flaws. Hearing what they say is never easy. But if I truly want to grow, then accepting their rebuke well is best.

Jesus cared enough about Martha to rebuke her in a loving way (Luke 10:38–42). She'd welcomed Him and the disciples into her home, but then she flew into a panic over meal preparation. Martha scurried around the house, all the while eyeballing her sister, Mary, sitting at Jesus's feet. "Lord, doesn't it seem unfair to you that my sister just sits here while I do all the work? Tell her to come and help me," she demanded.

Jesus's answer probably wasn't what she wanted to hear: "My dear Martha, you are worried and upset over all these details!" Then He said that Mary had discovered what really mattered.

This story doesn't give Martha's response, but we can assume she accepted it well and that she grew as a result. Here's why: She and Jesus interacted briefly after her brother died. If she'd resented Him for His rebuke, that probably wouldn't have happened. And it's unlikely she would have expressed faith in Him as she did (John 11:21–27). The fact that she welcomed Jesus into her grief and declared belief in His deity tells us that her faith had grown since the scene in her home.

Jesus loves us too much to let us behave in ways that grieve Him. He might convict us through the Holy Spirit, or He might speak through a friend. The extent to which we value Him and our personal growth will determine our response. —GRACE FOX

FAITH STEP: *Thank Jesus for loving you enough to rebuke you when necessary. Ask Him to help you receive rebuke well.*

WEDNESDAY, MAY 16

God's there, listening for all who pray, for all who pray and mean it. He does what's best for those who fear him—hears them call out, and saves them.
Psalm 145:18–19 (MSG)

MY HUSBAND, STEVE, WAS AWAY in Texas for work when he came down with food poisoning. Dizzy, dehydrated, and unable to keep anything down, he'd missed the day of work and was dangerously low on time to finish it before flying to Florida for two more jobs. He finally got a prescription that we hoped would provide some relief but then he threw up the first pill. The situation seemed desperate.

After the kids got home from school, I felt powerfully that the three of us needed to pray together for their dad. We sat down, and I began to talk to Jesus about Steve's need for healing and time he didn't have.

Jesus doesn't always say *yes* to our requests, but He does promise to give us what we need. Sometimes those difficult answers grow our faith in tough ways. I wasn't sure what He had in mind to teach Paxton and Calianne, but I was sure His answer would impact their faith.

Shortly after saying *amen*, I texted Steve. Almost immediately a reply text pinged: "In the past fifteen minutes I've been feeling much better! Getting ready to head out now."

I gasped. Jesus's answers sometimes take our breath away. He showed up when we needed Him. Steve needed a speedy recovery. The kids needed to see Jesus respond to their prayers. And I needed Him to look after my family.

We'll recall that day often as Jesus continues to grow our faith. He's working similarly in your life, too. —ERIN KEELEY MARSHALL

FAITH STEP: *What prayer request are you talking about with Jesus? Picture the scene in Heaven, and trust that He's responding with love. Read Psalm 107:28–32 and Philippians 4:6–7.*

THURSDAY, MAY 17

". . . So that He Himself will occupy the first place [He will stand supreme and be preeminent] in everything." Colossians 1:18 (AMP)

EVERYTHING ABOUT ME IS ENOUGH, several popular authors say. As a mom, I'm enough. As a woman, enough. As a wife, I'm enough just the way I am. I'm enough for what I've been assigned in life. And yet, in one critical respect, everything about me is less than.

Whatever in me registers as off the charts—imagination, perseverance, loyalty—has never seen the Jesus Chart.

No language on earth can adequately describe Jesus. I may be faithful, but He is more faithful. I may love people intensely, but Jesus loves them with inexpressible intensity. However nurturing I consider myself to be pales in comparison to His nurturing heart.

Above all. Beyond all. In all. All.

Colossians 1:15–20 (ESV) says it this way, in a biblical hymn: "He is the image of the invisible God, the firstborn of all creation. For by him all things were created, in heaven and on earth, visible and invisible, whether thrones or dominions or rulers or authorities—all things were created through him and for him. And he is before all things, and in him all things hold together. . . . He is the beginning, the firstborn from the dead, that in everything he might be preeminent. For in him all the fullness of God was pleased to dwell, and through him to reconcile to himself all things, whether on earth or in heaven. . . . "

I'm not intimidated by that reality. It bolsters me. This same Jesus—the El Shaddai (More Than Enough)—has invited me to share life with Him and has placed His resources at my disposal. Sounds like just enough, doesn't it? —CYNTHIA RUCHTI

FAITH STEP: *Copy this truth: Jesus + me = More Than Enough.*

FRIDAY, MAY 18

Think about the things of heaven, not the things of earth. Colossians 3:2 (NLT)

MY EIGHTY-SEVEN-YEAR-OLD GRANDMOTHER HAS LIVED with our family for over fifteen years. She mostly uses a walker to get around, and she often tells me, "The hardest job I've ever had is getting old." It's hard to get only a little done when you're used to being busy with kids, a household, and work your whole life. Yet I often see her reading her Bible and praying. I hear her singing praise songs to Jesus throughout the morning. With eight decades of life to look back on, she knows life is fleeting, yet she is joyful as she considers eternity with Jesus.

The older that Grandma gets, the more her thoughts turn to heaven instead of earth. She thinks about reuniting with her husband of fifty years and with old friends. She is eager to see Jesus face-to-face. As Philippians 3:20–21 (NLT) says, "But we are citizens of heaven, where the Lord Jesus Christ lives. And we are eagerly waiting for him to return as our Savior. He will take our weak mortal bodies and change them into glorious bodies like his own, using the same power with which he will bring everything under his control." My grandma is ready for her new body. Ready for living under a new kingdom where everything is under Jesus's control.

Even though it has been challenging caring for an elderly family member in addition to raising my children, it has been a joy. Sometimes I get so busy with the daily stuff that I tend to forget the eternal stuff. And that's when I'll hear my grandma's sweet voice lifting to heaven, "I'll fly away, Oh Glory." It's the reminder I need to hear to transform my mind in preparation for what's to come. —TRICIA GOYER

FAITH STEP: *Spend time with someone from another generation and ask this person to share what heaven means to her or him. Take time to consider living in a new kingdom where everything will be under Jesus's control.*

SATURDAY, MAY 19

Bring a gift of laughter, sing yourselves into his presence. Psalm 100:2 (MSG)

AN EVENT ON MAY 19, 2016, changed at least one woman's life. Donning a *Star Wars* Chewbacca mask she bought as a birthday gift for herself, Candace Payne, a 37–year-old Texas mom, decided to give her friends a few smiles. She recorded a four-minute video of herself wearing the mask, complete with her own hysterical laughter, and uploaded it to Facebook. It went viral.

According to Wikipedia, the "Chewbacca Mask Lady" video broke the all-time record for the most viewed Facebook live videos. Not only that, her fame soared from being an ordinary stay-at-home-mom to a household name within days. She has appeared on shows such as *Good Morning, America*, and Hasbro, the maker of the original *Star Wars* toy, presented her with her own action figure. All because she wanted to share a light moment with friends.

When I stumbled upon Psalm 100:2 in the Message translation, I immediately thought of the Chewbacca Mom incident. I'm more of an Elizabeth Barrett Browning kind of gal—even though two of my coauthored books in the past were humorous inspirationals. Yet I couldn't hold back the laughter while watching Candace Payne's Chewbacca video.

What would happen if I gave Jesus a gift of laughter? I smiled as I pictured myself not only singing but also laughing myself "into his presence." My thoughts continued. *What if I allowed the joy of Jesus's presence and of knowing Him to bubble up like an unstoppable, unquenchable, contagious gift to others around me?*

Holy laughter. No mask needed. —REBECCA BARLOW JORDAN

FAITH STEP: *Read a few Psalms this week, including Psalm 100, and let Jesus put an infectious smile on your heart.*

SUNDAY, MAY 20

The Son of Man came to seek and to save the lost. Luke 19:10 (ESV)

I SAT IN CHURCH HOLDING back tears. I'm not going into specifics here: First because it's too personal, and second because I'd like you to think about a hurt that still troubles your heart.

Mine bubbled up that evening at church while I was otherwise in a season of loss and heartbreak. I was sick of the weight of that burden but couldn't shake it, even as I remembered verses about Jesus's faithfulness.

Sometimes life hurts anyway. And many people live with pain much deeper than what I felt that night.

I also sat in the pew battling the guilt of trying to hide how low I was feeling. Guilt that I wasn't tough enough, that I was too emotional, that I'd drag others down if I didn't keep it together.

And then the teaching leader said something that pierced my soul. It got my attention with the hope I craved. Jesus pursues me.

In a moment I felt released from the pressure to fix things or manage them myself. I felt released from the lie that I had to do most of the pursuing in my relationship with Him. I'd been adding to my grief the total responsibility of pursuing Jesus, lest I lose Him.

Yes, we need to stick close to Him. But sometimes sticking close means surrendering, not chasing Him down. How comforting to realize Jesus is always after my heart.

Yours, too, in the midst of that sorrow, as you wonder if you'll ever feel like yourself again. Whether the source is a broken dream, or security; whether it's the loss of a job, or a loved one; or your health, trust, or faith. Jesus pursues you.

Jesus pursues you. —ERIN KEELEY MARSHALL

FAITH STEP: *Write yourself an IOU for the peace that comes from surrender (not more exhausting effort or guilt), payable by resting in Jesus's pursuit of you.*

MONDAY, MAY 21

Even when I walk through the darkest valley, I will not be afraid,
for you are close beside me. Your rod and your staff protect
and comfort me. Psalm 23:4 (NLT)

WHEN I WAS A LITTLE girl, bridges terrified me. I had nightmares about them. Whenever we drove over a bridge, I crouched down in the floor of the car. (Not sure what I would have done if cars had seat belts back then.) Then I grew up. Now I have no problem driving across a bridge—unless it's a narrow one. Or old and rusty. Or goes up high in the air. Or crosses over a large body of water.

Needless to say, I was not thrilled when we relocated to an area in southeast Louisiana with bridges everywhere. If I want to go pretty much anywhere, I have to cross one of two major bridges (both old). One spans more than a mile-and-half long, curves around and arches to a peak of one hundred and forty feet, crossing over a huge lake. The other bridge is almost as long and high, crosses over water, and on a safety scale of one to ten, earned less than one. I've seen a couple of other nearby bridges even more frightening.

Each time I cross one of these bridges, I pray; yet, I still grip the steering wheel with sweaty palms and hunch forward as I drive. Will the fear ever go away? I can't say, but one thing I do know: each crossing reminds me Who is close beside me. Just like a good shepherd, Jesus has promised to guide, protect, and comfort me no matter what I have to face. Only His presence can give me the courage to cross any bridge I come to, those on the highway and those in life. —DIANNE NEAL MATTHEWS

FAITH STEP: *Name the one thing that scares you most right now. Memorize part or all of Psalm 23 in your favorite translation and apply those words to your situation each time you confront your fear.*

TUESDAY, MAY 22

I'm writing out clear directions to Wisdom Way, I'm drawing a map to Righteous Road. . . . Guard it well—your life is at stake! Don't take Wicked Bypass; don't so much as set foot on that road. Stay clear of it; give it a wide berth. Make a detour and be on your way.
Proverbs 4:11, 13–15 (MSG)

TWO YEARS AGO FLOODING CAUSED massive damage in several states. Too often, a car entering a low area filled with water ended in either a close-call rescue or a drowning tragedy. Lately during flood seasons I've been hearing the National Weather Service emphasize the catchphrase, "Turn Around, Don't Drown." Until I researched those words, I had no idea that the slogan was trademarked almost eleven years earlier, or that most flooding fatalities occurred in cars. Yet drivers still ignore the warning signs.

Like those drivers, I detest detours, too. But too many times over the years I've also ignored other warning signs of danger: childish decisions I made when I refused to accept parental wisdom, or prideful moments when I clung to my rationalizations instead of paying attention to others' advice. Fortunately, my foolish mistakes weren't fatal, but occasionally they did set off a flood of misery. Ultimately, before I could expect any forward progress, I was forced to back up and turn around.

I hope that those rescued drivers learned a lesson. Through His Word, Jesus gives us clear directions with ample warnings to "turn around" so we "don't drown." I have learned to respect those warning signs. Jesus never leaves us on our own, trying to figure out the path by ourselves. He always allows us the opportunity to head again in a safer direction. —REBECCA BARLOW JORDAN

FAITH STEP: *Draw a road sign that says, "Turn Around, Don't Drown." Place that sign where you'll see it often.*

WEDNESDAY, MAY 23

*Fear not, little flock; for it is your Father's good pleasure
to give you the kingdom. Luke 12:32 (ESV)*

SHEEP LIKE GRASS AND HAY, but they love grain. When we shake a bucket of grain, they follow it where they wouldn't otherwise go. We feed grain before breeding and lambing, plus during lactation when a higher level of nutrition results in multiple births, fewer pregnancy complications, and faster growth in the lambs.

Making sure everyone got enough turned out to be a problem. With ground feeders, the bigger sheep threw their weight around and ate too much. The smaller, timid sheep got less, if any. All suffered from either excess or lack. The usually gentle sheep jostled to get to the grain and might have knocked down a child or taken out the shepherd's knees. For everyone's safety and to provide each sheep with what was needed, my husband calculated the recommended headspace for our flock and built a custom walk-through feeder. He ran it down the center of the barn so we were even able to divide the flock by their nutritional requirements.

It was an unqualified success. The sheep loved it and so did I! It was a pleasure to scatter grain down the trough and set cakes of hay at an angle along the racks before calling the sheep. They ate eagerly and appropriately, in safety and peace. I couldn't pull myself away from watching and took joy in their care.

Jesus was speaking to His followers when He said, "Fear not, little flock." Hearers would have been struck by Jesus's love. We, too, can seek our Shepherd's Kingdom, sure of that amazing love.
—SUZANNE DAVENPORT TIETJEN

FAITH STEP: *Think of a time when someone used an endearing term when addressing you. How did it make you feel? Address Jesus in prayer, really meaning the words when you say, "Dear Lord."*

THURSDAY, MAY 24

The Lord said, "Go over to Straight Street, to the house of Judas.
When you get there, ask for a man from Tarsus named Saul.
He is praying to me right now." Acts 9:11 (NLT)

CHICAGO'S O'HARE IS ONE OF the world's busiest airports. Only a divine appointment during my layover could have led me to a woman with a need for God's encouragement. Our polite conversation quickly turned personal.

Years before, she'd adopted two eastern European orphans. Now they were young adults and, sadly, trapped in addictive behaviors.

I knew with certainty that Jesus had orchestrated our meeting. You see, one of my American friends living in eastern Europe had adopted six orphans from the same region. She'd experienced the same fears. Knowing that my friend would gladly offer this gal wisdom and support, I promised to put them in touch by e-mail.

"May I pray for you?" I asked. She nodded.

"Our meeting was an answer to my prayers," she said as we parted ways. I couldn't have agreed more.

Perhaps Saul felt the same sense when Ananias knocked on his door. Struck blind by an encounter with Jesus three days prior, the only thing he knew to do was to pray. As he did, Jesus spoke to Ananias and gave him direct orders to find Saul.

The two men connected. As a result, Saul's sight was restored, the Holy Spirit filled him, and he was baptized.

Do you believe that Jesus is the master of divine appointments? I do. He knows our specific needs and whom to send to lend help or offer encouragement. —GRACE FOX

FAITH STEP: *Recall a divine appointment in your past. Ask Him to give you a divine appointment today and thank Him in advance for the privilege.*

FRIDAY, MAY 25

He will cover you with his feathers. He will shelter you with his wings. His faithful promises are your armor and protection. Psalm 91:4 (NLT)

MY SON, ADDISON, IS MY resident snuggler. Even though he is ten, he will still crawl in bed next to me and add his warmth to mine. As I throw the blankets over him, he tucks his head under my chin. His feather-soft hair tickles my face. He falls asleep in seconds, nestled in the crook of my arm. In that place of warmth and safety, Addison knows he is loved and cared for.

There is something so delicious about snuggling in with Mom and Dad, especially during the winter months here in the San Francisco Bay Area. The wind is whipping the trees, and rain is pattering against the windows. But weather doesn't matter to Addison. Storms come and go but as long as Addison is near us, he feels safe. He knows Scott and I are looking out for him. There is no reason for him to worry.

Just like Addison, we all long to be safe and loved. Jesus is the One Who offers us peace and comfort in the harsh winter days of life. When the days are dark, He invites us to come close. He longs to hold us near until our pounding hearts and worried minds are settled in the richness of His faithfulness. He opens His arms of protection to us, covering up our fear with His truth—the truth that He is caring for us and guarding us with His life. There is nothing that He wouldn't and hasn't done on our behalf. Whatever fears and changes life has for us, Jesus has one plan: to keep us tucked in close to His side, knowing that we are loved. —SUSANNA FOTH AUGHTMON

FAITH STEP: *Wrap yourself in a cozy blanket and have a talk with Jesus. Feel His love and protection surround you in this moment.*

SATURDAY, MAY 26

As the men were leaving Jesus, Peter said to him, "Master, it is good for us to be here. Let us put up three shelters—one for you, one for Moses and one for Elijah. . . ." Luke 9:33 (NIV)

NOW THAT MY GRANDDAUGHTER IS four years old, she's able to FaceTime with me. She carries the phone to her room after her mom calls me. I read her stories, pointing the camera at each picture. My puppets each pop up to chat with her. Sometimes we sing songs at the piano. I've even taken her out to the garden with me, so she can help me pick beans and tomatoes. I treasure these times of connection.

But now that she has a little brother, he sometimes crawls to her room, eager to join the party. Other times her mother wants to tell me something. My granddaughter doesn't like this idea. She says, "This is my time with Grandma," and firmly shuts her door.

Her desire to keep me to herself has reminded me of how often I'm tempted to be that way with my relationship with Jesus. I enjoy encountering Him in the Scripture. I cherish the personal moments of communion I've had with Him. Like the disciples, I want to set up a shelter and camp there indefinitely. As Peter said on top of the mountain with Jesus, "It is good for us to be here."

That wasn't Jesus's plan for His disciples. They needed to head back down the mountain and continue to share the Gospel with others. Their fellowship with Jesus wasn't a gift to be hoarded, and neither is ours. After receiving the joy and love that Jesus pours out to us in our times with Him, it is also good to share Him in the nitty-gritty world that waits at the foot of that mountain. —SHARON HINCK

FAITH STEP: *Linger in the presence of Jesus today in your prayer time. Then ask Him to bring to mind one other person you can share Him with.*

SUNDAY, MAY 27

The thief comes only to steal and kill and destroy. I came that they may have life and have it abundantly. John 10:10 (ESV)

THE SATAN WHOM JESUS DESCRIBES conjures up an image that might have been cooked up by Stephen King and Steven Spielberg. An epic villain, stealing jewels, killing heroes, destroying cities. Such a Hollywood vision is nearly comical and hard to take seriously.

I need only to remember Satan's debut in the Garden of Eden to get a more accurate and sobering perspective on his true nature and methods. Satan appealed to Eve's pride with deception and promises of greatness, planting seeds of doubt about God's goodness. In falling for the scam, Eve forfeited an untroubled life in paradise, in perfect relationship with Adam, nature, and God Himself.

Later, the devil tempted Jesus in much the same way. My pastor says the enemy always lures us in one of three areas: pride, pleasure, and possessions. Satan shows us the bait, not the hook, which leads to our downfall.

I face at least one or another of these temptations every day. Whether it's buying something I can't afford, judging a friend, or eating a plateful of cheese and crackers in bed at night, temptation is ever-present.

Giving in to temptation can steal our peace and joy, kill our relationships, and destroy our families. But in Christ we have the ultimate superweapon and the promise of deliverance from evil and forgiveness when we do fall. —ISABELLA YOSUICO

FAITH STEP: *Tempted? Pause to ask yourself what giving in will steal, kill, or destroy in your life.*

MONDAY, MAY 28

"Not that I speak from want, for I have learned to be content in whatever circumstances. . . ." Philippians 4:11 (NASB)

WE OFTEN HEAR PEOPLE TALK about the pursuit of happiness. Although it's not a horrible pursuit, it's an empty one. Life's real pursuit is contentment. I learned the secret of contentment the hard way. As a young woman, I was surrounded by the lure of wealth and material possessions. Life as a pro-athlete's wife was full of distractions. Better jewelry, nicer clothes, and beautiful homes. But as with any false advertising scheme, once you attain new things they lose their luster.

As soon as I got used to the "good life," it was gone as quickly as it came. We plunged into decades of working as many jobs as we could to keep afloat. So much for luster! During that time I thanked God for the difficulties we faced because my children got to witness parents who worked hard, praised God, and were content with what they had—not bitter about what they lost.

Now my life is a wild mix of several worlds. Part of the year I work in the villages of rural Uganda, loving people who have nothing but the torn shirts on their backs. I also sit in the stands of minor league baseball stadiums, loving the wives and girlfriends of players desperate to break into the major leagues. And sometimes I live among wealthy leaders in the film, book, and sports industries. No matter where we are or whom we are with, our lives mirror the struggle to be content—and the secret is in Christ. As we give our dreams, plans, and agendas over to Him, we begin to understand what it means to be content. —GARI MEACHAM

FAITH STEP: *Take a small notebook and title it "Contentment Commitment." Write about the areas in which you struggle and how you will invite Jesus into the struggle.*

TUESDAY, MAY 29

They burn incense to worthless idols, which made them stumble in their ways, Jeremiah 18:15 (NIV)

WHEN MY CHILDREN WERE SMALL, they were mystified that I so often knew when they were lying to me. "My other superpower," I told them. "That, and having eyes in the back of my head."

I knew what the truth looked like and sounded like from a child. When I heard hesitation or saw eyes darken or dart, my mom instincts sent up a red flag. "Lie alert! Lie alert!"

Jesus made it clear that He is "the way and the truth and the life. No one comes to the Father except through me" (John 14:6, NIV).

So many have forgotten that time-proven premise and adopted other belief systems as their pseudotruth. God the Father proclaimed centuries ago that when we fail to follow the Truth—His Son—we are susceptible to following and sacrificing our lives to lies.

If I believe my solutions are up to me, I'm falling for a lie. If I act out of character with the character of Jesus, I'm living a lie. If I lean on an unstable economy or shaky emotional structure, I serve and give priority to—sacrifice to—a lie rather than the One Who is Truth personified. If I resort to lies, I'm doing the liar's bidding.

"Truth is always the right choice," I told my kids. "Even when there are consequences, always default to the truth. Lies are too easy to trip over. And they rot your soul."

Now that my kids have children, they're using the same lines. And they have keenly calibrated lie alerts. I'm blessed that they also recognize the Truth when they see Him. —CYNTHIA RUCHTI

FAITH STEP: *If you've ever had a relationship with a compulsive liar, you know how liberating it is that a relationship with Jesus means all truth, all the time. The Way. The Truth. The Life. Make that the song your heart sings today.*

WEDNESDAY, MAY 30

For Christ himself has brought peace to us. He united Jews and Gentiles into one people when, in his own body on the cross, he broke down the wall of hostility that separated us. Ephesians 2:14 (NLT)

GROWING UP IN CALIFORNIA AND living much of my life in Montana, I didn't understand much about racial tension until I moved to the South. Little Rock, Arkansas, is known for racial tension. In 1957 when the U.S. Supreme Court ruled that segregation in public schools was unconstitutional, the governor of Arkansas still didn't allow integration. Governor Orval Faubus called in the state National Guard to block black students' entry into Little Rock Central High School. Protestors joined the National Guard, screaming and spitting at the nine students who attempted to enter the school. It wasn't until weeks later that the students were able to enter with the help of federal troops sent by President Dwight D. Eisenhower.

This is part of history, but from what I see in the news, racial tension is still real in our world. Yet just as Jesus brought peace between the Jews and Gentiles, today He continues to bring peace where hostility attempts to divide. When we let His love grow in us, we are able to love each other better.

I am a witness to this. My family attends a multi-ethnic church in Little Rock, and because of Jesus, blacks, whites, and people from other backgrounds worship together. As Colossians 3:15 (NLT) says, "And let the peace that comes from Christ rule in your hearts. For as members of one body you are called to live in peace. And always be thankful." When we allow Jesus to fill us with love and work through us, He will break down the wall that separates us. —TRICIA GOYER

FAITH STEP: *Do you know someone from a different background you'd like to know better? Reach out to them and share the love of Jesus.*

THURSDAY, MAY 31

God disciplines us for our good, in order that we may share in his holiness.
Hebrews 12:10 (NIV)

MY DAD AND I WERE talking about how we might help a couple we know. The wife is addicted to prescription drugs, and while the husband loves her, he's tried five different times to get her to come clean without leaving her and taking the kids. It's never worked. He finally decided to separate, hoping she will get the help she needs. And even though he has her best interest at heart (not to mention the family's), now he's considered the bad guy to his in-laws.

"That's the way most parents are," my dad told me. "I saw it over and over in my time as a school principal. Even when a kid is in the wrong, parents typically take his or her side."

"But it's not really taking the child's side!" I lamented. "It's making them do what's right!"

"I agree with you. But most don't see it that way."

This is the toughest thing about discipline as a parent, and about being disciplined, I suppose. When something hurts, it doesn't feel like love. But feelings can be deceptive. If the long game is health, safety, and happiness in a family, we can't enable dangerous behaviors. That's not love.

It's the same with God, Whose long game with us is to make us like Jesus. He loves us with unconditional love. But in the process of making us like Jesus, He may have to chisel away some sin. And it's painful. It may feel like punishment. But the truth is that He disciplines those He loves. —GWEN FORD FAULKENBERRY

FAITH STEP: *The image of Jesus is worth whatever price you have to pay to get it. Consider how you might submit to the Lord's discipline today, rather than fighting it, so that you can become more like Him.*

FRIDAY, JUNE 1

If you remain in me and my words remain in you, ask whatever you wish....
John 15:7 (NIV)

I'M TRIMMING THE AMOUNT OF "but maybe I'll need this" items from my packing process when preparing for a flight, but have not yet perfected the skill. My luggage was overweight. Again.

On the return trip, I'd reorganized what went in my carry-on bag versus what I could send through my checked bag. My "feels like forty-five pounds" technique turned out to be fairly accurate. So I pulled my Bible from my purse—the heavy, study-helps kind—and asked the airline representative if I could add my Bible to the checked bag before it hit the conveyor belt.

"Certainly." Then she added, smiling, "Although, it would make good reading material for the flight."

Her words held significant meaning for me. I don't want to be far from my Bible. Even the distance between the hold of the plane and where I would sit seemed vast. But her assessment described my need to keep my Bible close for the flight called life.

With technological advances, we're not as used to the idea of frequently consulting a manual as we navigate a difficult assignment. We may watch a tutorial on YouTube. Or click a link that solves a specific dilemma instantly. But life is a flight that requires constant reference to the flight manual—the Bible.

Jesus saw to it that His words would be recorded in the Bible as an expression of eternal truth and a record of His teaching and His love for us. Don't leave home without it. —CYNTHIA RUCHTI

FAITH STEP: *Did you learn how to spell the word Bible, like I did, from the song, "The B-I-B-L-E. Yes, that's the book for me. I stand alone on the Word of God, the B-I-B-L-E!"? Let that song be your background music today.*

SATURDAY, JUNE 2

Not that we dare to classify or compare ourselves with some of those who are commending themselves. But when they measure themselves by one another and compare themselves with one another, they are without understanding. 2 Corinthians 10:12 (ESV)

WHEN MY SON FIRST STARTED riding a bike, he had the habit of looking off to the left or right when he should have been looking, and going, straight ahead. He'd comically veer off track, sometimes plowing painfully into a shrub or curb, toppling over. (I've done the same in my car.)

While looking to others for healthy, helpful guidance in our journey can be a good thing, making comparisons is a trap that prevents us from being who we're designed to be. The Bible asserts that we are wonderfully made, each of us uniquely designed for a purpose that is as unique as we are. By looking at what others are doing, we can find ourselves living someone else's plan instead of our own.

Let's not minimize the consequences of comparison. Comparing ourselves to others, either positively or negatively, is simply no good. Not only does it result in distorting our relationship with others by promoting feelings of either superiority or inferiority, it can also prevent us from fully investing in God's plan for our own lives.

The wisdom of keeping our eyes on Jesus applies. So we can enjoy the luxury of an entirely personal God, one who knows us intimately and has a good, unique plan for our lives.

I want to stay in my own lane, and enjoy the ride while I go where He is leading. —ISABELLA YOSUICO

FAITH STEP: *Ask Jesus for a sense of vision of His plan for you even while you thank Him for what He's doing in and through other people in your life.*

SUNDAY, JUNE 3

The scepter will not depart from Judah, nor the ruler's staff from between his feet, until he to whom it belongs shall come and the obedience of the nations shall be his. Genesis 49:10 (NIV)

I LOVE REVISITING DEPICTIONS OF Jesus in the Old Testament. Here, Jacob is on his deathbed in Egypt. He pronounces blessings over each of his sons. Even though Reuben, Simeon, and Levi are older, the important blessing – being part of the bloodline of Jesus – wouldn't go to them. Israel promises that Judah will be a descendant whom all the nations will honor.

Jesus is the reason for this special family who were called apart. They will endure a troubled history, yet again and again God will preserve a remnant, and protect this line.

After all the generations who passed along this promise, I feel frustrated when I read how slow people were to recognize Jesus as King. Yet when I look at my own life, I find I'm guilty of the same. In Scripture, Jesus challenges me to take up my cross and follow Him, yet I'd rather take up a comfortable quilt and a picnic lunch. He invites me to seek first His kingdom, yet I often seek other things.

When we look at world conflicts, it's good to pray that all the nations would bow in obedience to Jesus and stop the cruelty and injustice. But this verse also reminds us to look to our own hearts and to allow individual obedience to the great Lion of Judah to guide us. The scepter was passed and is now in the hands of our Messiah. Let's bow before His throne, thank Him for the plan that took so many generations to unfold, and offer our service to the plans He is still unfolding in our world. —SHARON HINCK

FAITH STEP: *Doodle a picture of a king, including crown, throne, and scepter. Ask Jesus to help you honor His kingship today.*

MONDAY, JUNE 4

The day of the Lord's return will come unexpectedly, like a thief in the night.
1 Thessalonians 5:2 (NLT)

I REMEMBER LEARNING IN SCHOOL about the San Andreas Fault that runs most of the length of California and how, even back then, seismologists were predicting the Big One would shake that state at any time and dislodge the edge of it into the Pacific Ocean.

Recently, I heard of another fault line predicted to be worse.

The Cascadia Fault runs north of the San Andreas, seven hundred miles through the Pacific Northwest from Cape Mendocino, California, to Vancouver Island, Canada. That fault is getting more precarious because an oceanic plate, eighty miles out to sea and ten thousand feet below the surface, keeps slipping farther beneath a continental plate that isn't giving way. That continental plate will one day buckle and cause an earthquake and tsunami with devastation to make anyone want to escape.

In July 2015, the *New Yorker* published two articles anticipating these effects. The articles warned that the Pacific Northwest is woefully underprepared for that kind of disaster, but multiple warnings and scientific evidence have not motivated most people to act.

That inaction doesn't make sense. Just as well, the promises of Jesus's return, like a "thief in the night," don't phase most people either, even believers in Him.

Today's verse speaks to those who don't yet understand Jesus's saving grace, but it's also vital for believers.

Will I have regrets wishing I'd lived fully for Him? Will our reunion be as glorious as possible? —ERIN KEELEY MARSHALL

FAITH STEP: *Imagine meeting Jesus in five minutes. Would you feel like scrambling to adjust how you're living life today?*

TUESDAY, JUNE 5

The members of the council were amazed when they saw the boldness of Peter and John, for they could see that they were ordinary men with no special training in the Scriptures. They also recognized them as men who had been with Jesus. Acts 4:13 (NLT)

TODAY'S VERSE ASSUMED NEW MEANING for me during my recent trip to Nepal. Teaching at two Bible conferences gave me an opportunity to meet nearly 125 rural church leaders. One was a radiant nineteen-year-old woman.

A couple of years ago, she applied to a three-month Bible training program in Kathmandu. When she arrived, the director considered turning her away. Her clothes were dirty, her hair was unkempt, and she lacked basic social skills. She was too shy to speak and barely literate. But he sensed God telling him to allow her to stay.

Within one month, the awkward teenager blossomed into a bold and beautiful young woman. The secret? She learned how to develop a vibrant relationship with Jesus. She embraced the Word, believing in His promises and applying His commands. She talked with Jesus, and she delighted in His presence.

She returned home upon completing her training. There she faced severe persecution and narrowly survived a knife attack by a neighbor who cursed her for her faith. Despite the hardships, she has become an unstoppable evangelist. Every day she treks miles from village to village telling others about Christ.

Peter and John were ordinary individuals, and she's no different. They amazed the council, and she astounds her countrymen. The change factor, for her, was Jesus. —GRACE FOX

FAITH STEP: *Think of one person whose faith you admire. Ask that person to tell you how she or he came to know Jesus and the difference He's made.*

WEDNESDAY, JUNE 6

"But for you who fear my name, the Sun of Righteousness will rise with healing in his wings. And you will go free, leaping with joy like calves let out to pasture." Malachi 4:2 (NLT)

I RECENTLY BROKE BOTH OF my middle toes. One on each foot. Three weeks apart. You may be asking yourself, "What are the odds?" I have been asking myself the same question. Who knew walking depended so heavily on middle toes? The healing process has been incredibly slow. And I have been incredibly impatient.

Each morning I wake up, hoping that I will be able to put weight on at least one foot. I have been learning two things: (1) crawling really is an amazing workout, and (2) healing takes time. I have no control over the timeline. I have taped the offending toes to their unbroken sisters to stabilize them, lest they be jarred or further injured. I have spent hours on the couch with my feet elevated. I have found that both ice and ibuprofen do wonders for swelling. I am wearing orthopedic shoes, lovely Velcro contraptions, to minimize movement. And then I am sitting and waiting for my body to do the unimaginable work that it is designed to do. Heal. In the stillness. In the waiting. In the invisible. In the presence of Jesus Who loves me.

Sometimes we feel forgotten in our brokenness. But Jesus has healing for us. Whether it is toes or hearts, His purpose is to restore, renew, and resuscitate. Healing rarely happens in the time frame that we are expecting. More often than not, healing is a process of waiting, hoping, and being still. Soaking up His presence and the truth that the One Who heals will do so in His time and His way.
—SUSANNA FOTH AUGHTMON

FAITH STEP: *Is there an area of your life where you are waiting for healing? Offer it to Jesus, knowing that He has healing for you in His time.*

THURSDAY, JUNE 7

"Be dressed for service and keep your lamps burning, as though you were waiting for your master to return from the wedding feast. Then you will be ready to open the door and let him in the moment he arrives and knocks." Luke 12:35–36 (NLT)

THE MORNING OF MY BIRTHDAY, the doorbell rang. Still in my pajamas and barely coherent, I ignored the bell. Later when I was dressed, I peeked outside. A cute gift bag rested beside the door with a note from a friend. While I was delighted by the gift, I was disappointed that I'd missed my friend—because I wasn't ready.

Jesus taught His disciples to be prepared for His return—like servants with the lights on, ready to hear His knock. I've always understood this to mean a readiness for the ultimate last day, when He comes in glory. But I wonder if we can glean another sort of call from these verses. I'd like to wake each day with my heart tuned to hear from Jesus, ready to change course at any time. When something interrupts my plans, I'm more likely to dig in my heels. I rarely stop to consider whether Jesus might be asking for my attention—asking me to let Him into my day. I miss an opportunity for fellowship with Him—all because I wasn't ready.

Today, let's keep our hand on the doorknob, ready to respond when Jesus knocks. In our rushed commute, He may nudge us to offer a cup of coffee to a homeless man. During a chaotic day, He may point out a friend who needs a kind word. In the exhaustion of evening, He may ask us to pray for our spouse.

How exciting life will become as we keep our lamps burning, watching for the ways Jesus arrives in our day. —SHARON HINCK

FAITH STEP: *Think about the ways you get ready for each new day. Ask Jesus to help you keep your heart prepared for His arrival.*

FRIDAY, JUNE 8

*Forgetting what is behind and straining toward what is ahead,
I press on toward the goal to win the prize for which God has
called me heavenward in Christ Jesus. Philippians 3:13–14 (NIV)*

PEOPLE ARE SHOCKED WHEN I tell them that John and I have adopted seven kids, they think we are superstars...either that or they think we're crazy. Yet of all the traits of adoptive parents there are two that stand out. First, we are determined. Second, we are unified. We have to be, with seven kids we are greatly outnumbered!

Yet why would we choose to take on so much? My husband, John, summed it up one day when we were talking. "I don't want to get comfortable and stroll this walk of faith," he told me. "I don't want to get to heaven not having given it my all. I don't want to stand before Jesus and feel that I had anything left." His words reminded me of Paul, "forgetting what is behind and straining toward what is ahead."

Through life we are marketed a life of comfort, beauty, and ease. Catalogs display beautifully designed rooms and products. Commercials urge viewers to "take a break" or "work less and play more." I guarantee that adding more children to our family has made it impossible to keep my house clean or give myself a break, but I am certain that when we reach heaven John and I will be able to stand before Jesus, proud of our goal of doing our best to care for orphans and share Jesus's love. In the end, I believe, it will be worth it. Anything we do for others and for Jesus, and not ourselves, is worth it. Straining and running isn't easy, but it helps to remember that at the end of the run Jesus will be waiting there for us with open arms and a smile of joy on his face. —TRICIA GOYER

FAITH STEP: *Write a list of messages that come from marketing ads. Then write a list of Jesus questions. Ask Jesus to turn your heart to His desires.*

SATURDAY, JUNE 9

On the last day, the climax of the festival, Jesus stood and shouted to the crowds, "Anyone who is thirsty may come to me!" John 7:37 (NLT)

AS A NEW BEEKEEPER, I had to provide a safe water source for the bees. Before I took on this duty I thought, *No problem. There's a lake just down the lane.* Turns out it was more complicated. Bees can't drink from just any body of water. Top-heavy, they flip over and drown in deep water. Without a safe source, they'll go elsewhere—your neighbor's dog bowl or puddles. Thirsty, wandering bees wouldn't endear themselves to my neighbors.

First, I tried a birdbath. The bees checked it out, but rain overfilled it. I drowned some bees before my dog broke the birdbath. I tried dripping water onto a board under a spigot, but couldn't maintain the low flow. I finally found an automatic dog water bowl and filled it with rocks. The water level remains constant and the bees cling to the rock "islands" while they drink.

Water is life's most urgent need. My bees routinely risked everything for it. Jesus craved it during dusty ministry days and on the Cross when He cried, "I thirst!"

Thirst can be a gift, making us seek out what we need. Jesus's invitation at the festival was prophesied by Isaiah, "Is anyone thirsty? Come and drink—even if you have no money!...It's all free...Come to me with your ears wide open. Listen, and you will find life" (Isaiah 55:1–3, NLT).

Jesus knows how to meet our needs. He said, "Blessed are those who hunger and thirst for righteousness, for they will be filled" (Matthew 5:6, NIV). He's our safe supply. —SUZANNE DAVENPORT TIETJEN

FAITH STEP: *Remember a time when you were thirsty. Offer a prayer of thanks each time you drink today.*

SUNDAY, JUNE 10

Jesus wept. John 11:35 (NASB)

THE SHORTEST VERSE IN THE Bible just might be the most profound. "Jesus wept." God cried. Who is this God Who cries?

He's a God who knows all things, from the beginning to the end. And He's all-powerful. My friend, Char, likes to say there are no cracks in His love, which means He's all-loving. There are no instances in which God is not loving, no circumstantial cracks for us to fall through. Nothing escapes Him. Nothing can separate us.

It would seem that a being with this kind of power would never cry. I mean, what do you have to cry about if you already know everything and can change any outcome? It's a mystery.

I've heard the story of Jesus raising Lazarus from the dead all of my life. Every theologian has his or her own take on why Jesus wept. I think He wept for simple reasons. He was sad that His friend died and sad that His friends (Lazarus's sisters) were sad. It's a moment where we glimpse the vulnerability of being human—a God who fully enters into the experience of death, loss, and pain. A God like us, with us, in order to know us.

I need no other explanation of why Jesus wept. Because while it might be interesting to imagine that He cried from a place of infinite understanding—for reasons I can't fathom—it's more important to me that He understands my pain. He understands what it means to be human, powerless, and speechless in the face of death. To gaze into the chasm and see darkness staring back. Resurrection came for Lazarus and his sisters, but not before Jesus wept.
—GWEN FORD FAULKENBERRY

FAITH STEP: *In the deepest chasm of your heart, Jesus is there. Today do something that demonstrates you trust the God Who cries.*

MONDAY, JUNE 11

Therefore we are always confident and know that as long as we are at home in the body we are away from the Lord. For we live by faith, not by sight. We are confident, I say, and would prefer to be away from the body and at home with the Lord. 2 Corinthians 5:6–8 (NIV)

THE CALL CAME IN THE middle of the week. My eighty-nine-year-old dad had not been himself since a brief hospital stay for fluid in his lungs two months earlier. Now his new doctor had hospitalized him again, this time with a diagnosis of advanced lung cancer. Living several hundred miles away and having just moved, I needed a few days to reach his bedside. By the time I arrived, my dad was lying in his hospital room with eyes closed, morphine dripping through an IV to keep him comfortable.

For more than a week, I sat watch with my family. Eventually, his blood pressure dropped so low that nurses could not get a reading. I stood with my hand on his forehead, listening to his occasional soft, shallow breaths. "It's okay, Daddy," I whispered. "You can go on home to Jesus." The last bit of air softly left his lungs and the tiny twitch in his neck muscle ceased. My dad was no longer on this earth.

Despite my sadness, I had the comfort of knowing that my father's last breath ushered him into the presence of His Savior and the beginning of his new, glorious life. Death doesn't seem so scary when we understand that it means stepping into our heavenly home that Jesus has prepared for us. And the worst that life throws at us is not as frightening if we remember that the help we need is instantly available through prayer. Whether we live or die, Jesus is always just a breath away. —DIANNE NEAL MATTHEWS

FAITH STEP: *Listen to your breathing as you think about how close Jesus is to you now. Thank Him for His presence in your life and after death.*

TUESDAY, JUNE 12

And Jesus said to him, "'If You can?' All things are possible to him who believes." Mark 9: 23 (NASB)

WHEN I FINISHED A SPEAKING event this week a kind woman handed me a gift. It was a painted canvas with beautifully etched flowers and a jeweled bumblebee in the left corner. As I turned the painting over, I saw a handwritten note she'd taped to the back of the frame.

According to the laws of aerodynamics the bumble can't fly. Its body is too heavy for its wings. But the bumble doesn't know this fact, and so it flies anyway—for all to see. Remember this when you're losing hope; God's proof that the impossible can be. —A. S. Waldrop

As a woman who seems strangely attracted to impossible things—I felt inspired. If a flapping bumblebee can beat the odds, why can't we? I set out to understand the plight of the yellow-and-black flying fuzz balls and found that, theoretically, they should stay grounded. Their wings are so small that an airplane built with the same proportions would never get off the ground. They also carry large loads of pollen and nectar—sometimes as much as their body mass—simply to help sustain the rest of the bee colony. It's a good thing no one ever told the bumblebee she can't fly—or that she doesn't have the strength to carry her load. *She might panic and quit if she knew she was doing the impossible.* Jesus promises that *all* things are possible to those who believe. Even the bumblebee knows that impossible things happen when they set out to fly. When life feels overwhelming—keep flapping your wings. You're already doing the impossible! —GARI MEACHAM

FAITH STEP: *Put a fresh flower in a vase as a reminder that the lives around us bloom when we do the impossible.*

WEDNESDAY, JUNE 13

And I will give you a new heart, and I will put a new spirit in you.
I will take out your stony, stubborn heart and give you a tender,
responsive heart. Ezekiel 36:26 (NLT)

I CAN'T RESIST A BARGAIN, especially in a craft store. Recently I went to one with my sister. Shelves in a corner held beads and other items. I didn't need anything, but my sister and I rummaged through the bins anyway. And I found something on my mental shopping list: polymer clay. I used to have scads of the stuff but had given it away. Now I needed some to adapt a traditional bee feeder for use with a Kenyan hive. Polymer clay is firm but softens with hand-kneading and holds its shape after baking.

I found out at home why the clay was on sale. It was almost too old to be malleable. When my fingers got tired, my husband took a turn. Sore-handed, I shaped the pieces and heated them. I had no use for the rest—kept longer, the clay would be useless.

When the disciples asked Jesus why He taught the people with parables, He said, "...this people's heart has become calloused; they hardly hear with their ears, and they have closed their eyes. Otherwise they might see with their eyes, hear with their ears, understand with their hearts and turn, and I would heal them" (Matthew 13:15, NIV).

My heart, too, grows dull with disuse. I skim past a familiar Bible verse. I daydream when I think I know where the pastor is going with a sermon. There's a common thread here. Me. Turned inward. My heart closed to what Jesus might want to reveal.

O Jesus, keep me soft. Give me a tender, responsive heart.
—SUZANNE DAVENPORT TIETJEN

FAITH STEP: *Study the word "heart." Focus on what Jesus had to say about it. Ponder what it means to know something in your heart.*

THURSDAY, JUNE 14

We are children of God, and if children, heirs also, heirs of God and
fellow heirs with Christ, if indeed we suffer with Him so that we may
also be glorified with Him. For I consider that the sufferings of this present
time are not worthy to be compared with the glory that is to be revealed to us.
Romans 8:16–18 (NASB)

WE USED TO SING A song by Wayne Watson in a youth group I led when I was an intern. I remember a line that went, "Sometimes a rough and rocky road is going to take you to a beautiful place."

I was reminded of that line yesterday when my family took a hike together. Stone and I have four kids, ages sixteen down to four. We live on a ranch that backs up to the Arkansas River, and our hike took us down a very steep mountain to the shores of the river. It was a wild and woolly walk. I fell once while navigating a ravine full of vines and broken trees. Everybody got scrapes and sore muscles. But after pressing through the challenging course, we came to a place where the river opened up. We sat on a rock and picnicked under a canopy of trees, soaking in dappled sunlight.

The morning before our hike, I had a difficult conversation as a parent, laying down rules my teenager was not happy to follow. The rationale for the rules, and all of the concern that went with it, seemed neither understood nor appreciated. But still we pressed on.

It occurred to me, as I sat by the river, that this is life—the promise of life in Christ. Over and over again, a rough road takes us to a beautiful place. Therein lies my hope. He walks beside us; He leads us along and picks us up when we fall. Then, in His time, He reveals the glory. —GWEN FORD FAULKENBERRY

FAITH STEP: *Are you traveling a rough or rocky road today? Trust Jesus to lead you to a beautiful place.*

FRIDAY, JUNE 15

"*. . . and the two shall become one flesh.' So they are no longer two but one flesh.*" *Mark 10:8 (ESV)*

I MARRIED FOR THE FIRST time in my midthirties and my husband had been married before becoming a Christian. Let's just say we both had a complete set of unmatched luggage.

The first two years of marriage are often challenging under the best of circumstances, and ours were not. It was hard. The honeymoon ended even before it had begun.

Thankfully, I had enough Jesus under my belt not to bail, which is what I've done in previous relationships. In retrospect, I can also see how God conveniently orchestrated our circumstances so that bailing would have been practically impossible, even early on. He kept me still long enough to do what He needed to do.

Having lived alone most of the prior years, it was easy for me to focus on what was wrong with my husband, Ray, failing to recognize that our differences were by design. It was hard to appreciate that maybe, just maybe, our differences could complement each other.

Seeking guidance and comfort in God's Word, one simple truth quickly become apparent: merging two people into one flesh is messy business.

Think about it. Fusing hearts together and making one person out of two people is excruciating. In real life, such a radical procedure would take place over a long period of time.

God's design for marriage is fusion. By lovingly submitting to this process, our partnership can emerge stronger, more unified, and more complete. —ISABELLA YOSUICO

FAITH STEP: *Sit down with someone close to you, and list some of your differences and how they enrich each of you. Thank God for His methods.*

SATURDAY, JUNE 16

"the Father is in Me, and I in Him." John 10:38 (NKJV)

"IF THERE WAS ONE THING that I would wish my father was like, it would be...." How would you answer that? Someone read my blog titled, "Five Characteristics of a Perfect Father," and sent me an e-mail asking me that question. He indicated that many like him didn't have a perfect relationship with their fathers.

I responded that wishing our fathers were different doesn't serve a healthy purpose. Our parents are imperfect people with hurts of their own, many of which we may never discover. Most do the best they can with what they have. What is healthy is to grant forgiveness and to accept the truth that God is the only good, perfect Father.

Wishing doesn't change things. Forgiveness does. While fathers/ parents are still living, there is always hope to renew and refresh relationships with Jesus's help. But after they pass, we can still exercise love and forgiveness through Christ, even after experiencing pain or disappointments.

Jesus was the perfect example on earth, showing us what His Father God was really like (John 10:37–38). Through teaching parables, through His miracles, through His character and actions, and even through the "parenting" of His band of disciples while on earth, Jesus demonstrated the flawless attributes of the Father: unconditional love, unending grace, total forgiveness, undeserved mercy.

Jesus opened the way for a loving relationship with God the Father—one no earthly parent can give. He helps us see our parents through His loving eyes. —REBECCA BARLOW JORDAN

FAITH STEP: *Thank Jesus today for showing you what a perfect father is like. And thank Him for your parents, no matter how imperfect they are or were.*

FATHER'S DAY SUNDAY, JUNE 17

[Jesus said,] "I and the Father are one." John 10:30 (ESV)

IT'S HARD FOR ME TO look at my brother's hands. They remind me of my father's hands. Dad has been gone almost a quarter of a century. Missing him hasn't let up. I'm left with sweet memories and a persistent ache that Dad isn't present to watch the grandkids and great-grandkids grow, to marvel at technological advances (he was such a gadget guy), and rejoice that so many he loved know Jesus.

The ache intensifies when I look at the "architecture" of my brother's hands. Or hear a piece of music Dad loved. Or see his penmanship on a keepsake. But Dad lives on in the kindness I see in my brothers and sisters and their children, the insatiable appetite for learning in those he parented and grandparented, in the way my siblings show their devotion to their spouses.

I no longer purchase Father's Day cards. No place to send them. Maybe I should consider sending cards to my siblings this year for the way Dad's character qualities show up in them.

Imagine what Jesus would write in a Father's Day card to His Heavenly Father. "Dad, Abba, You're the Best!" "Thanks for always being on My side!" "I tell people that You and I are like this," He might write, with a picture of two raised fingers tight against one another.

In a way the human mind can't comprehend, Jesus assures us that He isn't just like His Father. He doesn't merely resemble God or reflect His character traits. Jesus and the Father are one. Though my brother's hands resemble Dad's, they're not the same. But in the case of Jesus and His Father, they are! —CYNTHIA RUCHTI

FAITH STEP: *Consider this. Jesus said, "I and the Father are one," after He said, "no one is able to snatch them [us] out of the Father's hand." John 10:29 (ESV). Same hands. How safe and cherished do you feel?*

MONDAY, JUNE 18

Who shall separate us from the love of Christ? Shall trouble or hardship
or persecution or famine or nakedness or danger or sword? . . . No, in
all these things we are more than conquerors through him who loved us.
Romans 8:35, 37 (NIV)

I ENJOY PLAYING VIDEO GAMES, especially with my daughter. It's fun
to collect coins and gems, to explore virtual lands, and to solve puz-
zles. However, in many of the games, there are bad guys that need
to be defeated to continue making progress. My eye-hand coordination isn't great, and I'm not fast enough to beat them. That's when I
pass the controller to my daughter. She's of the generation that grew
up with computers. She easily trounces the bad guys for me.

Every day, we face enemies we need to conquer. As we explore
our world and gather the blessings Jesus sends our way, we also run
into problems. Romans 8 shares a few of the trials we may face,
then reassures us that we are conquerors over those enemies. But
the last half of verse 37 is vital: "through him who loved us." Jesus
is the Mighty Warrior Who loves us and enables us to confront our
struggles. He is the One Who conquers.

Today I was stressing out over a work problem, putting more and
more effort into conquering it by using my own strength. I felt
defeated and weary. When I remembered that the love of Christ is
constantly and steadfastly at work on my behalf, fighting the battles
for me, the worry lifted. Let's start using frustration and stress as a
signal to hand over the controller to the One Who has conquered
sin and death for us. —SHARON HINCK

FAITH STEP: *Play a computer game. Or work on a crossword puzzle. When you*
get to an obstacle, consider Jesus's offer to let us turn to Him with your struggles.

TUESDAY, JUNE 19

Give thanks to the LORD, for he is good! His faithful love endures forever.
Give thanks to the God of gods. His faithful love endures forever.
Give thanks to the Lord of lords. His faithful love endures forever.
Psalm 136:1–3 (NLT)

I HAVE BEEN KNOWN TO overplay a song. Or as my husband, Scott, says, drive it straight into the ground. But really ... how else can you memorize the lyrics so that you sing it at the top of your lungs in the car? You have to play it over and over and over so that the words can work their way into your soul. So that you can sing without thinking and know the truth of it in the very marrow of your bones. My kids complain when I say, "Hey, let's play that one more time." But I don't just want to hear it over and over again. It's the only way I can truly understand it.

Repetition is a good thing. We need to hear about Jesus's love over and over before it begins to sink in. We need to experience His faithfulness repeatedly in our lives before we can begin to understand His character. We need to hear His voice time after time before we can recognize His truth in our hearts.

Jesus is singing a song of freedom and hope and peace over our lives. It is a tune that we need in our heads and in our hearts, so that we can begin to learn it ... and live it. His faithful love endures forever. It is never going away. Can you feel the truth of it? Can you hear the hope thrumming in between the chords? Can you understand the importance of knowing that Jesus loves you endlessly? He will never leave you or forsake you. Ever. Lean in, listen, and soak it up. —SUSANNA FOTH AUGHTMON

FAITH STEP: *Listen to the song, "No Longer Slaves," online and set it on repeat. Let the words penetrate your heart and know that Jesus loves you beyond measure.*

WEDNESDAY, JUNE 20

And the Good News about the Kingdom will be preached throughout the whole world, so that all nations will hear it; and then the end will come.
Matthew 24:14 (NLT)

MY FRIENDS, ORA JAY AND Irene, lived the first half of their lives as Amish. They were raised in a close-knit community where neighbors helped each other. Young women were taught to cook, sew, and garden. Young men learned how to tend their animals and land. Then this couple met neighbors who had a vibrant relationship with Jesus. Through Bible reading, they discovered God's Word was more about relationship than laws, and they realized that they could please Jesus without living under such strict guidelines of dressing plain or living without electricity. They learned to place all of their faith in Jesus for their salvation, instead of in their works and lifestyle. Yet they still loved all the same things: gardening, cooking, sewing, and caring for animals. That hadn't changed.

Ora Jay and Irene now run Cripple Creek Horse Ranch in Northwest Montana. He provides wagon, carriage, or sleigh rides to groups, and she cooks for guests on their property. They enjoy meeting the people on vacation who have come from all over the world, and they share the Good News of Jesus.

There are times we may question how it's possible to share the Good News about Jesus's kingdom with the world. The truth is that Jesus has given each of us unique abilities. We simply have to believe there are people whom we can connect with who need to hear the truth of what a relationship with Jesus means, as we do what we love best. —TRICIA GOYER

FAITH STEP: *Write down one gift or talent that brings you joy. Ask Jesus to open doors to reach others for Him.*

THURSDAY, JUNE 21

When you obey my commandments, you remain in my love, just as I obey my Father's commandments and remain in his love. I have told you these things so that you will be filled with my joy. Yes, your joy will overflow!
John 15:10—11 (NLT)

A YOUNG MOM INVITED ME to meet her at a nearby park. We spent an hour at the playground and then took her two sons for a walk around the lake in the center of the park.

At one point, the four-year-old ran ahead of us. We watched as he darted for a dock. His mom yelled for him to stop, but he didn't listen. She sprinted after him, grabbed his hand, and brought him back to where I waited with the baby in the stroller.

The woman knelt beside her son and explained his need to obey her. "You're not allowed on the dock without me," she said. "That's a rule you must obey because I want you to be safe."

Whether we're talking about a mother's safety rule or Jesus's teachings for life, the truth remains the same: obedience is for our benefit. He never issues commands to burst our joy bubble. His only motivation for telling us how to think and behave is to enable us to experience life to the fullest.

Just as he did to Eve in the Garden of Eden, Satan sows seeds of doubt in our minds, hoping to dupe us into disobedience. But let's remember the fallout from Eve's choice, and choose obedience instead. Doing what Jesus says—forgiving our enemies, praying without ceasing, giving thanks in everything, fixing our minds on pure thoughts, and more—brings freedom, peace, and joy—overflowing! —GRACE FOX

FAITH STEP: *Read Colossians 3:5—15. These verses contain numerous commands. How would obeying them produce joy in your life? In contrast, what would result from refusing to obey?*

FRIDAY, JUNE 22

Give him first place in your life. Matthew 6:33 (TLB)

IN THE SUMMER OF 2016, I read a story about a family of five killed in a car crash.

Jamison and Kathryne Pals and their three small children were traveling from Minnesota to Colorado in final preparation to become missionaries to Japan. Their picture showed faces lit with hope and joy, ready to share Jesus's love with faraway people.

Jesus could've used them here. They had such vision, energy, and willingness to uproot their lives. And their desire was to minister to unreached people—the heart of Jesus's Great Commission (Matthew 28:16–20). Few are willing to fully remove themselves, much less their children, from the comforts and dreams this world prizes, in order to do that.

Their story both inspires and haunts me. Their family and friends were clobbered with the unexpected pain of losing them from earth. And it hits me with the question of whether I live my daily life for Jesus first. Their story is filed squarely in the category of my mind titled "Doesn't Make Human Sense."

If we're to be tools for Jesus's Kingdom, why did He remove such willing tools from their usefulness on earth?

Then I felt Jesus's Spirit speak to mine. While He does want to do powerful things for His Kingdom through us, His always-and-forever primary goal is to make us fully His.

From what it sounds like, the Pals parents were His.

He wants us to be His own first, too. —ERIN KEELEY MARSHALL

FAITH STEP: *Take a look at joyofjapan.org to read about the Pals family. Thank Jesus that He wants you as His own.*

SATURDAY, JUNE 23

The bowl of flour was not exhausted nor did the jar of oil become empty, according to the word of the Lord. . . . 1 Kings 17: 16 (NASB)

ONE OF MY FONDEST MEMORIES is standing in my grandmother's kitchen while she made her famous Lemonade Cake. Truthfully, it was just lemon cake from a box—but the frosting was the crown jewel. She thawed bright pink lemonade concentrate from a can, and slowly stirred it into a fluffy mountain of powdered sugar perched in a bowl. As she mixed the lemonade with the sugar, a beautiful pink glaze began to form, and she let us take knives and coat the layers of cake to puffy pink perfection! To this day Lemonade Cake is our family favorite, but to me, that cake means so much more.

When I was a child, a car accident left my father paralyzed from the neck down. My siblings and I would often spend weeks with my grandparents so my mom could catch her breath. Although my grandmother ached for her paralyzed son, she created a haven for us. We woke to fresh griddle cakes with homemade syrup, snap peas and strawberries from her garden, and pink Lemonade Cake that melted in our mouths. Somehow her food brought our tattered lives comfort.

At times, even Jesus used food as ministry. He multiplied fish and bread for the masses, and gathered with His disciples at a last supper before He left the earth. I consider baking a cake to be one of my best ministries and, of course, my cakes are bright pink.
—GARI MEACHAM

FAITH STEP: *Think of someone who would love to receive a homemade cake or other treat. Make time to bake it and deliver it with joy.*

SUNDAY, JUNE 24

There is no fear in love, but perfect love casts out fear. For fear has to do with punishment, and whoever fears has not been perfected in love.
1 John 4:18 (ESV)

THE IDEA OF A GOD I should fear made me uneasy. Fear still wells up when I feel that I've failed. Can I love, trust, and feel safe with a God who's waiting to pounce on my mistakes? I've learned this notion of God is linked to my childhood. I was sometimes afraid of my dad, an alcoholic who was scary when he drank.

Normally charming and full of life and love, Dad's fragile ego would erupt unpredictably after a few drinks. He would criticize me sharply, leaving me in tears. I wanted so much to please him, but always seemed to fall short. I projected some of my earthly dad's traits onto my Heavenly Father, imagining God as a harsh taskmaster, impossible to satisfy.

The Bible offers perspective. The word "fear" in Hebrew is more accurately translated "reverent awe" of the sort due an exalted, powerful authority. Surely, God is that. Yet there is no denying that the Old Testament God also meted out terrifying punishments on wayward believers and unbelievers alike. How can I reconcile that awesome and fearsome God with the perfectly loving God we see vividly in the New Testament? Jesus is the answer.

Unlike our flawed earthly parents, our Heavenly Father is perfect. God is loving and just. Thankfully, as the eternal surrogate for the punishment we deserve, Jesus took the wrath of a fearsome God, enabling us to enjoy the loving parenthood of an awesome God without fear. —ISABELLA YOSUICO

FAITH STEP: *Write down your earthly dad's positive and negative traits. Write down the traits you attribute to our Heavenly Father. Reflect on them.*

MONDAY, JUNE 25

Not neglecting to meet together, as is the habit of some,
but encouraging one another....Hebrews 10:25 (ESV)

WHILE VISITING THE MONTEREY BAY Aquarium in California, I spent the tour with my mouth agape. So much wonder and beauty. An undersea universe, the work of a Divine Designer.

The work of God the Father, Son, and Holy Spirit's hands—present at the dawn of creation (John 1:2)—surpassed anything manmade. Like many people before and after me, I walked past the aquarium displays with a sense of awe. The indispensable purpose in the tiny hairs along the edges of a jellyfish's ruffles. The anemone's diversity of design. The reasons why some starfish are leathery and others crusty. The ballet of sea otters.

As much as I was taken with the sea creatures, I stopped to snap pictures of the placards by many of the exhibits. One said, "Anchovies move together as one in a shimmering school. They find safety in numbers. It's harder for predators to grab just one fish out of hundreds of flashing silver bodies." Safety in numbers.

The teachings of Jesus say, "Forsake not the assembling of yourselves together..." Could it be that part of His reasoning was the same impulse that makes anchovies move as one? Safety in numbers? We protect each other, look out for one another, provide an impressive-looking body that repels predators?

Jesus knew that some people would be called to solitary ministry, for which He designed unique protection. But He knew that most of us would find safety in one shimmering school of Jesus followers.
—CYNTHIA RUCHTI

FAITH STEP: *It's easy to assume that we're alone on this walk of faith. Remind yourself there's spiritual safety in numbers.*

TUESDAY, JUNE 26

The LORD is my strength and my shield; my heart trusts in him, and he helps me. Psalm 28:7 (NIV)

EARLY ON, BOTH MY GRANDFATHER and my father taught me how to watch for the gentle bobbing of the red-and-white ball near the end of my fishing line, and if the cork ducked under the water, how to pull in those wiggly creatures—mostly small catfish, drum, or perch.

But it was my husband who patiently showed me the fine art of bass fishing: the right plastic lures, how to set the hook, the difference between worm, lizard, and top water fishing. Growing up at a fishing camp, he had become what I considered to be an expert.

The other day while we were fishing, I snagged what felt like a huge bass. The tug-of-war began. "Hold your rod tip up!" "Give him time!" Great instructions, but my arms had grown weary from the battle. I had caught my largest fish, nearly eight pounds, last year. But he had taken the bait right beside the boat. This one had grabbed my lure at least twenty yards away.

In the end, my arms gave way as the fish ducked under the boat and wrapped himself around the trolling motor. You always hear about the one that got away. This one looked huge. And I was sick at losing him. But I couldn't catch him with my own strength. In this case, I should have handed the rod to my husband.

Jesus tells us we'll have much more serious battles in life—times where our strength is not enough. We may engage in our own tug-of-war, to reel in our problems by ourselves, only to realize in our failure that we should have depended on Jesus. He's standing by to help, if we'll only ask. —REBECCA BARLOW JORDAN

FAITH STEP: *Are you facing any problems that seem huge right now? Visualize handing them over to Jesus today, and let Him be your strength.*

WEDNESDAY, JUNE 27

... His very breath and blood flow through us, nourishing us so that we will grow up healthy in God, robust in love. Ephesians 4:16 (MSG)

I'D RESUSCITATED A LOT OF babies, but never a lamb. Until one day, I delivered a perfect but deathly still lamb out of our very best ewe. Slime slicked its curls, tinted yellow, a sign of a difficult birth. Drying and stimulation failed, so ventilation—breathing for the lamb—was the last resort. Yes, it was kind of gross, but it worked. When adults or older children need resuscitation, the heart is the focus, requiring compressions and shocks, but in babies (lambs or humans), the problem is almost always the lungs. Breathing has to begin for life to carry on. Often it's all that's needed. Recovery, as with this lamb, can be surprisingly fast and complete.

God breathed life into Adam's nostrils in the beginning. He had Ezekiel prophesy to the dry bones in his vision of Israel. They came together, whole again but not alive until God had Ezekiel call the breath from the four winds to breathe on them, so they'd live. God promised to put them in their own land and to place His spirit in them, so they would know He was the LORD. He promised them a king from David's house. They'd have one Shepherd (Ezekiel 37).

When the Shepherd came, it wasn't what they expected. Few recognized Him. He breathed His last on a Cross. When Jesus showed Himself to his followers that Sunday night, He spoke peace to them, then "...breathed on them and said, 'Receive the Holy Spirit'" (John 20:22, NLT). The One who spoke the stars into existence then breathed on them. It may have seemed like nothing happened. But it did. —SUZANNE DAVENPORT TIETJEN

FAITH STEP: *Breathe on your own hand. The sensation doesn't feel like much, does it? Ask Jesus to breathe on you.*

THURSDAY, JUNE 28

Just as our bodies have many parts and each part has a special function, so it is with Christ's body. We are many parts of one body, and we all belong to each other. Romans 12:4–5 (NLT)

THIS SEASON IN MY LIFE of broken toes and bed rest has changed my perception of how I should be living. I've found that pain and fear have stripped me down to my most vulnerable. I am having to ask for help. Up until this point, I never realized how much I hate doing that.

I like to do life in my own time frame and on my own terms. I want to be able to take care of the details of my life without asking anyone for anything. But Jesus is allowing me to sit in this uncertain place of not being able to do for myself and just...be. I am neck-deep in "I don't knows." I don't know when my feet will be completely better. I don't know how long it will be before I can go grocery shopping by myself. I don't know when I will really get walking with crutches down.

What I am beginning to understand is that....I need people. In fact, this is how Jesus designed life to be. We were supposed to lean on one another. Life is richer when we trust one another. When we care for others. Jesus created us to speak life and light and to build up one another. Our kindness toward others speaks volumes. Our willingness to step in and minister to somebody else mirrors the sacrificial love that Jesus has for us. This belonging to each other reveals the strength found in many, not the weakness of one. And that is powerful. —SUSANNA FOTH AUGHTMON

FAITH STEP: *Who do you belong to? Is there someone who needs to hear your words of light and life today? Write an encouraging note to a friend who needs one.*

FRIDAY, JUNE 29

In Him was life, and the life was the light of all people. John 1:4 (NRSV)

THE SOUNDTRACK FOR MORNINGS AROUND the Faulkenberry house is John Williams's theme from *Star Wars*. While the rest of us bustle around getting ready for work and school, Stella, our four-year-old who stays all day next door at Granny and Pa-Pa's, snuggles in a blanket in front of the TV and watches a *Star Wars* movie.

Some days it's little Anakin in the pod race she's cheering on. Other times it's Yoda or Han Solo or Obi-Wan. But her all-time favorite character is Luke. She studies him. I remember the day she figured out what makes Luke tick.

"Mommy, if you could be any character on *Star Wars*, which one would you be?"

"Anakin," I said without hesitation. "He's the one I relate to the most." She narrowed her eyes at me.

"Who would you be, Stella?"

"Obviously, I would be Luke."

"Why? Why not Leia?"

"Because Luke is the best character in all of the *Star Wars*. He's the bravest and the strongest. He never goes to the dark side because he has loveness in his heart." I pondered this.

"Don't be Anakin, Mommy." Stella wrinkled up her nose. "Anakin has hateness in his heart. That's why he goes to the dark side. But Luke brings him back. Because Luke only has love."

Only love, only light. I am always battling the dark side. But God is love. Jesus is light. And His love brings us back, over and over again. —GWEN FORD FAULKENBERRY

FAITH STEP: *Is darkness a temptation to you? It's true that you can't overcome darkness. But truer still that Jesus can. Choose light and love today.*

SATURDAY, JUNE 30

No, despite all these things, overwhelming victory is ours through Christ, who loved us. Romans 8:37 (NLT)

OCCASIONAL SHOUTS FROM THE NEXT room made it hard to concentrate on my book. After an especially loud outburst, I went to see what had happened. My husband grabbed the remote and replayed the last twenty seconds of the football game. The opposing team had scored a touchdown, leaving ten seconds on the clock. Then, with only four seconds left, one of our players sent a pass toward a teammate in the end zone, who leaped above several players to catch it. As I watched the unexpected ending, I silently acknowledged that I probably would have given up ten seconds too soon.

I hate that I have a tendency to give up too easily. But at least whenever I need a pep talk to help me keep going, I know where to turn. Long before any football coach urged his team to stay in the game, God set down the same message in the Bible. Jesus urges us to keep on praying, keep on seeking, keep on knocking. Other New Testament writers encourage us to persevere, press on, run our race.

Whether our natural inclination is to be a scrappy fighter to the very end, or to give up when it looks like we're defeated, Jesus gives us a reason to keep going through our difficulties. Since He conquered sin, evil, and death, we can live in victory over any situation that comes our way.

There may be times when we look like we are down, but we are never out, thanks to Jesus and His presence and His power within us. And who knows how He will demonstrate His power at the last second? —DIANNE NEAL MATTHEWS

FAITH STEP: *What makes you feel like giving up? A long-term, unanswered prayer request? A troubled relationship? A broken dream? Health problems? Memorize Romans 8:37 and recite it when you start to feel discouraged.*

SUNDAY, JULY 1

But if anyone loves God, he is known by Him. 1 Corinthians 8:3 (NASB)

BEING MARRIED TO THE SHORTSTOP for the New York Yankees certainly had its ups and downs. Because of my husband's job we were sometimes given perks that I was truly grateful for. But other times living in the public eye held many unrealistic standards.

One night we joined another couple for dinner downtown. Midway through the meal I noticed flashes and cameras going off. This wasn't unusual, but what made it strange was that the flashes were coming from outside. People walking by the front of the restaurant noticed that my husband and another ballplayer were eating inside, and the fans were snapping photos from the sidewalk, staging themselves to look like they were sitting next to the players at a meal. Up close the prank was evident, but from afar it looked like they may have been dinner guests! We laughed at the lengths people go to to pretend they know someone… but later I thought about how many people approach a relationship with Christ in the same way.

Some people don't feel worthy so they stay outside the glass, pretending to be at the table while purposely standing back. Would a "famous" Savior actually invite us to be His guests? He already has. We're known by God and invited to His table. We don't have to fake acquaintances—we're welcomed into an intimate relationship that never has to pretend. —GARI MEACHAM

FAITH STEP: *Think about a famous person you admire and imagine what it would be like to be close friends. Now imagine you're invited to intimacy with the God of the universe.*

MONDAY, JULY 2

He told them: "Take nothing for the journey—no staff, no bag, no bread, no money, no extra shirt." Luke 9:3 (NIV)

YES, I'VE SOMETIMES BEEN CALLED out for finding spiritual applications everywhere I look. But, in light of the practical stories and slice-of-life scenes that Jesus used in His teaching, I'm in good company.

I stood before the mackerel display at the Monterey Aquarium, tempted to pass it quickly. Yet another fish. Because of my husband's passion for fishing, I'm well-acquainted with fish, their habits, their habitat, their anatomy, and... their taste.

The mackerel swimming past the tank window seemed ordinary. But it was the shape that formed the life lesson for me.

"Smooth and streamlined, mackerel waste little effort as they swim." So the sign near the tank told me.

How much effort do I waste because I'm not streamlined? I stand in front of my closet, perplexed because I don't know which of my many outfits I should wear that day. I open the pantry thinking about the selections in the freezer and fridge, holding up my dinner preparation because I have too many choices. I thumb through my collection of Bible study materials, debating with myself about which one I should read that day. Soon, the time for study is gone.

Jesus told His disciples to travel lean. Streamlined. We assume He wanted to prove to His friends that He was their provider. But He may also have wanted to communicate that an accumulation of options would only weigh them down and create wasted effort as they swam upstream against the religious current of the day.

Noted, Jesus. Thank You. —CYNTHIA RUCHTI

FAITH STEP: *Toss one extraneous item each day for a month to streamline your closet, pantry, or calendar. Note how it draws you closer to Jesus.*

TUESDAY, JULY 3

Always be full of joy in the Lord. I say it again—rejoice!
Philippians 4:4 (NLT)

I RECENTLY TRAVELED TO NEPAL to provide Bible training for rural church leaders. Eight conferees came from the region that was the epicenter of a massive earthquake in 2015. One afternoon they spoke about the earthquake and how it affected them, but they didn't linger on details. Instead, they focused on the Lord's protection and of His providing food in the quake's aftermath. When they finished talking, the worship music began.

I watched and listened as the men raised their hands and voices heavenward. Smiles lit up their faces, and they burst into dance.

These folks are some of earth's poorest, and yet they model joy, I thought. *They prove that joy doesn't depend on material things and happy times. I have much to learn.*

I suspect one reason my Nepali friends experience true joy amid uncertainty is that they know their future is secure. They've applied Hebrews 12:1–2: "And let us run with endurance the race that God has set before us. We do this by keeping our eyes on Jesus, the champion who initiates and perfects our faith. Because of the joy awaiting him, he endured the cross, disregarding its shame. Now he is seated in the place of honor beside God's throne."

My friends keep their eyes on Jesus. Their faith in Him assures them of even greater joy ahead. They anticipate the day when they'll meet Him in person. Then they'll trade earth's temporary trials for heaven's eternal glory. Oh, that we would experience the same depth of joy!
—GRACE FOX

FAITH STEP: *Identify a joy-buster in your life. Ask Jesus to give you His perspective on the problem and to help you choose joy in the midst of it.*

WEDNESDAY, JULY 4

Keep your eyes on Jesus, our leader and instructor. Hebrews 12:2 (TLB)

YEARS AGO I SIGNED UP for a beginning piano class. The first night the instructor gave us handouts showing the notes for two songs and which fingers to use. Every day I practiced, until I could proudly play the melodies of "Yankee Doodle Dandy" and "Happy Birthday" with my right hand. The second week the teacher added the chords for the songs. *Poof*—my enthusiasm evaporated. Many class members had had lessons in childhood, and I felt like the only total beginner. While I struggled to put the right keys with the correct fingers, those around me could play them immediately. I left discouraged and tempted to drop out.

I've had similar experiences in my spiritual life. I've launched into a ministry filled with enthusiasm, until I compared my performance with somebody else's. Then I began to think that I would never be able to serve God as well as others. The secret to avoiding this type of discouragement is to fix our eyes on Jesus. We are called not to give a perfect performance, but to bring a faith that is daily being perfected through His power. When we consider Jesus rather than how we measure up against those around us, we won't "grow weary and lose heart" (Hebrews 12:3, NIV).

I didn't drop out. And besides mastering "Yankee Doodle Dandy," I learned the danger of not keeping my eyes focused where they should be. In piano class, I need to keep my eyes on the sheet music. In life, I'm better off keeping my eyes on Jesus. I just need to concentrate on doing my best to play the notes He has assigned to me. —DIANNE NEAL MATTHEWS

FAITH STEP: *Do you tend to compare yourself with others and get discouraged? During these times remind yourself to keep your eyes fixed on Jesus.*

THURSDAY, JULY 5

"Yes, I am the vine; you are the branches. Those who remain in me, and I in them, will produce much fruit. For apart from me you can do nothing."
John 15:5 (NLT)

RECENTLY MY HUSBAND AND I traveled with eight of our kids from Arkansas to Montana to visit family and friends. We hadn't seen many of them in years, yet it was easy to catch up. We shared the joys and the challenges we'd both been experiencing, and how Jesus was meeting every need in the midst of it all.

When John and I talk about the children we adopted, the work we've accomplished, or our ministry involvement, we always talk about Jesus. All these things are the result of Jesus at work in us. They are the fruit that is produced when we abide in Him. It's true for my friends, too. Some have lost family members, others have seen their kids make poor choices, but their peace and trust in Christ is also evidence of their abidance in Jesus, their vine.

The vine, in fact, is where believers meet, and our dependence on Jesus is what keeps our relationships strong. Jesus, our vine, supports and supplies our needs as individuals and as part of the body. And even when we travel two thousand miles to reconnect, the distance will not keep us from meeting in Christ together.

Sometimes it's easy to read the Scriptures and understand what they mean to me, but it's also important to look at them to see how the collective followers of Christ are affected. As branches, our dependence in Christ affects all the other branches. And together we can rejoice in all Jesus has done while we continue to trust in all He'll continue to do in us and through us. —TRICIA GOYER

FAITH STEP: *Think of believing friends who are having a hard time trusting in the true vine, Jesus. Pray for them to grow to depend on Him.*

FRIDAY, JULY 6

Consider the lilies, how they grow: they neither toil nor spin, yet I tell you, even Solomon in all his glory was not arrayed like one of these. Luke 12:27 (ESV)

I HAVE A PAIR OF socks that often gets compliments. I made them from my sheep's wool, carrying my hand spindle everywhere for the month or so it took to spin one skein of every color. Then it took almost a year to knit the intricately patterned socks. Some who saw me working on them asked why I didn't just go buy socks, while others asked me to knit *them* a pair. If I'd received minimum wage for the time it took, they'd have been worth hundreds of dollars. Money wasn't a consideration—I enjoyed every step in the process and ended up with lovely warm socks.

In Jesus's time, making clothing (or any kind of fabric) was even more labor intensive. It's likely that women were spinning or weaving whenever they weren't cooking or cleaning. Leisure time, as we know it today, was a foreign concept for most.

Jesus told His followers that life is more than possessions, and assured them that the Father knew their needs and would provide for them all. He told them not to worry about getting food and clothing because constant toil filled their waking hours.

Most of us buy our socks, but we have the same charge to put down our metaphorical spindles and relax. Jesus wants us to seek the Kingdom of Heaven instead of scrambling to take care of ourselves or store up treasures here. Jesus said life is more than constantly working to meet our physical needs. And if His Father dresses the lilies in more glory than Solomon, we can count on Him to take care of us, too. —SUZANNE DAVENPORT TIETJEN

FAITH STEP: *Give something away today. Loosen the grip on the "stuff" of life and build up treasure in Heaven.*

SATURDAY, JULY 7

And I saw the holy city, new Jerusalem, coming down out of heaven from God, prepared as a bride adorned for her husband. And I heard a loud voice from the throne saying, "Behold, the dwelling place of God is with man. He will dwell with them, and they will be his people, and God himself will be with them as their God." Rev. 21:2–3 (ESV)

MY WEDDING DAY WAS ONE of the best in my life. I woke that morning with so much joy in my heart, I thought I'd explode. As we were preparing for the ceremony in the church basement, one of my bridesmaids asked, "Aren't you nervous?" No. After all the months of preparation and the years of longing, all I had room for was joy and eagerness.

I love that Jesus describes the fulfillment of our relationship with Him as a wedding. As a bride I longed to join my groom, in covenant and celebration with our friends and family. As the Bride of Christ, we long to be reunited with Jesus face-to-face, to have our sinful nature cast off forever, to have no more separation.

There is another profound truth in these verses. Just as we wait with great anticipation, He also longs for us. Have you ever thought about how Jesus eagerly waits for the time when we dwell with Him? I often feel like I'm a problem to Jesus. I cause Him so much suffering. I feel like I disappoint Him with my attitudes and actions. It's hard to believe that He's eager for me to join Him in eternity. Yet He makes clear that He longs to dwell with us. He speaks of the new Jerusalem with the enthusiasm of a groom who adores his bride. —SHARON HINCK

FAITH STEP: *Look at some wedding pictures today (yours or someone else's). Thank Jesus for the amazing truth that He longs to spend all of eternity with you and also wants to be part of your day today.*

SUNDAY, JULY 8

"Therefore don't worry about tomorrow, because tomorrow will worry about itself. Each day has enough trouble of its own." Matthew 6:34 (HCSB)

SOMEONE REALLY WISE ONCE SAID, "Worrying is like praying for what you don't want to happen." I don't know that my worried thoughts can actually influence reality, but they can definitely make me miserable. I've consumed lots of time by fretting about things that never came to pass, sometimes spending hours working on solving a problem that never occurred. Meanwhile, whatever was right in front of me, whether a trouble, task, or triumph, went unattended. Silly and sad.

I don't have a magic formula for eliminating worry, except simply choosing to believe that this verse is true, as demonstrated by the many times I've worried needlessly only to have my fears never realized. Lest I beat myself up for my humanness, I can recall the trusty Israelites, prophets, and apostles who all seemed to worry about something, sometimes.

Jesus told the disciples that He was sending the "helper," the Holy Spirit Who would live inside of us, teaching us and reminding us of everything the Savior said. When the angst about anything threatens to overwhelm us, we can call on the very Spirit of Christ to still our worry and remind us that life is best lived one day at a time.
—ISABELLA YOSUICO

FAITH STEP: *Start a Fear/Fact Journal. Next time you find yourself worrying, make a note of the fear and allow yourself time to fret for five minutes. Then give it to Jesus. Sometime later, revisit your list and note the facts. If you're like me, you'll find that so much of what we worry about never happens or resolves itself.*

MONDAY, JULY 9

Such love has no fear, because perfect love expels all fear. If we are afraid, it is for fear of punishment, and this shows that we have not fully experienced his perfect love. 1 John 4:18 (NLT)

I HAVE BEEN STRUGGLING WITH learning how to walk on crutches. It has been scary since I have problems with balance. I have a distinct lack of upper-arm strength. I find myself caught up in this ocean of uncertainty, casting about for a safe place to land, both literally and figuratively. I am scared of falling, of losing control and not being able to navigate life in the way I am used to.

The other morning I broke down in front of our boys. I was trying to clean up the house, on crutches, before my mother-in-law arrived. My middle son, Will, asked me, "Mom, why are you so mad?" In a very loud, high-pitched voice, I said, "I am mad because there are so many things that I can't do that I want to do!" Then I began to cry. And Will said, "But Mom, can't we help you?" There it was. Love. This is what Jesus is trying to show me. I have been trying to figure out how I can possibly "do" life. And He is saying, "How about being loved? Loved by Me. Loved by your family. Loved by your friends." Love. Love. Love.

In the middle of being afraid, He offers His Love. Perfect love casts out fear. Love is our safe place to land when life is crazy. Recognizing that we need help. Understanding that we can't control outcomes. Resting in the truth that Jesus has us exactly where He wants us. And breathing in the truth that my friend, Laurie, speaks out, "God is good and I am loved." —SUSANNA FOTH AUGHTMON

FAITH STEP: *Trusting Jesus can be difficult when life seems out of control. What is an area of your life where you remind yourself that "God is good and you are loved"?*

TUESDAY, JULY 10

My dear friends, since this is what you have to look forward to, do your very best to be found living at your best, in purity and peace. 2 Peter 3:14 (MSG)

AS THE MIDAFTERNOON SUN WARMED my desk, I clicked off the social media site and felt a little guilty for letting it steal another fifteen minutes. Keeping up with everyone's sparkly online life was addicting but not always fulfilling.

I grabbed my purse and added two things to my shopping list that I'd seen ads for while online. A cherry pitter that removes six pits at once? Earbuds with retractable wires? Yes, please! I'd have time to pop into the kitchen store and the electronics store for both and make it home before my kids' school bus arrived.

While running my errands, I noticed all the new vehicles. When had Buick remodeled the Enclave? And the Lincoln Navigator was pretty. My car was nice...for a ten-year-old Honda Pilot.

I scolded myself for getting so distracted by material stuff, the latest and greatest to make life worthwhile, right? Strangely, as I waited in traffic and faced the discontent of desiring more than what I had, I felt my heart rate increase and my peace dissipate.

Is there some magic point in life when I'll be immune to striving for more? Or at least for more of the good stuff that disguises itself as the best, the best being closeness and contentment with Jesus?

Today's verse sums up how we're to live our days. Trying our best, yes. But look at what defines *best*: purity and peace. A heart that is satisfied to spend life loving Jesus and offering that love to others, being steadfastly sure that all will be well in Him.

This life is full of opportunities and distractions. *But Lord help me be preoccupied with You the most.* —ERIN KEELEY MARSHALL

FAITH STEP: *What derails the peace and purity of your faith? Memorize 2 Peter 3:14.*

WEDNESDAY, JULY 11

You are a hiding place for me; you preserve me from trouble; you surround me with shouts of deliverance.... Psalm 32:7 (ESV)

THE SIGN NEXT TO THE jellyfish tank in the large aquarium stopped me before I could focus on the fascinating creatures. "In a world without hiding places, jellies protect themselves by blending in."

Sometimes it feels like we're in a world without hiding places. Our pain can't escape notice. Our failures are paraded on the news or social media. Our mistakes are visible. Our need for solitude is met with a thousand opposing forces. Because of that truth, many try to protect themselves by blending in. A friend of mine was viciously attacked in a school locker room as a young child. In high school, the thought of a locker room made her physically ill. Rather than explain the reasons for her extreme discomfort, she stayed silent but skipped school every day when gym class was scheduled. All through high school. She barely graduated.

The locker room offered her no place to hide. But she couldn't blend in either. Jesus doesn't want us to camouflage our pain. Or skip life because it's hard. He's the Shelter we run to. But within the shelter of His embrace is an equipping station where we draw strength to survive out there in the exposure of the often unkind world.

He is our Hiding Place. If we stay close enough to Him, we are provided a cloak of invisibility that protects us from being vulnerable to attack. Jellyfish blend into the world around them. We blend into Jesus. —CYNTHIA RUCHTI

FAITH STEP: *Do you own a fish tank? Or did you as a child? Remember having to work hard to find where the well-camouflaged fish were hiding, though they were in plain view? Consider yourself protected by the holiest of Hiding Places today.*

THURSDAY, JULY 12

I want to drink God, deep draughts of God. I'm thirsty for God-alive.
Psalm 42:1 (MSG)

IN THE MIDDLE OF A hot summer day, we were experiencing a cool front, and the temperatures had dropped into the pleasant seventies. As I sat on the porch, a breeze blew through the patio. Eager to fellowship with Jesus, I opened my mouth for whispered conversation.

But before a word escaped, I froze, mesmerized. There, near the bird feeder, a hummingbird flitted from one side to the other, drinking the ruby-colored water. At first, it only took a few sips. But after a few minutes the bird stopped sipping and started drinking deeply. Obviously enjoying the sweet nectar, this time it perched for long periods of time on the feeder, its wings still.

I immediately thought of David the Psalmist's thirst for God. Earlier I had read where Jesus issued an unusual offer to those He taught in the temple one day: "If anyone is thirsty, let him keep coming to me and drinking!" (John 7:37, CJB). Jesus knew the desperation of a dry spirit, parched from lack of nourishment.

Like that hummingbird who returned repeatedly for "deep draughts," I, too, wanted to keep drinking from Jesus. I had experienced droughts in my life when I had settled only for quick sips of spiritual nourishment. But as I grew in Jesus, I knew my very existence and spiritual energy required more than that.

That day on my porch, I joined the psalmist and reflected on Jesus's offer as I whispered, "Jesus, I still want more—I want to drink deep draughts of You daily!" —REBECCA BARLOW JORDAN

FAITH STEP: *Place an empty glass nearby to remind you of your emptiness without Jesus.*

FRIDAY, JULY 13

He makes the barren woman abide in the house As a joyful mother of children. Praise the Lord! Psalm 113:9 (NASB)

HEARING THE NEWS I WAS pregnant with our first child was one of the happiest moments of my life. I couldn't believe I was going to be a mom, and my husband, Bobby, was thrilled, too. Though we were in the middle of a hectic baseball season, we set our sights on the due date and the joy to come. But soon into the pregnancy I began to bleed, and after full bed rest, ended up losing our first child to miscarriage.

At first I thought I was okay. No big deal. We'd try again soon and that would be the end of it. But listening to one of the wives complain each night at the games about being pregnant, just about did me in. I wanted to shout, "Don't you know how much I'd love to be in your shoes? Quit complaining!" Thankfully I bit my tongue and silently prayed that Jesus would give me the patience to believe He had good things in store for me as a mother one day. During the miscarriage I had opened my Bible to a Scripture that talked about God making me the joyful mother of children, but I didn't mark where the Scripture was—and though I tried to find it every day after the miscarriage, it remained hidden from me.

One day while journaling I felt as if the Lord promised that when I was pregnant again with another child, He would show me where that Scripture was. Five months later I found that Scripture (Psalm 113:9), and the next day I ran to the store to buy a pregnancy test. Sure enough, I was pregnant! Next to this verse in my Bible is the name of my first child...Brooke Nicole. It's a reminder of His promises. —GARI MEACHAM

FAITH STEP: *Use your Bible to mark the dates that God proves to be faithful. Soon your Bible will be full of your life monuments and markers.*

SATURDAY, JULY 14

*The heavens declare the glory of God; the skies proclaim
the work of his hands. Psalm 19:1 (NIV)*

ONE THING I ENJOY ABOUT my Facebook news feed is seeing the nature-oriented photos. My friend, Georganne, shared a picture of the summer evening sky with this caption: "View from a front porch rocking chair. I wonder if the world would be different if everyone gazed at the skies before bedtime." In the comments section, I related how at age fifteen, I gazed at the sky every summer night after seeing my first shooting star. I was convinced that we would have world peace if everyone would look at the nighttime sky. Georganne responded: "Exactly! I'm convinced that sky gazing does something very good for the soul."

I've always marveled at how the sky displays the majesty of God's creation. I love how the heavens remind me of Jesus all day, every day. Each morning the sunrise confirms that He has a plan and a purpose for me. Every evening the glowing sunset assures me that He will guard me through the night. In between, a sunny sky makes me think about His goodness, while thunderstorms represent His power. Clouds remind me of the peace that comes through a relationship with Him.

A bright star and angels in the heavens heralded the birth of Jesus; a darkened sky marked His death. Forty days after His Resurrection, His followers witnessed Him rising into the sky as He returned to heaven. An angel promised that one day He will return the same way. Yes, we have many reasons to do a little sky gazing, and as Georganne says, "It does something very good for the soul."
—DIANNE NEAL MATTHEWS

FAITH STEP: *Whenever you get a chance today, look up at the sky. Tell Jesus how what you see reminds you of Him.*

SUNDAY, JULY 15

"The thief's purpose is to steal, kill and destroy. My purpose is to give life in all its fullness." John 10:10 (TLB)

THE OTHER DAY I FOUND my four-year-old daughter, Stella, on the floor in front of her closet in a cluster of shoes. She'd try one on and toss it when it didn't meet her qualifications.

"Might I ask what on earth are you doing?"

"I'm finding the right shoes."

"Just pick some! It's time to go!"

"Mommy, I need to find the best pair for skipping!"

I can honestly say this was a new one. One Sunday after church she flung off her shoes as soon as we walked in the door and told me to throw them away because they were like tigers. When I gave her a puzzled look she explained how they bite and claw her feet. Needless to say, those shoes are no more. But skipping shoes?

My shoe philosophy is a lot more practical. I wear whatever matches, or what is most comfortable. Occasionally I'm fashion minded, pairing just the right boots with an outfit, or a dress with heels. But I've never really considered what shoes are best for skipping.

The thing is, we were going to the grocery store. There were no plans for skipping per se, but Stella's choice of shoes reflects her general outlook on the day. She didn't know and couldn't control what else was on the schedule. But she was planning on skipping.

I want my outlook to be more like that—to reflect more trust in Jesus when He says "I came to give life…in all its fullness." John 10:10 (NCV). If His purpose for me is abundance, I need to plan on joy, no matter what the day brings. —GWEN FORD FAULKENBERRY

FAITH STEP: *Make a to-do list for your day. Regardless of what's on it, don your skipping shoes before you step out, trusting that His plan for you is good.*

MONDAY, JULY 16

Let every detail in your lives—words, actions, whatever—be done in the name of the Master, Jesus, thanking God the Father every step of the way.
Colossians 3:17 (MSG)

I LOVE DETAILS. THEY WERE crucial in my nursing career. I look for details everywhere and include them in my own fiber art, even if no one else ever recognizes them. To me, little things matter.

Science recognizes this as well. When Edward Lorenz, a scientist in the 1960s, tried to take a shortcut by omitting the last three of six decimal places in his weather prediction program, the results were vastly different, giving rise to what is now called the butterfly effect. Can the tiny breeze from a butterfly's wings result in a tornado a continent away? Apparently so. Everything matters.

This comes as no surprise to God, Who made this interconnected world and has always been meticulous about details. His directions to Moses regarding the Tabernacle in Exodus and His detailed instructions to the Israelites in the book of Leviticus reveal this. David, too, gave his son, Solomon, comprehensive instructions regarding the construction of the first Temple. Eugene Peterson, translator of The Message, says, "There is immense significance in everything that we do."

Details matter to Jesus, too. He came to accomplish His Father's will—"not a single detail missed" (John 6:39, MSG), carrying out His Father's wishes "down to the last detail" (John 14:31, MSG). He told His Father, "I glorified you on earth by completing down to the last detail what you assigned me to do" (John 17:4, MSG).

And little you and me? When we follow Jesus, we can be "sure that every detail in our lives of love for God is worked into something good" (Romans 8:28, MSG). —SUZANNE DAVENPORT TIETJEN

FAITH STEP: *Offer Jesus moments in your day. Then live those moments.*

TUESDAY, JULY 17

"I have told you these things so that you will be filled with my joy. Yes, your joy will overflow! This is my commandment: Love each other in the same way I have loved you." John 15:11–12 (NLT)

WHILE WATERING THE FLOWER BOX on our front porch, the spray suddenly stopped. I squeezed the handle more firmly, checked the setting, and wiggled the hose. Finally I found a kink in the line that had stopped the water from flowing. Once I untangled the hose, the water sprayed freely, and I was able to finish watering my flowers and herbs.

There are times when joy seems like a meager drip in my life, even though I know Jesus promises to give it in abundance. When I realize that I've stopped raining joy on those around me, it's a good signal for me to check for blockages and tangles. Jesus linked His promise of joy with His command to love others in the same way He loved. Often when my joy dries up, I discover that I've begun to focus so much on my own needs or hurts that I've stopping letting Jesus's love for others flow through me. The knot grows tighter, my spirit shrivels, and I have nothing to pour out into the lives of others.

My first response when I recognize lack of joy in my heart is to try harder. Like twisting the nozzle or squeezing more intensely, this does no good if I'm not open to the Source. I need to remind myself that I can run to Jesus, ask Him to change my heart, to live in me, to connect me to the Source of joy, so I can love others as He does.

Like the generous spray that waters my flowers, joy flows naturally when He forgives the sins that block our relationship. Because of Him, we can open our hearts to His love again and overflow with joy. —SHARON HINCK

FAITH STEP: *Water a plant today. Think about anything in your life that is blocking the free flow of Jesus's love, and ask Him to restore your joy.*

WEDNESDAY, JULY 18

For if anyone is a hearer of the word and not a doer, he is like a man who looks intently at his natural face in a mirror. For he looks at himself and goes away and at once forgets what he was like. James 1:23–24 (ESV)

MY NEW HOME HAS A mirror on the closet door in the bathroom, right behind the vanity mirror. It also has much better lighting than in my old home, with a sunny skylight above the master bath sink. You can see everything. The other day I got a good look at myself, and I have to admit, my bathing suit rear view was a little disappointing. It made me think: *What's with all that cellulite? And am I really getting bags under my eyes at fifty? Maybe I should have used more sunscreen.*

I also caught glimpses of blemishes that my mirrors and lighting don't show. Mainly I saw ingratitude for many of my blessings, including my husband. *Hasn't he been running both kids to school every morning so I can make my deadline? Didn't he just fold yet another pile of never-ending laundry? And he thinks I'm really beautiful, despite the cellulite, and tells me all the time.*

There are many examples in the Bible where we are urged to embrace gratitude and humility, like in Matthew 23:12 and Ephesians 5:20. Those verses help us recognize who we really are, even on our very best days, and what we are charged to do. Jesus vocally confronted hypocrisy because it is the heart of pride. The call to humility and gratitude sets us free from the spiritual blindness that so often prevents us from enjoying our lives and everyday blessings.
—ISABELLA YOSUICO

FAITH STEP: *Next time you find yourself criticizing anyone or anything, take a moment to ask Jesus to help you to reflect on three positive aspects of that very person (or thing) who's troubling you.*

THURSDAY, JULY 19

Then Jesus called the children over to him and said to the disciples,
"Let the little children come to me! Never send them away!
For the Kingdom of God belongs to men who have hearts as
trusting as these little children's." Luke 18:16 (TLB)

ON THE NEWS RECENTLY I watched a video clip of six-year-old Jordan Warrick being baptized in the church baptistery in Louisville, Kentucky. According to the pastor, Jordan had been looking forward to this for a long time. Evidently too long.

Before the pastor could finish his usual words, Jordan yelled, "I'll do it!" and hit the water headfirst, self-dunking his body. Mouths flew open and laughter filled the church as friends and family watched in disbelief. When his father's video of the baptism was posted on Facebook, it went viral.

Maybe that's the kind of attitude or spirit Jesus was referring to when some parents came to Him one day, asking Him to bless their children. His disciples tried to shoo them all away, but Jesus stopped them. Welcoming their cherub faces, He used them to teach the disciples a lesson: "Let the little children come to me!"

Trusting, eager hearts—like the children gathered around Jesus—make up the Kingdom of God. Jesus loves the bold anticipation of a new disciple committed to Him, ready to say, "I'm a Christone," and get on with the business of living for Jesus. Childlike faith knows where blessings and answers lie: in Jesus.

Later that week as I observed a smiling, senior adult being baptized in our own church's baptistery, I thanked Jesus that He is not concerned with age. His salvation is for everyone willing to come to Him like a little child. —REBECCA BARLOW JORDAN

FAITH STEP: *Ask Jesus to give you a childlike spirit, always eager to follow Him.*

FRIDAY, JULY 20

Jesus replied, "I am the bread of life. Whoever comes to me will never be hungry again. . . ." John 6:35 (NLT)

I ENJOY SAMPLING DIFFERENT VARIETIES of bread when I travel. In the Middle East, I dip pita bread in lentil sauce. In Nepal, I fold *roti*—a flatbread that resembles a tortilla shell—and use it to scoop curried vegetables. In eastern Europe, I smother rolls in cheese curd and forest berry jam for breakfast. And for dessert, I like warm crepes stuffed with cooked apple slices.

Bread is a staple in most cultures. In biblical times, *lechem* was such a significant part of the diet that the term referred to food in general. Perhaps that's why Jesus called Himself the Bread of Life. He knew people would understand the symbolism. He, like bread, is vital for sustenance.

It's possible that Jesus also used the symbolism to teach people that He wasn't an ordinary religious teacher or leader. As manna in the desert came from heaven, He came to meet our need. Jesus said, "I tell you the truth, Moses didn't give them bread from heaven. My Father did. And now he offers you the true bread from heaven. The true bread of God is the one who comes down from heaven and gives life to the world" (John 6:32–33).

Nothing less than the Bread of Life satisfies our spiritual hunger. We might try to fill our appetite with a career, money, material possessions, or even relationships, but these things are like empty calories—they might quiet our hunger pangs for a while, but they won't nourish our souls. They'll never meet our craving for unconditional love, forgiveness, and purpose.

Jesus alone feeds us so we'll never hunger again. —GRACE FOX

FAITH STEP: *Incorporate bread into one of your meals today. As you eat it, thank Jesus for being the Bread of Life. Ask Him to give you an appetite for Him.*

SATURDAY, JULY 21

Get rid of all bitterness, rage, anger, harsh words, and slander, as well as all
types of evil behavior. Instead, be kind to each other, tenderhearted,
forgiving one another, just as God through Christ has forgiven you.
Ephesians 4:31–32 (NLT)

SCOTT AND I RARELY LEAVE our three boys at home alone even though our oldest is fifteen. It wouldn't be safe...for them...or the neighborhood. They tend to go at it. The same was true for me and my siblings when we were left on our own. We would get into fights. I have two sisters and a brother. We weren't kind to one another. We weren't loving. We weren't thoughtful. In fact, we could be mean. If there was a disagreement and Mom wasn't around to sort it out, it got ugly.

When I didn't get my way, I often resorted to screaming, hair pulling, and scratching, followed by punching, kicking, and throwing toys. It was every boy or girl for himself or herself. Learning how to be kind takes some work. It doesn't come easily.

Our natural tendencies are selfish; just ask any two-year-old. But Jesus isn't keen on violence or name calling or trash talking. He wants us to treat one another with the utmost kindness. Each of us is special to Him. Jesus longs for us to treat others with the same genuine love and care that He gives us. When we show each other mercy, the world changes. We begin to resemble Him when we are kind to one another. Peace steps in. Love abounds. Relationships flourish. Cultivating kindness and forgiveness not only changes us, it changes everyone we come in contact with. —SUSANNA FOTH AUGHTMON

FAITH STEP: *Be strategic about being kind. Ask Jesus to show you the people who need your compassion and forgiveness today and reach out.*

SUNDAY, JULY 22

Then Jesus told his disciples a parable to show them that they should always pray and not give up. Luke 18:1 (NIV)

WHEN I LOOK AT MY prayer list and find blank spaces in the "Answered on This Date" column, the following parable becomes a bedtime story that comforts my soul so my sleep is undisturbed despite the blanks. It's a "bedtime" story Jesus told in the daylight.

He said: "In a certain town there was a judge who neither feared God nor cared what people thought." Luke 18:2 (NIV). The story describes an interchange between the judge and a widow who'd been wronged. She asked for justice. The judge refused. Providing justice for an uninfluential widow held no priority for him.

She kept asking. And asking. And asking.

Finally, the judge gave in. She bothered and embarrassed him. He gave her what she needed so she'd leave him alone.

At first reading, I wondered what Jesus could have meant by using that example. Our Judge is not unjust. He exudes compassion. He not only respects but cares for our every need. Begging seems to disrespect both God and our humanity.

But Jesus tells us specifically at the beginning of the story that He wants us to find within it encouragement to pray continuously and not grow discouraged.

He bookends the story with this poignant line: "When the Son of Man comes, will he find faith on the earth?" Luke 18:8 (NIV). Jesus is faithful to us, faithful to answer quickly or to hold us tightly if the answer is slower in coming. The real question is, "Will *we* be faithful to ask, to keep asking, and to trust Him?" —CYNTHIA RUCHTI

FAITH STEP: *What request is lingering on your prayer list? Put a gold star next to that request—an award for endurance—and keep praying.*

MONDAY, JULY 23

"So don't be anxious about tomorrow. God will take care of your tomorrow too. Live one day at a time." Matthew 6:34 (TLB)

IT FELT LIKE AGES SINCE my husband and I had gone on this two-mile mountainside hike. At times we trudged up winding tree-lined paths, being careful not to stumble over roots and jutting rocks. Other parts of the trail took us through open spaces with easier walking but no shade in the hot sun. At one point I figured we must surely be close to the end, but my husband informed me that we had only walked about a half-mile. My heart sank, but I knew he had a keen sense of distance. After that, each time I asked for an update, I dreaded the answer.

I prefer the kind of trail with markers to delineate each tenth of a mile. Some nature trails even offer a brochure with a map to show your exact location and what lies ahead. Wouldn't it be nice if life worked that way? How much easier it would be if we had markers that showed our progress and how much farther we had to go to reach our destination. And a map would be nice to reveal what type of terrain or obstacles we could expect ahead.

Jesus understands how discouraged we get from obsessing over the unknowns in our future. That's why He advises us to focus on one day, one moment, at a time. We can ask for wisdom to deal with a difficult business meeting, healing words to offer an estranged relative, or maybe strength and stamina to get through today's chemotherapy treatment. Regardless of the challenges we currently face, we can always trust Jesus to give us, not just our daily bread but whatever we need to end each day on a victorious note. —DIANNE NEAL MATTHEWS

FAITH STEP: *Each time you're tempted to worry about the future, remember Who holds it in His hands. Pinpoint the challenge you're facing right now and ask Jesus to supply what you need today.*

TUESDAY, JULY 24

So I say, walk by the Spirit, and you will not gratify the desires of the flesh. For the flesh desires what is contrary to the Spirit, and the Spirit what is contrary to the flesh. They are in conflict with each other, so that you are not to do whatever you want. Galatians 5:16–17 (NIV)

OVER THE SUMMER THREE OF my children, eight years old and under, loved playing out front with their friends. We live in the back of the subdivision at the end of a cul-de-sac so it's typically safe. The problem is all of the trouble my little kids get into without direct adult supervision. Most of the time my neighbor or I are there, but there are times when we need to slip inside the house. It's during these times when one of the kids decides to cut someone else's hair or tackle each other on the asphalt. Without the watchful eye of an adult, little children tend to turn to mischief quickly.

The truth is I find myself doing what I ought not to do when I'm not mindful of oversight from the Holy Spirit. I make unwholesome media choices or choose to pretend I didn't see a friend at the grocery store instead of opening myself up to her. My flesh wants to gratify myself, hide my flaws, and not get too wrapped up with the needs of others, but this is not what Jesus's Spirit wants.

Walking by Jesus's Spirit is not complicated, but it does take surrender. It means pausing to pray and asking Jesus to meet you and fill you in the moment. Then it's listening to His still, small voice inside that urges you, not only to cease to do evil but to learn to do well. Only Jesus's Spirit will tell us what to cherish and cultivate in our hearts. When we give Him permission, He will guide us in doing what He desires in our lives. —TRICIA GOYER

FAITH STEP: *Pause this moment and ask Jesus's Holy Spirit to help you to stop following your own desires and instead strive to follow His.*

WEDNESDAY, JULY 25

*For our light and momentary troubles are achieving for us an eternal glory
that far outweighs them all. 2 Corinthians 4:17 (NIV)*

MY HUSBAND AND I WERE staying at a friend's cabin on the banks
of Lake Superior. We strolled the beach, admiring the beautiful
smooth stones covering the shore. Waves rolled in, rubbing rocks
against each other. Over the years the water had shaped granite
and quartz into stunning rounded sculptures. Glimmers of crystal
sparkled in the sunlight.

We collected a few samples to bring home. The agates and the
fragments of precious minerals shine because their surrounding
rock was first broken open by storms and pounding waves, and
their surface was then polished by the constant action of abrasion.

I used to growl at this verse in 2 Corinthians. In my opinion,
my troubles weren't light or momentary at all. We live in a world
where the free-will choices of other sinful humans can cause injustice and suffering, where disease can attack out of the blue, where
disagreements can separate us from those we love.

Jesus has great compassion for our pain. He is able to bring His
transformative grace into our most hurtful experiences. This verse
doesn't mean we should buck up and pretend the pain isn't so bad.
It simply reminds us that one day we'll look back and discover the
long-term gifts that He produced in the midst of the abrasive sand,
the crashing waves, and the day-after-day pressures. On that day,
when we glimpse the eternal glory, we'll agree that glory outweighs
any pain. —SHARON HINCK

FAITH STEP: *Set a few smooth stones on your kitchen table as a centerpiece and
use them as a reminder that the abrasive struggles in your life will be used by our
Savior for glorious purposes.*

THURSDAY, JULY 26

Since everything here today might well be gone tomorrow, do you see how essential it is to live a holy life? Daily expect the Day of God, eager for its arrival. The galaxies will burn up and the elements melt down that day—but we'll hardly notice. We'll be looking the other way, ready for the promised new heavens and the promised new earth, all landscaped with righteousness.
2 Peter 3:11–13 (MSG)

MY FAMILY VISITED THE KENNEDY Space Center and had the rare opportunity to watch an Atlas V reconnaissance rocket launch from Cape Canaveral, Florida. From our viewing site, we could feel the rumble of 1.5 million pounds of thrust that would carry the rocket to its orbit 22,000 miles over the equator. The launch simulator showed us what that much force feels like.

We saw the Space Shuttle Atlantis up close and read about its many missions and the millions of miles it traveled.

In a word, it was *awesome*. Or maybe *awe-inspiring*. While I was there, I wondered how many other people were seeing Jesus, Lord of the Universe, behind it all. What a missed opportunity it would be to spend hours marveling at humanity's advancements into space but to overlook Jesus, the One who died and rose to save us and to give us eternal life—life that extends limitlessly beyond what we humans could ever discover ourselves.

Today's Scripture reminds me that everything we see is temporary and, as remarkable as this world is, the Redeemer's glory is so much greater. —ERIN KEELEY MARSHALL

FAITH STEP: *Spend part of an evening gazing at the night sky. Ask Jesus to reveal more of Himself to you as you look for Him in the world.*

FRIDAY, JULY 27

Wash me clean from my guilt. Purify me from my sin. Psalm 51:2 (NLT)

MY HUSBAND AND I RECENTLY went on a guided fishing trip. After eight hours out on the water, we were famished, having had no food since our predawn doughnuts. One man familiar with the area suggested a restaurant. But first, we had to clean up—really clean up. Not knowing the boat would travel at forty-five mph for long distances, I had left my hair loose. Now it was a mass of tangles. My clothes were dirty and soaked in sweat. My legs had been splattered by bits of yucky stuff when our guide dressed the fish with an electric tool. After we showered and changed clothes we met our friends in the hotel lobby. One of the wives commented, "Y'all clean up good."

Some people think they have to "clean up" before they can have a relationship with Jesus. I'm so thankful that's not the case. He extends His forgiveness, mercy, and grace to anyone willing to accept them. Once we admit our need for a Savior, Jesus goes to work cleansing us from the inside out. He washes away the penalty for our sin so that we can receive eternal life. Then, He begins transforming our thoughts, attitudes, and behavior so that we can reflect His character.

This transformation is a lifelong process. At times we still get dirty living in a sin-marred world. But that's no reason to avoid Jesus, allowing guilt or shame to hinder our fellowship with Him. He has given us a wonderful promise in 1 John 1:9: "But if we confess our sins to him, he can be depended on to forgive us and to cleanse us from every wrong...." (TLB) Whenever we slip up, Jesus stands ready to give us a fresh start. If we ask Him, He will do what we cannot do for ourselves: clean us up completely. —DIANNE NEAL MATTHEWS

FAITH STEP: *Prayerfully examine your heart for anything you need Jesus to clean up. Meditate on 1 John 1:9 and thank Him for His promise to purify you.*

SATURDAY, JULY 28

No power in the sky above or in the earth below—indeed, nothing in all creation will ever be able to separate us from the love of God that is revealed in Christ Jesus our Lord. Romans 8:39 (NLT)

LIFE CHANGED DRASTICALLY FOR A friend's family when leukemia struck his sixteen-year-old daughter. He and his wife never expected this. Who does? Nor did they foresee months of weekly eight-hour drives to the nearest children's hospital for chemotherapy. Circumstances forced them to adjust work schedules, find a place for their other daughter to stay when they were away, and trust the Lord to provide for extra expenses.

Our friend sent regular e-mail updates to prayer partners. I marveled at his positive outlook. This was understandably a very difficult time, yet he kept his focus on the Lord and His promises, and he always listed reasons to praise Him.

In my travels, I've met other people who walk similar paths, but not all navigate the journey as well as my friend. They question Jesus's presence and purposes. They doubt His power to heal or to bring about something good from suffering. Sometimes they feel as though He doesn't love them anymore. Nothing's further from the truth.

Suffering is common to humankind. When our turn comes, let's remember that circumstances are not the barometer of Christ's love for us. They change from day to day, but His love remains constant, steadfast, tried and true.

Nothing—not even the circumstances that flip our lives upside down—can separate us from Christ's love. Amen. —GRACE FOX

FAITH STEP: *Get two pieces of paper. Draw a stick figure of yourself on one. Draw a heart shape and write "Jesus's love for me" on the other. Glue them together and use it as a bookmark.*

SUNDAY, JULY 29

The book of the genealogy of Jesus Christ, the son of David, the son of Abraham. Matthew 1:1 (ESV)

SO BEGINS THE GOSPEL OF Christ, followed by a list of names. Beyond a mere biographer's introduction, with this list God communicates His loving mercy, understanding, and grace.

Jesus's family tree included adulterers, murderers, drunks, cowards, lonely widows, the disabled—undesirables by the world's standards. However, many also claimed a singular virtue or moment of simple and often reluctant greatness that earned them a spot in Christ's story, the greatest story ever told. What a comfort!

One of my favorite authors, Isabel Allende, writes fantastical, multigenerational sagas that cover the lifetimes of dramatically flawed people within epic tragedies to beautiful effect. I sometimes borrow this device in thinking of my own family.

My mom was mentally ill and my dad was an alcoholic. My lineage also includes adulterers, illegitimate children, and assorted other not-so-secret sins, wreaking havoc on generations.

Before Christ, my own story and sense of self were overshadowed by what seemed to be my inescapable genealogy. Yet, both my parents were also remarkable people who imparted in me gifts that I appreciate more and more each day.

My newfound understanding of the Gospel tells me that just as God deliberately wove an eternal tapestry with a motley crew of wayward humans, He is weaving a brilliant tapestry of my life, touching others in the process. The backstory may be a jumbled mess, but the tapestry is coming along nicely. —ISABELLA YOSUICO

FAITH STEP: *Be creative in drawing your family tree. Thank God for using all of the members to weave the tapestry of your life.*

MONDAY, JULY 30

There is no fear in love; but perfect love casteth out fear: because fear hath torment. He that feareth is not made perfect in love. 1 John 4:18 (KJV)

I'VE NOTICED THAT MANY OF the things I'm initially afraid of aren't as scary up close. For example, the first time I went snorkeling I was terrified. My husband, Stone, and I were in Egypt in this tiny village on the Red Sea. I wanted to snorkel there because it had a reputation of being one of the best places for snorkeling in the world. *But what if a shark ate me? Or I got stung by some deadly coral? What if I drowned? What if I got lost and no one ever found me and my parents never knew what happened?*

"Honey. You need to do this. We can hold hands. Seriously, I promise you will love it." This from a husband who grew up in Hawaii and had no fear of snorkeling. "Fish are our friends," he said.

So I tried it. And it was one of the best experiences of my life. I was transported into a new world. It was amazing.

I've had similar experiences in other places, and with people I first thought were scary. My piano teacher's dog was as big as a horse, but all he wanted was to be loved. The meanest professor in law school turned out to be a big teddy bear when I got to know him. It's a recurring theme.

We see this dynamic with Jesus as He walks through life. He reaches out to people who others—and especially religious people— fear. The woman at the well. Lepers. Foreigners. Tax collectors. Prostitutes. Even the thief on the Cross. When He brings them into proximity, the fear fades. Perhaps we should follow His example.
—GWEN FORD FAULKENBERRY

FAITH STEP: *Is there a person or group you most fear? Find a way to connect with them. Give love a chance to work its magic.*

TUESDAY, JULY 31

Look at me. I stand at the door. I knock. If you hear me call and open the door, I'll come right in and sit down to supper with you. Revelation 3:20 (MSG)

WHEN I WAS DIAGNOSED WITH a heart rhythm disturbance, I was told I needed a pacemaker. We explained this to my granddaughter, Mara, and answered her questions. After the procedure, her other grandmother found her crying. When asked what was wrong, Mara said, "Will Grandma have to ask Jesus into her heart again?" At eight years old, she'd misunderstood and, thinking I'd had a heart transplant, was worried about my salvation.

We laugh about it now, but I'm still touched by her concern. It's curious that some people who've had heart transplants report unexpected changes like craving foods they never liked, appreciating different styles of music, or showing aversions to sounds that never bothered them before. Some who met the donors' families discovered that the changes reflected the likes and dislikes of their donors. Scientists are researching what they call cellular memory to discover whether emotions or moods can be stored in parts of our bodies other than our brains.

The Bible refers to the heart as the center of our spiritual life.

We believe when the Father draws us to Jesus (John 6:44). And when we open the door of our hearts, Jesus comes in.

Like those with new physical hearts, we can't help but be changed. "Let the word of Christ... have the run of the house. Give it plenty of room in your lives" (Colossians 3:16, MSG).

Give Him free rein! —SUZANNE DAVENPORT TIETJEN

FAITH STEP: *Is it hard to believe that Jesus is right there inside of you? What might this mean for you as you walk through your day? Ask Him to show you.*

WEDNESDAY, AUGUST 1

In the temple [Jesus] found people selling cattle, sheep, and doves,
and the money changers seated at their tables. Making a whip of cords,
he drove all of them out of the temple, both the sheep and the cattle.
He also poured out the coins of the money changers and
overturned their tables. John 2:14–15 (NRSV)

A FRIEND OF MINE TOLD me how different his two sons are. One is so gentle that my friend has to teach him to defend himself against bullies. The other one is such a fireball that my friend worries he is too aggressive, and works with him on being more kind.

As we discussed these differences, I told my friend I think these issues sometimes become complicated by our ideas of what is "Christian." What I meant is that it seems easier for most people to relate to the gentleness of Jesus than this Jesus who makes a whip of cords and turns over tables. Perhaps it's our focus on the narrative of the Cross and how He suffered for us. I don't really know the reason—I just know it's easier for me to accept. By nature I'm more like my friend's gentle son. And while that probably seems sweet at first glance, it has caused me enormous problems.

Somewhere along the line I got the idea that being gentle was all a Christian should be. That translated into my being a doormat at times—an easy target for bullies. I thought it was being like Jesus not to fight back, to let people abuse me, and I was so wrong. It was only as an adult that I embraced what a fireball Jesus could be as well. When I created more of a balance between the two extremes, I became a healthier person. —GWEN FORD FAULKENBERRY

FAITH STEP: *Are you naturally softer or more assertive? Too much of either good thing is not Christlike. Pray and ask Jesus to help you find a balance, to make you more like Him.*

THURSDAY, AUGUST 2

For the sake of Christ, then, I am content with weaknesses, insults,
hardships, persecutions, and calamities. For when I am weak,
then I am strong. 2 Corinthians 12:10 (ESV)

SQUIRRELS ARE THE BANE OF my garden. This year we finally grew a
wonderful crop of tomatoes after several years of unhelpful weather,
bugs, and other problems. The first plump tomatoes began to turn
red, and I grabbed my gardening basket, excited to harvest.

Instead I found all the best tomatoes had huge bites taken out
of them. Others had been plucked, gnawed, and then discarded.
Later when I looked out of the window, I saw the culprits at work.
I chased them away, muttering about the wretched pests.

Then I remembered a visit from a New Zealand friend. One day as
we sat on the front steps chatting, she noticed squirrels leaping across
the yard. She was transfixed. "They are like little dancers. Look how
their tails move so gracefully." She explained to me that New Zealand
doesn't have squirrels. She found beauty where I hadn't seen any.

Sometimes our lives feel pestered by insults, hardships, and calamities. We may even feel wearied by dealing with a few squirrelly people
in our midst. Yet in Christ, there can be beauty within the struggles.
Our struggles and weakness remind us to lean on Him. And when we
turn to Jesus, we are strengthened by His faithful love and guidance.

Later that day, when I was confronted by additional hardships,
including physical pain and emotional discouragement, I asked
Jesus to help me view all challenges with new eyes. With His help, I
was able to embrace the words of the apostle Paul, "For the sake of
Christ, then, I am content." —SHARON HINCK

FAITH STEP: *Spend a moment observing a squirrel today. Ponder how some-*
times the things that annoy us can become beautiful through Jesus.

FRIDAY, AUGUST 3

But as he who called you is holy, you also be holy in all your conduct, since it is written, "You shall be holy, for I am holy." 1 Peter 1:15–16 (ESV)

THE BEACH IS LITTERED WITH things that once were something different—a pebble that used to be a much larger rock or a piece broken off a cliff an ocean away, an empty crab claw, a bit of frosted glass that at one time had a life as a container.

I walked a beach a few weeks ago that had stretches of sand interrupted by stretches of ocean litter. Piles of seashells—the hollowed houses of evicted clams. Human refuse like plastic rings from six-packs and water bottles not decomposing fast enough.

The remains of lives lived and purposes now silent.

Life, too, is littered with debris. We rake the beach of our personal histories. But another storm hits and the sand is piled with fronds and driftwood and seaweed that no longer floats but lies in rotting piles.

How does Jesus handle what washes up on the shores of our lives? He delights in beauty, so He likely pockets the stones shaped like hearts. But the human refuse?

He knelt and washed the disciples' feet when they accumulated the dust of this world. So Jesus is the one collecting the worthless things so He can dispose of them. If we let Him.

Like the disciple who argued against having his feet washed, we often resist letting Jesus do His cleanup work in us. It can pile up, inviting critters and bugs and becoming a tripping hazard for others, unless we step aside and let Him have His way.

Theologians call the process sanctification—continually being made more holy, more like Him. —CYNTHIA RUCHTI

FAITH STEP: *Sit for a moment after reading this. Imagine Jesus washing your hands, your feet, your mind of all that has washed ashore. Thank Him.*

SATURDAY, AUGUST 4

Who then will condemn us? No one—for Christ Jesus died for us and was raised to life for us, and he is sitting in the place of honor at God's right hand, pleading for us. Romans 8:34 (NLT)

HAVE YOU EVER ENCOUNTERED A situation so daunting or complicated that you didn't know how to pray through it?

I recently experienced a relationship hiccup when a friend misunderstood something I'd said and took offense. I initiated two conversations to try to resolve the conflict, but they failed. It seemed that the more earnestly I prayed about it, the stronger the tension between us grew. One day I took a long walk and talked with Jesus about it. Mostly my prayers sounded like this: "Help! I don't know what to do."

Don't be afraid or discouraged, I sensed Him say. *Trust Me. I'm praying for you.* The latter four words changed everything.

I'm always encouraged when other people tell me they're praying for me, but knowing that Jesus intercedes on my behalf takes things to a new level of reassurance. His prayers are offered in wisdom and faith, and they're always according to God's will, in my best interest, and for His glory.

Day and night, Jesus intercedes for His followers. He's mindful of our human frailties and aware of the temptations and trials we face. He knows when we need wisdom, patience, courage, creativity, strength, rest, and the ability to forgive and to control our tongue. The mere thought makes me want to wave a victory banner even as I continue to wait for Him to bring resolution to my relationship hiccup. —GRACE FOX

FAITH STEP: *Draw a picture of today's key verse. (Don't worry if you're not a Michelangelo!) Even drawing a simple sketch will trigger fresh insights about what the verse means.*

SUNDAY, AUGUST 5

In the beginning was the Word, and the Word was with God, and the Word was God. John 1:1 (NIV)

AS A NOVELIST, I STRIVE to create new worlds. I spin stories that I hope will feel real, have an emotional impact on readers, and reflect truth. When I write in the fantasy genre, the idea of creating a "story world" is especially challenging. I grapple with shaping the geography, the history, the scientific principles, the flora and fauna, and the characters who inhabit this new universe. My mom joked with me the other day: "No wonder your head hurts, you're making a new world."

Ultimately, though, my efforts to use words to invent a new world are only a poor shadow of the creative power of Jesus, the Word. We see Him, with the whole Trinity, present at the beginning of time. He spoke and the world spun into being. This simple truth reveals many things about the nature of Christ:

Jesus is eternal, the beginning and end. That means He can help us deal with our pasts and that He steers our futures.

Jesus is creative. As part of the Triune God, He devised a universe out of nothing, with all its endless beauty. That means He has fresh answers for our problems.

Jesus is powerful. A simple word from Him formed skies and oceans. His breath gave soul to us. This means that when danger frightens us, we can trust in our strong Shepherd, who gave His life to save us and has defeated the enemy of sin and death.

When I dwell on this verse, deep gratitude wells up in my heart, and becomes a prayer. "Lord, you spoke and life began. Please speak over my heart and bring me new life." —SHARON HINCK

FAITH STEP: *Create something today — a sculpture of clay, or a poem, or a song, or a painting. As you form it, thank Jesus for creating, preserving, and loving you.*

MONDAY, AUGUST 6

Faithful is He who calls you, and He also will bring it to pass.
1 Thessalonians 5:24 *(NASB)*

AFTER A TENSION-FILLED SIX-HOUR RIDE to the African airport, my entire mission's team missed their flight home, and I felt responsible. Many things contributed to the missed flight: the wrong size van sent for the ride, heavy traffic, and new airport security in Uganda—things beyond my control. But I slipped right into my "blame" place and began to berate myself. Crouched on the floor of the hotel bathroom, I let out bellowing sobs. I hoped no one in the neighboring rooms would hear me, but I'd reached a point of no return. "I can't do this." "I'm not equipped." "Someone else can do this better than me!"

In the midst of my sobs I remembered something I wrote on a sticky note and placed in my Bible years ago. "If He calls me to it—He will equip me for it." I repeated this phrase out loud and, Kleenex box in hand, left my room to lead our team through the next challenges. It's tempting to think we aren't called or equipped for the tough things we face: parenting, marriage, career changes, health upsets, financial decisions—but Jesus is faithful and will bring every big challenge to pass. Our skill set is irrelevant and can actually get in the way of fresh faith. He's leading us to new opportunities to trust, not to fall apart. Even if we need a few minutes on a bathroom floor to remember! —GARI MEACHAM

FAITH STEP: *Grab a note card or a sticky note and carry this message with you today: If He calls me to it—He will equip me for it!*

TUESDAY, AUGUST 7

I gave up all that inferior stuff so I could know Christ personally, experience his resurrection power, be a partner in his suffering, and go all the way with him to death itself. Philippians 3:10 (MSG)

MY HUSBAND AND I HAVE moved a lot. We enjoyed the years we lived in Illinois and Utah. But when he got a job in southeast Texas, I felt excited to be moving closer to Tennessee where we'd both spent the first thirty years of our lives. I told my friend, Kathryn, that I looked forward to getting back to the South, although I'd never wanted to live in the Deep South. Kathryn, who'd spent the first eight years of her life in Mississippi and Alabama, said, "Hey, if you're gonna go south, deep is the only way to go!"

We laughed over her comment, but I later decided it might be a good motto as I faced another move—and then another one soon afterward to south Louisiana. A reminder to fully embrace our new location, to jump in and explore all it offered. Sometimes that proved easy (fresh seafood and friendly people); other aspects were difficult (extreme humidity and the danger of flooding). But I'm still making an effort to adapt to our new home state rather than treat it as just another stop along the way.

I want to have that same committed attitude toward Jesus, too. I don't want to be His follower in name only, or to be satisfied with a superficial relationship. I believe that the choices we make every day determine how close our relationship with Him is. Are we studying His Word and doing our best to obey it? Do we talk things over with Him throughout our day? Once we experience the closeness that He desires, we'll surely say, "When it comes to knowing Jesus, deep is the only way to go!" —DIANNE NEAL MATTHEWS

FAITH STEP: *Tell Jesus you want to know Him on a deeper level. Ask Him to show you which steps you need to take to nurture your relationship.*

WEDNESDAY, AUGUST 8

You, friends, are well-warned. Be on guard lest you lose your footing
and get swept off your feet by these lawless and loose-talking teachers.
Grow in grace and understanding of our Master and Savior, Jesus Christ.
Glory to the Master, now and forever! Yes! 2 Peter 3:17–18 (MSG)

BACK IN HIGH SCHOOL I went on a summer youth-group camping trip to Matthiessen State Park in Illinois. It's a beautiful area, and we took time to explore some of the canyons, creeks, and waterfalls.

In order to reach one waterfall, we hiked through a creek for a half mile or so. The water was mostly calm, but in one spot there was a four-foot drop between two boulders that we had to maneuver around, gripping rocks to keep from being swept down the rapids.

I was petite, so standing against the current required a lot of effort. My feet slipped on the mossy rocks, and down I went.

Fortunately, I was able to grab hold of one of the boulders and reach up for help. The water's force would've pulled me under, but I was rescued in time.

Losing our footing of faith can happen swiftly when we aren't on our guard. Spending time with God, reading the Bible, praying, and being in fellowship with other Christians helps us to grow and to understand Him. Maintaining those habits is like packing on spiritual muscle that helps us stand firmly against fears, worries, goals, and temptations that contradict what Jesus really wants for us.

Following Jesus's path will include beautiful experiences. But when we face slippery spots, living in Him will provide the strength and steadying handholds we need. —ERIN KEELEY MARSHALL

FAITH STEP: *When have you slipped in your life's journey? Maybe a decision you regretted or a time you wished you had trusted and rested in Him more? Choose your footing today, and trust Him to be your sureness.*

THURSDAY, AUGUST 9

"Come to me, all you who are weary and burdened, and I will give you rest."
Matthew 11:28 (NIV)

WE HAD JUST RETURNED FROM a wonderful wedding anniversary trip, the finale to a yearlong celebration. Reluctantly, I looked at a hastily scrawled to-do list. A mountain of work waited for my attention, but my spirit sagged, and my energy lagged. Over six hundred e-mails, an empty refrigerator, and a looming writing deadline faced me. How would I ever catch up?

For several days I attempted to make a dent in the workload, but weariness would overtake me. I almost nodded off in my prayer time. Writing taxed my brain muscles, and grocery shopping zapped my energy. One morning, I gave up and lay down at noon—for just a few minutes—I told myself. Four hours later, I woke up, rebuking myself for being lazy.

I couldn't understand what was happening until I looked up "jet lag" on my computer. According to one article, it could last the same number of days as the time zones we had crossed in traveling. We had crossed five. I thought back to the day we returned from our trip. The first night home, I slept thirteen hours—but it still wasn't long enough. I sighed with relief and gave my body permission to catch up.

Jesus knows our makeup. He created us with precision. I understood in a fresh way Jesus's invitation to find rest in Him. Our bodies do get tired. And physical weariness can affect every part of our being. Instead of questioning our spiritual or emotional condition, sometimes all we truly need is rest, sweet rest in Jesus. —REBECCA BARLOW JORDAN

FAITH STEP: *Examine your workload alongside the amount of sleep/rest that you allow your body each week. See if there is some room for adjustment.*

FRIDAY, AUGUST 10

My grace is enough; it's all you need. My strength comes into its own in your weakness. Once I heard that, I was glad to let it happen. I quit focusing on the handicap and began appreciating the gift. It was a case of Christ's strength moving in on my weakness. 2 Corinthians 12:9 (MSG)

THREE YEARS AGO EVERYTHING CHANGED for me. I needed a routine medical procedure and was told it was scheduled for the coming Friday. I was on call for newborn emergency transports that weekend and no one else could cover my call, so I requested that the procedure be rescheduled for the following week. That's why I was in an ambulance instead of at home recovering from outpatient surgery that Saturday. I lost the hearing in my right ear after an abrupt pressure change when the back doors opened. Although my hearing loss, which was originally thought to be total and permanent, improved enough that a hearing aid helps, I still struggle with balance and cognition.

My mother used to say, "No good deed goes unpunished." I have to say it irked me that this happened because I'd been trying to do a good thing rather than just accepting the appointment as scheduled and calling in sick. I knew I wasn't indispensable. The hospital would have survived without me.

I wonder, though, where following Jesus enters the picture in the specifics of my life, and this incident in particular. Was He caught off guard and surprised by what happened? I don't believe He was. Jesus knows me and knows I follow Him. I came to a fork in the road and made a decision that had consequences.

I am different now. Weaker, but depending more on Him.

His grace is sufficient. —SUZANNE DAVENPORT TIETJEN

FAITH STEP: *Paul's weakness kept him from pride. Imagine your weakness being the place where Christ's power rests in you. What might that look like?*

SATURDAY, AUGUST 11

Don't copy the behavior and customs of this world, but let God transform
you into a new person by changing the way you think. Then you will learn to
know God's will for you, which is good and pleasing and perfect.
Romans 12:2 *(NLT)*

EVERY SWIMSUIT I HAVE EVER owned has been bought after trying on about seven hundred of them. But recently I found an ad online for a tankini that looked promising. They asked that you measure yourself with a tape measure and choose your size accordingly. The suit was only seventeen dollars. Cheap and easy...my love language.

Yesterday it arrived. I opened it and started laughing. Apparently, they measured the top half of my swimsuit at about a women's size eighteen. And the bottom half? A kids' size 3T. I could donate it to a preschooler. My son, Will, saw the bottoms on the table and said, "No, Mom. Just no." You can understand Will's concern. I should have known better. There are no shortcuts in swimsuit shopping. Or in life, for that matter.

The life that we long for comes when we submit every inch of ourselves to Jesus. No shortcuts allowed. It is not easy. It is not cheap. But the end result is total transformation. We can live on our own terms but it never gets us what we want or need. We want to be His, transformed by His love and grace and right thinking. We want to be found in the center of Jesus's palm, fulfilling the life that He has for us. It just doesn't get any better than that.
—SUSANNA FOTH AUGHTMON

FAITH STEP: *Where are you in your walk with Jesus? Are you trying to take shortcuts? Ask Jesus to show you His plan and path for your day as you welcome transformation.*

SUNDAY, AUGUST 12

"For this is what the Lord, the God of Israel, says: There will always be flour and olive oil left in your containers until the time when the Lord sends rain and the crops grow again!" 1 Kings 17:14 (NLT)

A WIDOW HAD ONLY A handful of flour and a little oil left in her kitchen. But as she was gathering sticks outside for a fire in order to prepare a last meal for herself and her son, the prophet Elijah approached her and asked for a drink and a little bread. The woman apologized: She didn't have enough to feed him. But Elijah persisted. He told the woman to first make him a biscuit and then to prepare a meal for herself and her son. The woman obeyed, and from that day on until God sent rain, she had a daily supply of oil and flour.

Just as Jesus fed the multitudes with only a few loaves and fishes from a young boy, we have seen Him turn a little into more than enough. As a young couple who lived not only from paycheck to paycheck, but who had to stagger their bills for payment, and who had no savings account for vacations, college, or children's weddings, and few resources for future retirement, we've experienced Jesus's provision for us repeatedly in times of drought—often in miraculous ways. Through the years we've given back to Jesus out of our limited resources, watching Him multiply the rest.

I began writing with only a flame in my heart and little training, simply offering Jesus what I had. But He has been more than faithful to take that desire and turn it into downpours of blessings.

When you give to Jesus whatever you have, trusting Him with the outcome, the promise in Philippians 4:19 will always stand. He truly will provide for all our needs. —REBECCA BARLOW JORDAN

FAITH STEP: *Today offer Jesus whatever you have. Then watch and see how He will use your limited resources for His glory.*

MONDAY, AUGUST 13

But grow in the grace and knowledge of our Lord and Savior Jesus Christ. To him be the glory both now and to the day of eternity. Amen. 2 Peter 3:18 (ESV)

LAST SUMMER, MY HUSBAND, DAUGHTER, and I went to the state fair. We arrived in time to watch the horse-riding competitions. I've always loved horses and gentle rides. However, the riding we saw was on a completely different level. Sitting in the front row, I felt the energy of the horse as it galloped past, leaning into the curve and kicking up dust. Teams of riders then charged around barrels, weaving tight patterns in perfect timing.

The power and skill of both horse and rider astounded me, and I clapped until my hands were sore. When the announcer introduced the next competition, children rode in and wove their ponies between poles. I realized that I was watching the early process of developing the skills for barrel racing.

The stages of growth in the riders reminded me of our spiritual journey. When we begin our walk with Jesus, we are like those children on their ponies, enjoying the ride.

As we confront new obstacles, He deepens our faith. We learn to adjust our balance, lean into Him more, and focus on Him. Like a rider galloping at full speed, we learn to take more risks in our faith and trust Him in difficult times. Sometimes we fall. Our mistakes make us even more aware of our need for His grace. Other times we dig into the Word. Scripture, fellowship with others, and time in prayer all help us grow in our knowledge of Jesus.

Let's heed the invitation of 2 Peter 3:18 and grow in both "the grace and knowledge of our Lord and Savior Jesus Christ." —SHARON HINCK

FAITH STEP: *Watch a video of rodeo events and think about the steps of growth involved. Ask Jesus to help you grow in Him today.*

TUESDAY, AUGUST 14

They have stumbled off the ancient highways and walk in muddy paths.
Jeremiah 18:15 (NLT)

SCROLLING THROUGH PICTURES ON MY phone, it was easy to be distracted by scenes of Mount Hood, Mount St. Helens, Cannon Beach. I flipped through images of a week at a beach in South Carolina and a fondly remembered vacation in Charleston.

It was good to be reminded of where we'd been.

Someday my husband and I are going to pack our bags, get in the car, and head for destinations unknown. It will be a vacation unlike the others, which were carefully researched, planned, and mapped out. We'll stop at every location that catches our interest rather than adhering to a schedule. We'll choose the slowest route. We'll check out places that aren't on every tourist's must-see list.

But side roads don't work well on *spiritual* journeys.

In the book of Jeremiah, the prophet often warned people to return to God's ways. But the people replied, "We will continue to live as we want to, stubbornly following our own...desires." Jeremiah 18:12 (NLT).

A few verses later, veering off His path sounded like this: "My people...have deserted me;...They have stumbled off the ancient highways and walk in muddy paths." Jeremiah 18:15 (NLT).

God's way is Jesus. *The* Way. He is a faithful path. But that doesn't make the trip boring. Ask anyone who has followed Jesus. Heartening sunrises with mercies new every morning and sunsets with the promise of the sweet sleep of a soul at peace. And curves and cliff edges that have us clinging to His robes. Boring? Never.

Life with Jesus is always a grand adventure. —CYNTHIA RUCHTI

FAITH STEP: *Take a look at your travel itinerary for today; your heart's pursuits and habits. Can you confidently say they stick to the main road—the Way—the path Jesus carved and invites us to follow?*

WEDNESDAY, AUGUST 15

So now we can rejoice in our wonderful new relationship with God because our Lord Jesus Christ has made us friends of God.
Romans 5:11 (NLT)

SOMETIMES AN INTRODUCTION CAN CHANGE a person's life. It happened to me at the outset of my writing career. At the time, I intended to develop a line of greeting cards, so I produced ten samples and sent them to a publisher with high hopes of landing a contract.

An editor, in a rejection letter, dashed those hopes, but he introduced me to a well-known card designer who gave me some tips.

That designer and I became friends. When his wife developed cancer, he asked me to join their prayer support team. Later I wrote his story for a widespread publication, and countless readers received encouragement through it.

I'm forever grateful to that editor for making my friendship with the card designer possible. But I'm far more grateful to Jesus for making my friendship with Almighty God possible!

We can try to gain access to God by being good people. We can hope to develop a relationship with Him by obeying rules, or volunteering time. But our efforts fail without Jesus Christ.

Jesus said, "I am the way and the truth and the life. No one can come to the Father except through me" (John 14:6, NIV). His death and resurrection provided the means for us to enter into a relationship with God and to enjoy friendship with Him forever.

This relationship is too precious to keep to ourselves. Let's pray for the loving boldness needed to introduce others to Jesus so that they might enjoy friendship with God, too. —GRACE FOX

FAITH STEP: *What does true friendship look like to you? List three characteristics of a good friend and then consider how Jesus demonstrates those qualities.*

THURSDAY, AUGUST 16

The eternal God is your dwelling place, and underneath are the everlasting arms. Deuteronomy 33:27 (ESV)

THERE ARE NO WORDS TO describe some moments in life. For example, after a day and a half of driving, we pull into the driveway at our daughter and son-in-law's house. As soon as I step out of the car, the front door swings open and two little bodies come flying out. I lean forward, stretch out my arms, and suddenly my granddaughter and grandson are plastered against me. Then I go into the house and greet whoever is holding the baby. When I stretch out my hands, the baby leans toward me. No words.

If an ordinary nana feels such joy when her grandchildren hurl themselves into her arms, can you imagine how Jesus must love it when we run to Him? When we feel weak, His arms support and strengthen us. During times of grief and hurt, His arms comfort us. If we're lonely, He wraps us in tenderness and love. And the best part of all? His arms are always there. Everlasting arms ready to hold us up through each season of life.

When I read the story of Esther approaching her husband to intercede for the Jewish people, I can't help but contrast King Xerxes with our King of kings. Esther knew that anyone who approached the king in his inner court without being summoned would be executed, unless the king held out his golden scepter. But we are invited to approach our loving Savior with confidence that we will receive grace (Hebrews 4:16). When I remember the times I've run into Jesus's nail-scarred arms, there are no words to describe those moments. —DIANNE NEAL MATTHEWS

FAITH STEP: *What do you need from Jesus's everlasting arms right now? Try to visualize His pleasure when you run to Him, trusting Him to hold you up.*

FRIDAY, AUGUST 17

We urge you, brethren, admonish the unruly, encourage the fainthearted, help the weak, be patient with everyone. 1 Thessalonians 5:14 (NASB)

EVERY AUGUST I'D RETURN TO my third-grade classroom to begin the ritual of preparing for the start of the school year. Desks were neatly placed, quotes about reading hung on the walls, and twinkle lights gave the room a dreamy glow. When my room was ready I'd say, "I'd be a fantastic teacher if kids didn't have to come in and mess up my room and my plans!"

The truth is that people, like children, are messy. They have habits and behaviors that we must learn to nurture rather than ignore. When our lives rub against lazy or needy people, it's tempting to try to "fix" them and then be on our way—but Scripture invites us to something deeper. To walk alongside the weak, frightened, lonely, and fainthearted, we need the power of patience. Patience is the fruit of the Spirit we'd like to skip, because the only way to grow this fruit is to be annoyed and tested.

I once worked with a woman whom everyone backed away from. She was needy, she was lazy, and she seemed to push her work onto anyone else she could find to take it. Every day as I pulled into the parking lot I asked Jesus how I could affect her life with His discipline and grace. Wouldn't you know I was placed with her on a long-term project that demanded a lot from both of us. During this time I was able to teach her the respect of sharing loads. We soon thrived as a team, and people began to enjoy her quirky personality. Without patience and intentional love, she never would have become the woman she longed to be. It showed me yet again the great power of Jesus's tender care. —GARI MEACHAM

FAITH STEP: *Ask God for one person to love whom others may find annoying.*

SATURDAY, AUGUST 18

Let us throw off everything that hinders and the sin that so easily entangles. And let us run with perseverance the race marked out for us, fixing our eyes on Jesus, the pioneer and perfecter of faith. Hebrews 12:1–2 (NIV)

IT WAS WINDOW-WASHING TIME AT the Marshall household. I woke up that Saturday morning thinking I'd do some mirrors and picture glass, and then suddenly I was washing away fingerprints from interior French doors, windowpanes, and trim. By that point, I decided, why not go outside and get it all done?

It had already been a long day when I noticed the renewed sparkle of our home and was motivated to finish the job. The afternoon sun was hot and made it difficult to keep streaks from showing. But I kept on. I finished two sides and moved toward the back. Along that outside wall, tall windows offer a glimpse into our kitchen. And along those windows is a row of rosebushes. They're vibrant pink, with lovely blooms that seem to last forever. Those bushes were between the windows and me, but I saw enough space to wedge myself into so I could clean the outside glass.

It wasn't enough to keep me from the thorns! Dozens of them, all poking, painful nuisances. I was entangled.

Isn't that how the enemy works? Even when we're doing our best to clean out old habits and distractions that keep us from seeing Jesus clearly, we feel the thorns of temptations, attitudes, worries, and other problems that try to trap us.

I finished the windows, but I got a reminder to watch for the enemy's snags, and to appreciate Jesus's help in taking on the enemy's thorns for us. —ERIN KEELEY MARSHALL

FAITH STEP: *Bring your camera on a walk in search of roses. Post a picture and ask Jesus for help to keep from getting entangled by the enemy's thorns.*

SUNDAY, AUGUST 19

This will be a Sabbath day of complete rest for you, and on that day you must deny yourselves. Leviticus 23:32 (NLT)

THERE ARE FEWER THINGS HARDER for a busy mom than to sit down, sit still, and rest. As a mom with ten kids—eight in the home—there is always something to pick up, clean, or cook. There is always someone who needs help or attention. The idea of rest, truly resting, seems impossible even on Sundays. Half of the day is spent getting everyone ready for church and attending it. The other half of the day is spent attempting to prepare for the week ahead. Yet for all of us busy people, rest is exactly what we need.

The Lord first spoke of Sabbath rest to the Israelites who had just escaped from Egypt, where they'd been slaves for hundreds of years. As slaves, they didn't know what rest was, but God wanted them to realize that their lives were no longer just about work and duty. He invited them to be His people, not because of what they did, but because He'd chosen them. The Sabbath rest applied to the first day of the week, and to appointed holy days. And knowing the human heart, God knew they'd have to deny themselves.

As a wife and a mom, rest feels like denying myself. When I do take a break, that means I can't check items off my list, or feel content with a pile of folded laundry, or gaze around at a freshly cleaned room. Resting is denying my need to achieve, yet it's also realizing that I'm enough on my own even if I'm not productive for a day. When I decide to rest, I acknowledge that it's not what I do, it's who I am in Jesus Christ that matters. —TRICIA GOYER

FAITH STEP: *Right now, plan ahead for Sunday to be a day of rest for you. Find ways to clear a large chunk of time just to be present with Jesus—without achieving anything.*

MONDAY, AUGUST 20

It's wonderful what happens when Christ displaces worry at the center of your life. Philippians 4:7 (MSG)

I HATED THAT MY PARENTS were worriers when I was growing up, and I told myself I'd be a more carefree mother. I'd let my kids climb trees without saying, "Be careful!" and wouldn't imagine worst-case scenarios. Then they began to have accidents. By the time the ER staff greeted my son, Zachary, by name on our third visit in two months, I'd turned into my mother. I tried to keep my three kids safe by anticipating anything that could go wrong, believing I could somehow keep them from harm.

Needless to say, it didn't work. I annoyed my children, modeled fear, and allowed worry to take over more territory in my life. The children have flown the nest now, but I still waste energy and inner peace worrying. It's bad for my health, shows a lack of faith, and does absolutely no good.

David, the man after God's own heart, said, "Do not fret—*it* only *causes* harm (Psalm 37:8 NKJV). Worry weighs us down and is a symptom of wanting our own way. Worry turns us inward and takes our focus away from Jesus. God's Word always condemns worry, and never encourages it.

Jesus didn't worry. We don't have to, either. Here's how: "Instead of worrying, pray. Let petitions and praises shape your worries into prayers, letting God know your concerns. Before you know it, a sense of God's wholeness, everything coming together for good, will come and settle you down" (Philippians 4:6–7, MSG).

Sounds good to me. No worries! —SUZANNE DAVENPORT TIETJEN

FAITH STEP: *Jot down every worry you have. Then put it out of your mind. During your prayer time, use your list of worries to shape your prayers.*

TUESDAY, AUGUST 21

Delight yourself in the Lord, and he will give you the desires of your heart.
Psalm 37:4 (ESV)

SOME PEOPLE (WINK) HAVE USED and abused this verse to "hustle" God. "God," I'd bargain, "I am delighting in you by reading my Bible, praying, and serving at church, so give me what I want."

In my ongoing negotiations with God, I have often tried to get Him to do my bidding by my pretend obedience, worship, delight. I'm not talking about all-out lying, like a scam artist bilking millions. I'm talking about obeying, praying, because I want things to go my way, because somewhere in my heart I believe I'll get demerits if I don't. I'd try hard to conjure "delight in the Lord", when I'd really rather "delight in a pedicure". How foolish of me! God sees right through my manipulation. Remember the Pharisees? Am I so different?

Sometimes God gently reveals this to me, and I've chosen to stop whatever practice simply as an act of faith in a God of grace.

I delight in my children. Just holding them fills me with deep satisfaction. This delight is not manipulative. It's spontaneous and true. But it's also not enduring, even with my precious kids. I still get up to check e-mail. Likewise, I cannot contrive to delight in the Lord. Getting to a place where He is genuinely enough for me happens only when there's nothing else for me to consider. But there's always something else. When I have soaked up so much of Him and shed so much of me, usually the hard way, the desires of my heart gradually change, as they have.

Thanks to Jesus, I don't have to try so hard or even try at all. He blesses me because of His gracious love and Christ's perfect delight, not mine. —ISABELLA YOSUICO

FAITH STEP: *Are you hustling God? Admit that to Him and talk to Him honestly about your desires. Then leave the results in His capable hands.*

WEDNESDAY, AUGUST 22

"Your old men will dream dreams, your young men will see visions."
Joel 2:28 *(NASB)*

IT WAS ONE OF THOSE days you wish you didn't have to endure. While working in Uganda, my mission team missed their two-day flight back to the United States, and we were faced with the possibility of not getting home for another week. To make matters worse, every hotel within miles of the airport was booked solid. We had no way to get home and nowhere to stay. In the midst of this frustration we remembered the name of a hotel we hadn't tried. Nearing the midnight hour, one of my staff members listlessly dialed the number, expecting the same response. To our surprise, the hotel manager said he had room for our team, so we stuffed ourselves back into our van and drove to the address.

After settling our team members into their rooms, the hotel manager asked to speak to me privately. He explained that immediately before we called he was awakened from a deep sleep by Jesus Christ. He told me that Jesus explained there were people in trouble, and he was to help them. I almost fell off my seat! We both had chills on our arms as he spoke, and to top it off, he was a Muslim man married to a Christian woman. "Why would Jesus show Himself to me?" he kept asking. All I could say was, "He loves and trusts you, and He heard our prayers for help."

Before leaving the hotel a few days later, my team gathered around our new friend and prayed for him with joyful thanksgiving. I've never forgotten his kindness, nor the revelation that God can speak in any way He chooses—even in the dead of night to a man who hasn't yet embraced Him. —GARI MEACHAM

FAITH STEP: *When was the last time you heard something about Jesus that knocked you off your feet? Thank Him today that He is alive, real, and active all over the world.*

THURSDAY, AUGUST 23

"The Spirit of the Lord is upon me, for he has anointed me to bring Good News to the poor. He has sent me to proclaim that captives will be released, that the blind will see, that the oppressed will be set free, and that the time of the Lord's favor has come." Luke 4:18–19 (NLT)

I TEND TO BUCK THE rules. I have had this tendency since I was a small child. Just ask my parents. I caused them no end of consternation. I saw rules as a barrier to my freedom. Rules shaped my view of how I saw Jesus. He was all "don't dos" and "can't haves" as far as I was concerned. What fun is that? It wasn't until my college years that I realized that, without Him, I would destroy myself. I was all good intentions and bad choices.

I slowly began to recognize that His ways weren't a barrier to my freedom. They were the only way to freedom. His laws weren't a blockade to fun; they were my jumping-off place into the safety and protection of His wide arms. Jesus's intentions for me weren't a load of backbreaking rules. His intentions were to liberate me from sin. To set my feet on a path of freedom. To unleash a new creation from the prison of bad habits and self-destruction. He was beating back my soul-crushing desires and selfish thinking so that I could live free in Him.

I am still learning this as I lean in and know Him more. Jesus is all about freedom. Freedom from addiction. From pain. From suffering. From heartache. From sin. From loneliness. From fear. How can we not see that? How can we not embrace it? His way of living is so beautiful and life-giving. Let's hold on to Him with both hands and let Him set us free. —SUSANNA FOTH AUGHTMON

FAITH STEP: *Go for a walk or a run. Open your arms wide. Imagine yourself receiving all the freedom that Jesus has for you.*

FRIDAY, AUGUST 24

"As for me, I know that my Redeemer lives, And at the last He will take His stand on the earth." Job 19:25 (NASB)

I UNDERSTAND THAT THIS EARTHLY life includes problems and troubles, but honestly, some seasons of our lives are especially hard, aren't they? My husband and I have just passed through a year that seemed to bring one crisis after another: unexpected job termination, serious illness and hospitalization, the turmoil of relocating again, the death of a parent. If I include my extended family, that adds other major crises to the list.

During such unsettling times, it's easy to get shaken by the uncertainty of life, especially when our minds are filled with questions. *Why is this happening? How will I ever get over this? What does the future hold? Will my life ever resemble "normal" again?* Surely these questions also filled Job's mind during his period of severe trials, when it seemed that everything good was stripped away from him. Yet even in the midst of expressing his grief, confusion, and pain, he occasionally burst forth with a statement of faith. Regardless of his feelings and circumstances, one thing Job knew: He had a living Redeemer whom he would see face-to-face one day.

It's okay to question why things happen to us. While we may never understand all the reasons during this lifetime, we can cling to what we do know: Jesus loves us so much that He died for us. He holds our present and our future in His hands and is working out everything for good. Meditating on these truths puts our earthly trials in perspective. —DIANNE NEAL MATTHEWS

FAITH STEP: *Make a list of your favorite Bible verses. Choose a few to be your designated statements of faith for when you go through a "Job" season of life. If you find yourself struggling to pray, begin with one of these affirmation verses.*

SATURDAY, AUGUST 25

"You profane me when you say, 'Worship is not important, and what we bring to worship is of no account,' and when you say, 'I'm bored—this doesn't do anything for me.'" Malachi 1:12 (MSG)

BOREDOM HAS RARELY, IF EVER, entered my vocabulary. Perhaps I owe that to my pastor father, whose motto was, "Always have something to do today, something to do tomorrow." I remember a few of his side hobbies: growing an orchard, restoring old Model T cars, and helping build missions. The joyful duty of pastoring filled his days, as well as, of course, being a dad.

My mom kept busy, too. A piano teacher, substitute schoolteacher, collector of small antiques, reader of a gazillion books, great cook. All that and being a pastor's wife and pianist/organist for many of their pastorates. And being a mom.

Following their pattern, I've always enjoyed a variety of interests in life. But I changed my father's slogan to, "Always have something to look forward to today, something to look forward to tomorrow." Anticipating what Jesus may bring on any given day helps balance all my activities. I do procrastinate with less pleasant tasks. But I never want the tyranny of something urgent to block the joy of my journey.

Through the prophet Malachi, God accused the high priests of presenting imperfect sacrifices. They had become bored with worshipping God. They failed to understand the joyful purpose of Christ-centered living (Matthew 23:23).

Our lives are consumed with worship. Boredom could mean that we are failing to see Jesus's perspective in life. But if we let Him, Jesus wants to put joy in our journey. —REBECCA BARLOW JORDAN

FAITH STEP: *Make a list of things that bring you joy. Include at least one of those activities daily, along with spending time with Jesus.*

SUNDAY, AUGUST 26

A thorn was given me in the flesh, a messenger of Satan to harass me, to keep
me from becoming conceited. Three times I pleaded with the Lord about this,
that it should leave me. But he said to me, "My grace is sufficient for you,
for my power is made perfect in weakness." Therefore I will boast all the
more gladly of my weaknesses, so that the power of Christ may rest upon me.
2 Corinthians 12:7–9 (ESV)

SCHOLARS THEORIZE THAT PAUL MAY have suffered from an eye ail-
ment. I think Paul's thorn could just as easily have been fear, glut-
tony, drunkenness, or something else less plain-vanilla. Whatever
the case, Paul knew God and himself enough to know that God was
allowing the affliction to remain in Paul.

Jesus removed a few of my thorns when I became a Christian,
some so swiftly and completely that there was no denying Who did
it. Other failings have improved over time.

But I have a few defects and weaknesses that linger. I've thought
to myself, I'd be much more effective if I were, well, perfect.

Here is where Paul nails it. My weaknesses are the best things I
have going for me. If it wasn't for them, you can be quite sure I'd
be ready to take the reins of my life, and maybe yours, too. Yikes!

My failings keep me humble, and sometimes so broken that I cry
out to Jesus. When I reach that point, I see Christ's grace rush in
and something wondrous happens. I feel a deep sense of peace and
freedom, and I also see God using me in a remarkable way.

In my flesh, I have contempt for weakness. Viewed in the light of
Christ and Paul's retellings, I, too, can boast of the weakness that
allows Christ to work through me. —ISABELLA YOSUICO

FAITH STEP: *Take a few minutes to write about the thorns Christ has taken from*
you and those He's left behind. Thank Him for both!

MONDAY, AUGUST 27

Observe how Christ loved us. His love was not cautious but extrava-gant ... [not] in order to get something from us but to give everything of himself to us. Love like that. Ephesians 5:2 (MSG)

LOVING PEOPLE IN A WAY that makes them feel cherished is an art form. Cherished is how my brother and sister-in-law made me feel during a recent weekend visit to their home. They anticipated my every need and extended themselves to make sure I not only had a place to pillow my head but a comfortable place to pillow my heart as well.

They went out of their way to meet my quirky dietary requirements. If I started to feel thirsty, almost before I could voice it or head to the sink to get a drink of water, one of the two of them was at my elbow with an array of options. They remembered how much I'd enjoyed a local restaurant on my last visit, knew my favorite music, insisted on carrying my bags even though I could have done it, and rearranged their schedules to accommodate mine. They set a place for me at the table so I could catch the best view. They listened unhurriedly. Loaded with their own concerns, they volunteered to shoulder mine, too.

When the weekend was over, they packed leftovers and treats to send home with me. Before we parted—and this is the most cherished moment—they wrapped me in their embrace and prayed for me.

It was at Jesus's feet that they learned the art of cherishing others. They'd experienced His extravagant love, watched how He antici-pates our needs, and determined to pattern their caring after His. Aiming for something higher and purer than hospitality, they dem-onstrated what we all need: to feel cherished. —CYNTHIA RUCHTI

FAITH STEP: *Somebody in your circle of friends and family is thirsty for a sip of Living Water, hungry for a bite of Bread, longing to know the extravagant love of Jesus. Are you the cherisher who will show them what it looks like, tastes like?*

TUESDAY, AUGUST 28

So now there is no condemnation for those who belong to Christ Jesus. And because you belong to him, the power of the life-giving Spirit has freed you from the power of sin that leads to death. Romans 8:1–2 (NLT)

I LOVE CONNECTING WITH OLD friends. On Facebook I'm "friends" with people I haven't seen since elementary school. And recently we had our family photos done by a friend whom I've known for twenty-five years. At the end of the photo session, Jessica and I reminisced about how we first met and marveled at how much has changed in our lives. It's wonderful to have such a long history with some-one... well, unless there are things in your history you wish to forget.

Sometimes when I connect with an old friend, I cringe over all they know about me. About my poor relationship choices or the fistfight I got into after one homecoming football game. People who've known me a long time know about my teen pregnancy, too.

It's also amazing that while those memories are still there, the condemnation is not. Because I've given my life and heart to Jesus, all the sin that used to bind me no longer holds me captive. Because of Jesus I have freedom and life in the Spirit. I'm not just fixed up; I'm new and clean. And I also make different choices.

As 1 Corinthians 1:30 says, "Christ made us right with God; he made us pure and holy, and he freed us from sin" (NLT). This is not only a message for me, but for all my friends who are still carrying the burden of sin and condemnation. Because they know where I've been and what I've done, they're also an eyewitness to the transformation Jesus brings. Knowing this reminds me not to hide from my past, but to tell those in my past that they can be transformed by Jesus, too. —TRICIA GOYER

FAITH STEP: *Reach out to an old friend this week. See the renewal of your relationship as a chance to share all that Jesus has done in your life.*

WEDNESDAY, AUGUST 29

*Jesus saith unto him, Go thy way; thy son liveth. And the man
believed the word that Jesus had spoken unto him, and he went his way.
And as he was now going down, his servants met him, and told him, saying,
Thy son liveth. John 4:50–51 (KJV)*

THE LAST TIME I WAS in Berlin, I saw a mural painted on a building that read "Believing is seeing." It was in German, but I loved it. It's a good way to describe faith, as the evidence of things unseen. We witness this in practice by the nobleman in John 4 who comes to Jesus asking for a miracle. He believes—and then he sees.

How often I demand that it be the other way around. As an academic, I'm trained not to accept any argument that is presented without evidence. First you show me evidence, then I might believe your claim. There is no risk involved in this; as long as the evidence is sufficient, the point is proven. No chance I'll be fooled or look stupid for believing. No way I'll have hope and then be disappointed. I'm in control of the outcome. Every time.

As He did with many human concepts, Jesus turns this idea upside down. He invites us to see beyond a scientific dimension into a spiritual one. Faith doesn't defy logic. It transcends it.

Case in point: If seeing is believing, I will approach my illness with the fear of disappointment until I see my test results. But if believing is seeing, I can move forward in confidence that I am healed. I don't get to choose how He does it, or whether it's even physical healing that He's accomplishing in me. But I trust that He heals me, because Jesus calls Himself my Healer.

For a believer, the difference between these approaches is peace that transcends our understanding. —GWEN FORD FAULKENBERRY

FAITH STEP: *What do you most want to see? Frist, believe.*

THURSDAY, AUGUST 30

When Jesus saw his mother standing there beside the disciple he loved, he said to her, "Dear woman, here is your son." And he said to this disciple, "Here is your mother." And from then on this disciple took her into his home. John 19:26–27 (NLT)

MY HUSBAND AND I SPEND months preparing for our annual eastern European ministries. We host a booth at mission conferences, process application forms, sort and pack donations, organize teaching materials, train volunteers, and purchase airline tickets. Add a myriad of household chores prior to departure, toss in a few short nights, and we're tired before we reach the airport.

Our usual flight leaves at 9:00 p.m. Because we're early risers, we've already been awake for fifteen hours by the time our plane takes off. We'll travel for more than twenty hours to reach our final destination. I can't sleep on airplanes, so my body aches with fatigue by the time we arrive in Budapest.

It takes effort and prayer not to become self-focused when I'm overtired. I rely on supernatural strength to answer volunteers' questions and ensure their needs are met before I go to sleep.

Jesus never succumbed to a self-focused attitude. Even as His life ebbed away. Despite pain that defied imagination, He acknowledged His mother standing near the cross. Then He saw the disciple John, and He connected the two. By doing so, He ensured that His mother's needs would be met after He was gone.

No one would have blamed Jesus if He'd overlooked this act of kindness, but doing so was not in His nature. He came to serve. And He stayed true to this mission until death. —GRACE FOX

FAITH STEP: *Stand at a window and look outside. What do you see? People driving or walking to and fro? Ask Jesus to love people through you and to give you strength to remain others-focused, especially when you're tired.*

FRIDAY, AUGUST 31

"My sheep listen to my voice; I know them, and they follow me.
I give them eternal life, and they will never perish.
No one can snatch them away from me." John 10:27–28 (NLT)

NOT ONE OF MY FRIENDS or family members will sit by me when we go to see a suspenseful movie. They even refuse to sit next to me in a good, old-fashioned drama. I tend to become totally engrossed in the movie, especially if the actors are in trouble. I begin interacting with the characters by yelling out to them. This is why no one wants to share popcorn with me.

My movie behavior is not a new development. When *Titanic* came out what seems like ages ago, my family took a vote to see who would have to sit with me. They didn't want to be associated with me when I was shouting out for people to "Jump!" and "Swim!" and "For goodness' sake, help those people get into the lifeboats already!"

I think Jesus is yelling out to us in the same way when He watches our lives play out. He interacts with us when we make choices and decide on our paths. He wants to save us. He calls out, "Come to Me!" and "Let Me save you!" Unlike my ineffectual, movie-screen yelling, Jesus has words for us that can change our lives, words of truth and hope and light. Words that can and will shape us into the people that He intends for us to be.

Jesus has a plan and a path for us, and if we listen for His voice of love, He will direct us. He will guide us. He will save us. His words are like oxygen, sustaining us no matter what we are going through. If we listen for His voice, He will always rescue us.
—SUSANNA FOTH AUGHTMON

FAITH STEP: *Read John 10 and then take some time to listen to Jesus's voice. What is He saying to your heart?*

SATURDAY, SEPTEMBER 1

*Now may the God of hope fill you with all joy and peace in believing,
so that you will abound in hope by the power of the Holy Spirit.*
Romans 15:13 *(NASB)*

MY STAFF AND MISSION TEAM had just ended a day of service in Kamuli, Uganda, when we entered our office. Toward the front was a row of stately women sitting on a bench. They were wearing perfectly creased dresses with posture that held them upright and proud. They'd been there for hours waiting for our return. Lily introduced her nine-year-old daughter, Rachel, and said she wanted to share her story.

She'd been married to a harsh man, and after the birth of their first child she had developed an infection that forced her to travel to the hospital for care. Lily was turned away because she didn't have enough money for the treatment. She decided to see an alternative medicine man several miles away. He told her he could help, but the payment would be a sexual relationship. Lily refused. He forced himself on her—leaving her assaulted and traumatized. A few months later, she realized she was pregnant with his child, and had AIDS. Little Rachel began weeping as she explained that she was born with AIDS, and her mama's husband abandoned them. Rachel whispered that she'd asked Jesus for help this year, and knew that He would somehow answer. Our hearts broke as we heard this story, but we knew our mission. We promised we'd do all we could to get Rachel back into school and healthy. And we kept that promise.

Today Rachel is leading her class in her studies, and sings love songs to Jesus all throughout her day. —GARI MEACHAM

FAITH STEP: *Do you know someone who needs hope today? Stop right now and pray for them, text them, or send a kind note.*

SUNDAY, SEPTEMBER 2

When the cool evening breezes were blowing, the man and his wife heard the LORD God walking about in the garden. So they hid from the LORD God among the trees. Then the LORD God called to the man, "Where are you?"
Genesis 3:8—9 (NLT)

HIDE-AND-SEEK CAN BE A FUN children's game, but in real life, our efforts to run and hide from Jesus can be tragic. Imagine, if when our Lord walked into the garden and discovered that Adam and Eve were missing, He simply left them to their choices, their sin, their knowledge of evil, and all of the consequences. Thankfully, He called to them. He kept pursuing, initiating a relationship.

Jesus's life was the ultimate act of searching out and restoring the relationship between humanity and God. Yet even today, I find myself hiding from Him. Early in the morning, the pages of my Bible call to me. Yet I hide myself in distractions. I turn on the radio or television, boot up my computer, listen to other voices. As much as I long to know Jesus and be known by Him, my sinful nature would rather drown Him out.

In the cool of the evening, the struggles of the day swirl through my head. Jesus invites me in to conversation, to prayer time that will deepen our relationship. Instead I turn first to a friend or family member. Or I research the problem. I might gather advice from experts but hold back from laying my troubles at Jesus's feet.

Today when Jesus calls, "Where are you?" darkness or dullness in our hearts may urge us to hide from His light. Instead, let's answer His call. Let's pour out our confession, our need, our praise—and trust in His steadfast love. —SHARON HINCK

FAITH STEP: *Play a game of hide-and-seek. Thank Jesus that when we try to hide from Him, He continues to find us and draws us into a relationship with Him.*

MONDAY, SEPTEMBER 3

*"Here I am! I stand at the door and knock. If anyone hears my voice
and opens the door, I will come in and eat with that person,
and they with me." Revelation 3:20 (NIV)*

IT'S THAT TIME AGAIN WHEN pools close until next summer. But
some in our house still have a little pool water clogged in their ears,
and we're trying to unclog them. It's not fun! When no amount of
hanging upside down and shaking your head is working, the feeling
slowly eats away at your patience.

My husband's ears have been the worst. We tried all the tricks
of olive oil drops, garlic oil drops, over-the-counter swimmer's
ear drops, bulb syringes to wash out whatever's clogging those ear
canals. Finally after a month, he was able to flush it out his right ear,
but he's still fighting a clog in his left. He's ready to hear again, and
I'm ready to stop repeating myself!

I've realized watching him these past weeks that the limits of our
hearing—or any of our senses—don't limit our connection to Jesus.
The deaf can hear His Spirit whisper to them. The blind can see Him
with their hearts. The mute can praise Him with their inner voice.

I've watched Steve listen closely for Jesus's direction every day,
even while his clogged ears have driven him up the wall. His sen-
sitivity to Jesus's voice is not limited by the weaknesses of his ears.

Isn't that amazing? And reassuring! There's a place inside of us
that is for Jesus only, a place in our spirit and soul that no one and
nothing can block—as long as we're looking and listening for Him.

He knows just how to reach each person, even those with serious
limitations. If you listen for Him knocking on the door of your
heart and open it to Him, He will come in and be with you.

Can you hear Him? —ERIN KEELEY MARSHALL

FAITH STEP: *What has Jesus been saying to you lately? Ask Him for a listening spirit.*

TUESDAY, SEPTEMBER 4

So that the tested genuineness of your faith . . . may be found to result in praise and glory and honor at the revelation of Jesus Christ. 1 Peter 1:7 (ESV)

AT AN AUTHOR FRIEND'S BOOK signing in a library, I sat in one of the side chairs and observed her interactions with the crowd.

In deference to the public library setting, my friend didn't try to turn the event into a preaching opportunity. She talked about her books, the characters and their heritage, the connections to the area, and the characters' journeys, and then fielded questions.

One attendee asked, "It's obvious from your stories that you are a woman of faith. Would you tell us about that?" She did. My friend wasn't stumped by the question, because her life matched the faith of the characters she writes about.

In our interactions with the public—at work, at the gym, at neighborhood gatherings—will our answers to questions like that reveal genuine faith in Jesus? Or will our answers make it obvious that we know Him in name only, not as the very vitality of our lives?

Fake faith is as see-through as plastic wrap. It can't hide what's inside. The Bible tells us that our faith is often proved authentic during the tough times in life, when we don't have a chance to think but have to respond immediately. "These [trials] have come so that the proven genuineness of your faith—of greater worth than gold, which perishes even though refined by fire—may result in praise, glory and honor when Jesus Christ is revealed" (1 Peter 1:7, NIV).

Jesus longs to see our words, actions, and hearts align with His. If any of the three are skewed or unmatched, it's an inauthentic faith.
—CYNTHIA RUCHTI

FAITH STEP: *Words. Actions. Heart. What adjustments are you willing to make so that your faith comes into clear focus—genuine, and easily read by others?*

WEDNESDAY, SEPTEMBER 5

He is before all things. Colossians 1:17 *(HCSB)*

MY NINE-YEAR-OLD DAUGHTER, ADELAIDE, IS a natural teacher. She has her own desk, fully supplied, and a chalkboard in her room, along with a massive bookshelf. She pilfers papers and worksheets from her teacher aunt. She teaches her sister, her cousins, her dog. Sometimes, she teaches her stuffed animals.

When the children's program at our church needed something new, she and her cousin, Sophia, came up with a great idea for a Bible study, led by them, complete with lessons and activities.

I said if they were going to propose such a thing to the church, then they had to plan. I told them they needed twelve lessons and activities. A list of supplies. And they would also have to enlist adults besides me as chaperones.

They got right to work. Adelaide hauled down our Children's Bible Story book and they perused its pages, marking their favorites. They pinterested ideas for crafts. They created worksheets. And they circled items in a supply catalog and made a budget. The only thing they could not get was adults on board.

I told Adelaide, with regret, that I just didn't see how I could do it by myself. She was disappointed but understood. As I washed dishes, she sat down nearby with her Bible Story book.

"What are you doing?"

"I'm taking out all of the markers, you know, where we picked the stories, since we're not going to do it." Her words stung. "No. Don't do that—please. We'll figure out a way." My little girl undoing plans for teaching others about Jesus? I had to make this happen. What else mattered? —GWEN FORD FAULKENBERRY

FAITH STEP: *Let the above verse clarify things for you today, and every day.*

THURSDAY, SEPTEMBER 6

Even before he made the world, God loved us and chose us in Christ to be holy and without fault in his eyes. God decided in advance to adopt us into his own family by bringing us to himself through Jesus Christ. This is what he wanted to do, and it gave him great pleasure. Ephesians 1:4—6 (NLT)

MY DAUGHTER LASHED OUT AT her younger brother, but the anger in her eyes quickly turned to fear. She rushed to her bedroom and something in my mind told me to follow. I found her in her room packing her backpack. I asked what she was doing. "I'm packing." She said it so plainly. It broke my heart realizing how often she'd been sent away to a new foster home because of her behavior.

"Home Sweet Home" seemed like a foreign concept to our daughters, and they had a hard time believing it when my husband and I said, "This is your forever home, we are adopting you, and you will be ours." Our children would sway between attempting to be good enough to deserve our love and acting really bad because they were so sure they were going to be kicked out anyway. It was only after a lot of love, therapy, and daily care that they understood that we meant what we said.

Seeing my children's journey has reminded me of my own. When I first joined Jesus's family, through the confession of my sins, I swung between striving to be good and doubting He loved me. My daughters have helped me to understand more how Jesus *chose* me. He adopted me and brought me to Him for His great pleasure. Adoption is something I'm still trying to understand, and something I'm forever grateful for. —TRICIA GOYER

FAITH STEP: *Write up a certificate of adoption. Seeing it, how does it make you feel to be part of Jesus's forever family? Pray and ask Him to help you to understand the truth of adoption more deeply.*

FRIDAY, SEPTEMBER 7

And all who have been united with Christ in baptism have put on Christ, like putting on new clothes. Galatians 3:27 (NLT)

AS MY GRANDDAUGHTER ENTERED THIRD grade, her family moved to a school district with a strict dress code. Students wore pants in khaki, black, or navy; polo shirts in a handful of colors; and plain dresses with polo-style tops. No jeans or glitzy accessories allowed. Lacey hated the limited wardrobe at first, but I think she grew used to it and felt a unity with the other students. I'm sure it took her less time to get ready for school back then, as opposed to now as a seventh-grader in a school with much looser guidelines.

Growing up I never had to wear a school uniform, but as a believer in Christ I do have a dress code to follow. Once we are united with Jesus, He calls us to lay aside our old, sinful nature and put on His character. Colossians 3:12–14 lists the specifics of our new wardrobe: tenderhearted mercy, kindness, humility, gentleness, patience, and forgiveness. And the perfect finishing touch to our outfit? "Above all, clothe yourselves with love, which binds us all together in perfect harmony" (verse 14, NLT).

Obviously, I need help with my wardrobe. Some days I find that I've clothed myself in pride instead of humility, self-centeredness instead of kindness, and resentment rather than forgiveness. We never know what the day ahead will bring. It's only when we are wearing the character traits of Jesus that we'll be able to respond to people and circumstances in ways that honor Him and bring good to others. We would be wise to stick to the dress code He's given us. —DIANNE NEAL MATTHEWS

FAITH STEP: *Write the character traits in Colossians 3:12–14 and keep the list nearby. As you get dressed, ask Jesus to help you to put on His character.*

SATURDAY, SEPTEMBER 8

Thomas said to him, "Lord, we do not know where you are going. How can we know the way?" John 14:5 (ESV)

I DROVE HALFWAY ACROSS THE United States recently and had difficulty finding my way home. I'm a pretty good navigator with a paper map but I've started to depend on my smartphone's navigation system. I won't do that again.

First, my phone couldn't seem to figure out where I was. Then I touched the arrow that centered the map around my location; it put me (represented by a little blue circle) in another state entirely. I pulled over and turned location services off and on. When that didn't work, I rebooted the phone. Finally, my blue dot was in the right place.

The computerized helper in the phone had trouble understanding me when I recited my home address so I typed it in. Then the smartphone decided that I didn't live at the address I provided and gave me directions to somebody else's house.

I gave up on the phone and pushed the car's internal navigation button. The representative said my car wasn't showing up on her screen. Would I mind a slight delay while technical support installed an update into my system? I wouldn't.

It's confusing to lose your way. Thomas may have thought Jesus left out some important information when Jesus told the disciples, "You know the way to where I am going" (John 14:4, ESV). Jesus said, "I am the way" (John 14:6). The only way.

They, and each of us, would have to obey Jesus's first command, "Follow me." —SUZANNE DAVENPORT TIETJEN

FAITH STEP: *What directs the steps in your daily walk? What role do other people's demands and expectations play? How do we follow someone we cannot see? Contemplate this. Ask and then trust Jesus to show you the way today.*

SUNDAY, SEPTEMBER 9

Samuel then took a large stone and placed it between the towns of Mizpah and Jeshanah. He named it Ebenezer (which means "the stone of help"), for he said, "Up to this point the LORD has helped us!" 1 Samuel 7:12 (NLT)

FEAR GRIPPED THE ISRAELITES WHEN they learned that the Philistine army was advancing toward them. They begged Samuel to ask God to rescue them, so he sacrificed a young lamb and prayed on their behalf.

God answered by speaking with a mighty voice of thunder from heaven. This threw the Philistines into mass confusion and enabled the Israelites to overpower them. Samuel celebrated the victory by placing a large stone between two towns as a permanent visual reminder of God's faithfulness.

After reflecting on this story, I found a small rock outside and placed it on the windowsill in front of my kitchen sink. I see it several times a day. It's my Ebenezer stone, my stone of help, my reminder to celebrate Jesus and walk in the victory He accomplished on behalf of all who place their faith in Him for salvation.

Because of Christ's death and resurrection, fear cannot paralyze us. Discouragement cannot cripple us. Doubts cannot destroy us. Jesus conquered the enemy of our soul, and he can never, ever defeat us! "Overwhelming victory is ours through Christ, who loved us" (Romans 8:37).

How easy it is to forget this life-altering truth. Troubles hit, and we lose sight of the promise that's ours to claim. But our forgetfulness doesn't change the facts—Jesus has fought the battle and won.

"Up to this point the LORD has helped us," said Samuel when he set the Ebenezer stone in place. Up to this point, He's helped us, too. And He'll continue helping us, day by day. —GRACE FOX

FAITH STEP: *Find a small rock and put it wherever you'll see it often. Every time you look at it, thank Jesus for accomplishing your eternal victory.*

MONDAY, SEPTEMBER 10

Not that I am speaking of being in need, for I have learned in whatever situation I am to be content. I know how to be brought low, and I know how to abound. In any and every circumstance, I have learned the secret of facing plenty and hunger, abundance and need. Philippians 4:11–12 (ESV)

I SUFFER FROM BOUTS OF discontent, times when I seem to focus on what's lacking in my life rather than on what abounds, which, by most standards, is plenty. Take where I am today. We recently moved to the Florida Gulf Coast, a physical paradise and the fulfillment of a dream for me and my husband, Ray.

Many of our prayers have been answered. We found a wonderful, affordable home in a beautiful community. Our children are adjusting more quickly than we hoped. Ray and I are also meeting wonderful people with whom we already feel close affinity. I have made some excellent freelance contacts. Ray has landed a gratifying job. We found a great church just minutes away. We can clearly see God's hand in so many things.

Yet I find something to long for. If only our community had basketball courts for my ten-year-old athlete. If only my husband's job paid more. If only we had room for a kayak. This speaks to the misguided expectation of perfection I have that will never be, this side of heaven. Unlike Jesus, Who lived a simple, sacrificial life, I grumble through even the best of times.

Gratitude fills my half-empty cup. By focusing on the many promptly answered prayers and their virtues, I can see more clearly that my cup overflows. —ISABELLA YOSUICO

FAITH STEP: *If you haven't already, start a prayer journal, handy for noting prayers and concerns. When prayers are answered, check them off, and make a point of thanking Jesus for those blessings, every day.*

TUESDAY, SEPTEMBER 11

"Therefore go and make disciples of all nations, baptizing them in the name of the Father and of the Son and of the Holy Spirit, and teaching them to obey everything I have commanded you." Matthew 28:19–20 (NIV)

RECENTLY, I REPOSTED A BLOG on Facebook that I had written a few years earlier called, "If Only We Had Known." It's a poem that reflects the familiar what-if exercise we writers often use to give wings to our thoughts. I read that poem again as others' memories of 9/11 filled the media airwaves. If we could have known the events of that day, how would we have acted differently?

None of us know what a day will bring. Life is fragile, a breath compared to eternity. But we can do something now—while there is still time. The apostle Paul encourages us to "make the most of every opportunity" (Ephesians 5:16, NLT).

The disciples, too, struggled with tragedy: Jesus's death by crucifixion. I wonder if they experienced what-if thoughts. If they hadn't left Jesus in His time of need, or if they had tried harder to fight Jesus's enemies, could they have prevented His death? But of course, we know the answer. Jesus gave His life willingly. No one took it from Him. He died so we could live.

Both then and now, our task is the same as what Jesus told the disciples after His Resurrection, before ascending to heaven. In His time on earth, Jesus encouraged His followers to comfort, encourage, and love others.

But, above all, Jesus said to "make disciples." We can help in preparing others for real life—here, and in the hereafter.
—REBECCA BARLOW JORDAN

FAITH STEP: *What are your memories of 9/11? Ask Jesus for opportunities this week to share His comfort and to point others toward Him.*

WEDNESDAY, SEPTEMBER 12

In this way stand firm in the Lord . . . whatever is true, whatever is honorable, whatever is right, whatever is pure, whatever is lovely, whatever is of good repute, if there is any excellence and if anything worthy of praise, dwell on these things. Philippians 4:1, 8 (NASB)

I'VE GONE THROUGH A SEASON of discouragement lately. But between mass shootings, the refugee crisis, friends' problems, and my own personal issues with finances, marriage, parenting, and a full-time job, I've had a serious case of the funk. I take medicine for depression, and try to get exercise and rest, but for some reason this funk has been exceptionally hard to shake.

I'm not alone in this phenomenon. A student came to my office yesterday and shared the same feeling. He lost his factory job and came back to school to better himself for his family. School is challenging, and so is work and parenting. And he's got all kinds of disadvantages he didn't choose. Still, he's working hard.

"Sometimes it just feels like it's not worth it, you know?" He asked me. "Like I'm taking a step forward and then two steps back. I feel like I'm trying so hard to be a contributor, to make a difference, and hardly getting anywhere."

After that conversation I watched the last movie in *The Hunger Games* series. Katniss goes through unspeakable horrors and ends up on a grassy knoll holding her baby. She tells her baby that it's hard to keep the darkness from overcoming her—but she makes a list of all of the good things, and she dwells on that. It's her stand against evil. The same principle applies when we are discouraged. Standing firm in Jesus, we set our mind on the good, and in Him we will overcome. —GWEN FORD FAULKENBERRY

FAITH STEP: *Brainstorm all of the good things you can think of. Post the list.*

THURSDAY, SEPTEMBER 13

[Jesus said,] Your Father knows what you need before you ask him.
Matthew 6:8 (ESV)

I COMMITTED A RIDICULOUS SIN the other day. Not unpardonable, but falling into the "What were you thinking?" category.

I gave Jesus counsel.

A problem confronted my family. One that seemed closer to impossible than merely perplexing. In prayer, I suggested several imaginative ways Jesus could use to solve that problem for us.

That's right. I offered Jesus the benefit of *my* wisdom. Makes me cringe to write this. I should know better by now. It took me far longer to list the possibilities in prayer than it would have for me to simply lay the need before the One Who created the idea of imagination, Who knows the end from the beginning, Who has my—and your—best interests at heart, and Who is the only One with the power to make a difference. The sovereign Lord.

Yet it's so natural for us to think we're helping Jesus when we offer scenarios that might work. How much mental energy have I expended trying to put together my own plans He merely needs to rubber-stamp?

The Bible tells us He knows what we need before we even approach Him with our request or dilemma. A friend of mine said that when she finally realizes that all He wants is for her to come to Him—no need for a list of possible solutions in hand—it's as if she hears Him say, "Well, honey, now I'm so glad you asked."

Those are the words I need to hear. So I'm relinquishing my *Counselor to the Almighty* hat in favor of the simplicity, humility, and surrender of laying my need before Him. —CYNTHIA RUCHTI

FAITH STEP: *Have you offered Jesus solutions He could use to fix a dilemma? Picture yourself in the counselor's chair, with Jesus on the couch. Trade places.*

FRIDAY, SEPTEMBER 14

"But the greatest among you shall be your servant." Matthew 23: 11 (NASB)

FOR SIXTEEN YEARS I WORKED in elementary schools, either as a teacher or a consultant, and I'm not sure who learned more—me or my students. Each day "life" lessons proved to be far more powerful than whatever textbooks could teach, and I learned some of my best lessons from our school janitor, Donnie.

A small man in stature, Donnie was a giant to the entire student body. Anytime there was a problem we called on Donnie. He kept that school humming when it came to maintenance, but we also asked for Donnie's help with some of our troubled children. He taught our bullies to help the younger children by pairing them for tasks in the lunchroom. He showed our restless kids how to listen by teaching them to plant trees on the playground. And he offered the best advice to anyone who asked.

One day I took my lunch outside and sat near the dumpsters against a brick wall. My husband had lost his job, and I couldn't face another lunch hour of small talk and forced conversation. As Donnie came out to empty trash in a dumpster, he saw my slumped body against the wall and asked how he could help. After I shared my story, his eyes filled with bright tears and he said "Jesus has never let us down, and He won't start now!" His quiet confidence lifted my mood, and I realized that this man of small stature was a giant of faith.

Sometimes it's tempting to overlook the humble people around us. Donnie's impact at that school was every bit as important as the teachers, principal, and school administrators. —GARI MEACHAM

FAITH STEP: *What does a "faith servant" look like to you? How do the words faith and servant fit together in a culture that pushes getting ahead and getting attention?*

SATURDAY, SEPTEMBER 15

"Call to me and I will answer you and tell you great and unsearchable things you do not know." Jeremiah 33:3 (NIV)

IN SEPTEMBER 2016, I READ a new story about Nessie, the Loch Ness Monster. I've always been a skeptic, but I've got to admit that this report included a compelling picture. The headline suggested it was the most convincing photo ever taken of the supposed behemoth. Sure enough, a head and two humps were clearly visible above the water's surface. The photographer was hunting red deer and happened to shoot the picture instead. And no one has proven that it's impossible for generations of some large animal to hide in those deep Scottish waters.

Scientists are learning more about the loch, or lake, itself. They know that the loch is deeper than originally thought. In 2013, an earthquake created a new trench and a new hiding place. But there's more we don't know.

It's surprising to me that we don't fully know the depths and hideaways of the earth. Creation has lots of unsearched places.

Sometimes Jesus can seem unsearchable. Reclusive. Unknowable. Sometimes teasing us with snapshots of His presence and work among us. He was born, He died and left, and He's away from us physically until He returns for His followers.

But Jesus is knowable. He sent His Spirit to live in believers, and He wants to reveal Himself to us so we can know Him. All it takes is an open heart.

Discovering *all* the depths of Jesus is a wonder for eternity!
—ERIN KEELEY MARSHALL

FAITH STEP: *Search the Loch Ness Monster online to gain perspective on how much greater are the depths of Jesus, and the relationship He wants to have with us. Ask Him for a heart to see Him clearly.*

SUNDAY, SEPTEMBER 16

And yet, O LORD, you are our Father. We are the clay, and you are the potter. We all are formed by your hand. Isaiah 64:8 (NLT)

I REGULARLY TEACH OUR KIDS' class at church. We have a wide variety of ages from preschool through fifth grade. As I welcome kids to the class, I will often have a table set up with an activity or craft. One they all seem to enjoy is Play-Doh. There is a rush to the table to grab a favorite color. We have to remind the preschoolers that Play-Doh is for hands…not for hair or pockets or our neighbor's ears.

After the ground rules are laid, creativity is unleashed. The wild sculptures abound. Flowers and puppies are crafted with small, determined fingers. I usually make a snake—I am excellent at rolling out a lean serpent with a forked tongue. There are multiple do-overs as the kids smash their creations to form completely new masterpieces. There's also a lot of chatter at the table. The artists discuss their work. They even share stories about their art and its purpose. They are in their element with imagination and dough as their tools. They are the image of Jesus at work, bubbling over with excitement at the prospect of getting His hands on us and our lives.

He is so patient, shaping and forming our days. Creating new out of old. Bringing forth the form and work that He purposed us for in the first place. He gives repeated do-overs. He lovingly works us over, molding our hearts to mirror His. It is beautiful, hard work that He is doing. And we are safe in His capable hands as we become the person He destined each one of us to be.
—SUSANNA FOTH AUGHTMON

FAITH STEP: *Get some clay or Play-Doh. Imagine Jesus's hands at work on your heart, mind, and spirit as you create and re-create. He is shaping you with His love.*

MONDAY, SEPTEMBER 17

Let us go right into the presence of God with sincere hearts fully trusting him. For our guilty consciences have been sprinkled with Christ's blood to make us clean, and our bodies have been washed with pure water. Hebrews 10:22 (NLT)

MY DOG, RUE, LOVES TO watch our chickens. She's practiced being calm around them and has to leave if she gets too excited or shows any sign of aggression. She was doing very well until the other night when she poked her nose through the electric net fence. She got zapped, howled, and turned tail for the cabin.

The worst part of it is that she thought I did it to her. She hid under my husband's desk chair all evening. When I called her to me, she slunk down, head low and eyes doubtful.

I wonder how many times I've mistakenly thought God was punishing me when hard things happened in my life. Israel, too, felt threatened by Jesus when He came. The Israelites misunderstood His motive and didn't see His love.

He tried to teach them. He told them His Father was like the shepherd who left his ninety-nine sheep in order to find one that was lost, and like the father who ran to embrace his long-lost spendthrift son. Jesus embodied God's love.

Many refused to see and Jesus mourned, "How often I wanted to gather your children together, just as a hen *gathers* her brood under her wings, and you would not *have it!*" (Luke 13:34, NASB). Their unbelief broke Jesus's heart.

Ours would do the same. He died to save us. He loves us. It's safe. Go to Him. —SUZANNE DAVENPORT TIETJEN

FAITH STEP: *Use your imagination to picture yourself approaching Jesus. See Him smile and throw His arms wide. Now run into those arms.*

TUESDAY, SEPTEMBER 18

Jesus replied, "I tell you the truth, you want to be with me because I fed you, not because you understood the miraculous signs. But don't be so concerned about perishable things like food. Spend your energy seeking the eternal life that the Son of Man can give you. For God the Father has given me the seal of his approval." John 6:26–27 (NLT)

AN ACQUAINTANCE CALLED ME AND wanted advice and encouragement. I listened to her dilemma, helped her brainstorm solutions, and did all I could to remind her that Jesus had not stopped loving her. After I got off the phone, I felt wistful. She hadn't asked about my life. This often happened when she called. She vented, asked for support, and then scampered away, never taking time to really connect or listen.

I wanted to rejoice that Jesus had made me available to serve someone else, but part of me wished we had a more reciprocal relationship – a sharing of our lives. Then I realized how often Jesus must have felt that way during His time on earth. He responded to needs around Him, listened, cared, healed, and provided. Yet often people grabbed up His healings or His miracles of fish and loaves without understanding what He longed for—relationship. Throughout human history, God has expressed His desire to be in a relationship with us. I don't want to be like the followers who only cared about what earthly provision they could get from Jesus. I want to pursue a relationship with Him, truly seek to know Him, and invite Him into every part of my life.

Today, let's do more than tell Him our woes, pour out our petitions, and then scamper away. Let's sit in His presence, ask His guidance, and thank Him for being a steadfast Friend. —SHARON HINCK

FAITH STEP: *Think about the ways you have deepened a relationship with a friend. Then ask Jesus to show you ways to strengthen your relationship with Him.*

WEDNESDAY, SEPTEMBER 19

"And surely I am with you always, to the very end of the age."
Matthew 28:20 *(NIV)*

WHEN MY DAD PASSED AWAY a few months ago, I took my mom to the Social Security Administration so she could apply for survivor's benefits. After we answered all the questions and showed the proper documentation, the representative handed us a copy of the application to sign. We noticed that she had written on one line: "Husband and wife were living apart at the time of death." Naturally we thought this had to be a mistake and called her attention to it. The woman explained that they notated it that way since my dad had been in the hospital before he died.

My mom felt upset about this, and I didn't blame her. In the previous months my mom had taken care of my dad at home as he struggled with health issues. He spent the last twelve days of his life in a hospital bed. During that time my mom barely left his side. The day after his passing marked their sixty-ninth anniversary.

My parents took their wedding vows seriously, including the line "until death do us part." Such an example of marital faithfulness shines brightly in today's culture when so many choose casual relationships and multiple partners. Yet even the best earthly commitment pales in comparison to the vow that Jesus has made to those who believe in Him. He promises to love us unconditionally for "better" and for "worse." He guards, guides, and provides for us. Best of all, His promises extend beyond this life. Rather than allowing death to separate us, Jesus vows to carry us into eternity, where we will never be parted. —DIANNE NEAL MATTHEWS

FAITH STEP: *Tell Jesus how much His promise to always be with you in life and after death means to you. Then write out your commitment to Him.*

THURSDAY, SEPTEMBER 20

"Ask, and it will be given to you; seek, and you will find; knock, and it will be opened to you." Matthew 7:7 (NASB)

JESUS USES ACTION WORDS TO describe the essence of prayer: ask, seek, and knock. I've pondered these words for decades and have come to realize that asking prompts us, seeking confuses us, and knocking just plain irritates us! The question is why did Jesus use these words as a prayer model? Why not just stop at "Ask and it shall be given to you"? Perhaps the maturity and strength of faith come in the seeking and the knocking.

When our savings dwindled and my husband and I were both working several jobs to keep our family afloat, we prayed for years that he would be chosen to be a major league coach rather than a minor league instructor. The salary would help us get ahead and not have to work so hard. But instead of this being a quick answer to a heartfelt prayer, it took us sixteen years of praying to land his first major league coaching assignment. During those years I grappled with the seeking and knocking phase of prayer. I felt that we'd sought and knocked until our knuckles were bloody and blistered.

In times of struggle it may seem like God has gone radio-silent...crickets...no response and no fuzzy messages of hope. But rest assured, He hasn't forgotten us or ignored our seeking and knocking prayers. He's simply creating the perfect circumstances, timing, and posture to display our heart's desire. Soon our seeking and knocking will turn to knowing and praising—and we'll be wiser and more faithful because of it. —GARI MEACHAM

FAITH STEP: *Write the word tenacity next to Mathew 7:7 in your Bible, and remember this definition: tenacity is the absolute certainty that what you hope for will transpire.*

FRIDAY, SEPTEMBER 21

*Count it all joy, my brothers, when you meet trials of various kinds,
for you know that the testing of your faith produces steadfastness.
And let steadfastness have its full effect, that you may be perfect
and complete, lacking in nothing. James 1:2–4 (ESV)*

WHO COUNTS IT ALL JOY when they face trials? Seriously? I desperately want a life of ease and comfort, and tend to bristle at trials of any size. Still, having lived out my faith for a number of years, more or less gracefully, I believe the truth of this verse with all my heart. I see better how I can enjoy the very practical benefits of its promise. The trials keep coming, but I definitely don't sweat the small stuff like I used to, and I enjoy life more than many. In this life, we'll have trouble, Jesus said. But *how* we face the inevitable challenges of life can improve our lives.

Most of the time, I sail through the routine trials that used to rob me of my joy and peace, and cast a shadow over my whole day. A broken appliance, computer glitch, or traffic jam would make me grumble all day. Bigger problems? Oh boy. I have given months to believing that a trial was the end of the road, some deep condemnation of my potential. Now I see many of my problems as opportunities for growth and I benefit, in turn, by helping others.

The promise of this verse hinges on faith that has been tested through life lessons, big and small. Gold, iron, diamonds, steel, and clay are all formed and strengthened by heat and pressure. Sometimes the trials of life can feel like a pressure cooker, exhausting our will and even breaking our very spirits. But the positives of trials come through submission, however painful, seeking and believing God's ultimate good purpose in anything that He allows. —ISABELLA YOSUICO

FAITH STEP: *Write down some of the trials you've faced. In retrospect, can you see how they've blessed you or others? Catalog some of those benefits.*

SATURDAY, SEPTEMBER 22

"I am the true grapevine, and my Father is the gardener. He cuts off every branch of mine that doesn't produce fruit, and he prunes the branches that do bear fruit so they will produce even more." John 15:1–2 (NLT)

TEN YEARS AGO, MY MOM planted a rosebush in our backyard. Each spring its old-fashioned roses overtake the side of the gardening shed. They are light yellow, edged in apricot and crimson. The blooms are fragrant and as big as my hand. The bush itself towers over the top of the eight-foot shed. I love everything about it. But it didn't get that way on its own. My mom shared the secret of pruning with me.

Every autumn when the last bloom drops to the ground, I go to town with the pruning shears. I deadhead all the old blooms. I trim off shriveled branches. And then I pare the bush way back. It looks pretty sad after I trim it up. Shorn. Spindly. Empty.

Pruning isn't my favorite gardening practice. I don't love getting pricked by thorns or hacking away at tough branches but I know if I let it go, then new growth can't take place. I actually stunt its potential if I don't cut off the dead portions.

Jesus feels the same way about our lives. He wants to trim out all the old growth. He is persistent when it comes to trimming the "dead" areas of our lives. The diseased parts of our souls, the unhealthy thinking, the areas of our lives that are limiting us? Those have to go. He wants to unleash the potential of growth in our lives. He wants to do a new work in our hearts and our minds. And, I think we should let Him. —SUSANNA FOTH AUGHTMON

FAITH STEP: *Take a walk outside and study the plants and trees. Growth is what Jesus is all about. Ask Him what areas He would like to prune out of your life.*

SUNDAY, SEPTEMBER 23

As he approached Jerusalem and saw the city, he wept over it. Luke 19:41 (NIV)

WAS "JESUS WEPT" (JOHN 11:35) one of the first Bible verses you memorized, too? I was blessed to be raised in a home full of faith, rich in love, and well-versed in the importance of the Bible for daily living. I filled my young mind with truths from the Bible. I'm amazed how, these many years later, random verses will resurface when I most need them.

I don't recall, though, getting a ribbon or star for Luke 19:41. It isn't a verse I stopped to ponder until much later in life. Even as a child, I could understand Jesus weeping over the loss of a good friend—Lazarus—as He did in the traditional "Jesus wept" verse. But weeping over a city? I glanced over the concept. Until recently.

The city mentioned in this passage—Jerusalem—had heralded His approach with proclamations of peace and glory in the highest (v. 38). The Bible tells us that Jesus's tears accompanied these words: "If only you knew on this of all days the things that lead to peace. But now they are hidden from your eyes" (v. 42).

Like me, you may have shed tears over the direction you see a child, or a church, or your country taking. Like Jesus, you may cry out, "If you...had only known...what would bring you peace...."

Another brief verse of often-memorized Scripture provides the answer: "He is our peace" (Ephesians 2:14, KJV). Peace isn't a strategy or a diplomatic move or a negotiation. It is Jesus. Just Jesus. He weeps—and we weep—over the heartbreak of those who do not know Him. —CYNTHIA RUCHTI

FAITH STEP: *Make it part of your devotional time today to pray: "I invite You, Jesus, to break my heart with the kinds of things that break Yours, trusting too in Your ability to mend the broken."*

MONDAY, SEPTEMBER 24

Creation itself also will be delivered from the bondage of corruption into the glorious liberty of the children of God . . . For we were saved in this hope.
Romans 8:21, 24 *(NKJV)*

THIS MORNING WE RAN LATE and my daughter, Adelaide, missed the bus. As I drove her to the high school, making myself late for work, I practiced mindfulness in order to rein in my anxiety. I looked at my daughter's face in the rearview mirror. I paid attention to the trees with their changing leaves, like a color guard lining the streets. I admired a group of herons by the river. I waved at people.

As I turned into the parking lot of the school, it seemed to be a little slice of heaven. Tucked into a pocket between rolling hills, it feels safe. And yet, if I gave you a snapshot of what I saw next, you'd see an ugliness on the landscape like an old wound.

A hateful symbol towered over a beat-up silver car. It unfurled from a wooden pole attached to the car, parked in front of the school and thus unavoidable for all who entered. The truck in front of me stopped, and one of a tiny number of black students got out, slung her backpack over her shoulder, and walked past the flag through the doors of the school.

I groaned. By the time I got to work my stomach ached. I wanted to let the girl and her parents know that I saw, and I care. I thought about ways to address this in the community, and the consequences. I began to feel hopeless.

Some days I feel so overwhelmed by the darkness I see in the world that I would despair if it wasn't for Jesus. Jesus is the Light. And we are saved because of the hope we have in Him.
—GWEN FORD FAULKENBERRY

FAITH STEP: *Use whatever influence you have to increase the Light today in the lives of others.*

TUESDAY, SEPTEMBER 25

My dear brothers and sisters, take note of this: Everyone should be quick to listen, slow to speak and slow to become angry, because human anger does not produce the righteousness that God desires. James 1:19–20 (NIV)

HEAVY STOMPING POUNDED UP THE stairs, followed by a child's cry. I hurried in that direction and found my six-year-old holding her foot. Her thirteen-year-old sister had been sent upstairs to clean her room, and was apparently frustrated by the task. She took out her frustrations on her little sister by stepping on her.

I never really considered myself an angry person, but adopting children who've previously faced trauma stretched me to my limit. I reminded myself of the phrase, "Hurting people, hurt people." Still it was hard not to get angry whenever I saw our new daughters acting out. It took self-control to discipline in love.

Even though I was holding in my anger, it simmered inside. I had a hard time connecting with my thirteen-year-old in particular, and I could feel distance between us. I knew she could feel it, too.

One evening I sat down and wrote out all that bothered me about my daughter's actions. Then I held that paper up to Jesus and asked how He saw my daughter. With each of my complaints, Jesus showed me His thoughts: how my daughter had been neglected, ignored, lied to, abused, and forgotten. As I pictured her life through Jesus's eyes, my heart softened. When she woke up the next morning I gave her a huge hug and I meant it.

Our relationship changed. She still acted out, but I handled it in love, and her poor responses happened less often. Jesus can help each of us with even the anger we try to hide. —TRICIA GOYER

FAITH STEP: *Do you have anger that you've been holding inside? Write it out, and then hold it up to Jesus. Ask Him to show you His point of view.*

WEDNESDAY, SEPTEMBER 26

"Keep on asking, and you will receive what you ask for. Keep on seeking, and you will find. Keep on knocking, and the door will be opened to you. For everyone who asks, receives. Everyone who seeks, finds. And to everyone who knocks, the door will be opened." Matthew 7:7–8 (NLT)

MY SON, JACK, IS AN asker extraordinaire. He is persistent when it comes to asking my husband, Scott, or me for something that he needs or wants. And while he uses steady pressure applied on a daily basis, his approach varies. There is the gentle ask. Then comes the constant reminding. And then Jack usually resorts to some action, like placing the car keys in our hands to encourage us to take him somewhere or bringing us to the computer to view the wanted item. He is relentless. He knows that if he keeps it up long enough, he will get results. They may not always be the results he wants, but they are results nevertheless.

I need to learn from Jack about the power of persistence when it comes to asking. I ask Jesus for things all the time but maybe prayers are not just words to be spoken. Maybe they are actions to be taken. Maybe we should take more of Jack's approach when we pray. We should pursue Jesus's answers relentlessly and fervently. Not just casually throw up a prayer here and there.

It seems that Jesus really likes persistence because it reveals our heart. It reveals our resolve and our motives. It shows Jesus that we want His power, His resources, and His wisdom to intersect with our lives. And the best part? He promises to answer.

—SUSANNA FOTH AUGHTMON

FAITH STEP: *What are you praying about right now? Talk to Jesus about it every day this week and ask Him if there is a way that you can take action to show Him your resolve.*

THURSDAY, SEPTEMBER 27

But soon it was time for the Jewish Festival of Shelters, and Jesus' brothers said to him, "Leave here and go to Judea, where your followers can see your miracles! You can't become famous if you hide like this! If you can do such wonderful things, show yourself to the world!" For even his brothers didn't believe in him. John 7:2–5 (NLT)

IN A PERFECT WORLD, OUR friends and family would provide a safe place for us to share our dreams and hopes. They'd be the sanctuary where we could confide the visions that Jesus plants in our hearts no matter how impossible or illogical they seem. They'd be our greatest cheerleaders, instilling us with the courage and confidence we need to pursue our calling.

Sadly, a perfect world doesn't exist. Sometimes the people with whom we ought to be able to share our innermost thoughts are the most critical. They laugh, they mock, and they scoff when we dare share anything intensely personal. They might say something like, "You want to do what? What are you thinking? You can't possibly do that!"

If you've experienced this, then know that Jesus empathizes. Fully God and fully man, He was part of a human family that struggled with negative sibling interaction. Perhaps His brothers were jealous of His growing notoriety, or maybe they thought He was crazy. Perhaps He embarrassed them, or they felt He posed a danger to their family. Whatever the case, they clearly felt no respect for Him and His life's purpose. But their influence could neither sideline nor stop Him.

Jesus responded to their mocking with respect, and then He pursued what He knew to be right. Maybe we should do the same, my friend. —GRACE FOX

FAITH STEP: *The shepherd boy, David, encountered negativity when he said he'd fight Goliath. Read his story in 1 Samuel 17:17–51.*

FRIDAY, SEPTEMBER 28

You crown the year with your bounty. Psalm 65:11 (ESV)

AUTUMN HAS BEEN IN THE breeze the past few days. A yearly relief from the muggy midnineties! It calls me outside because the sun no longer seems angry.

I actually get the same boost to my spirit in the first days of summer, when I can bypass heavy, chilly-weather clothes for shorts and a sleeveless top. Even my feet are thrilled to breathe in flip-flops. And then there's rediscovering the pool every late May.

I grow a little weary of each season toward its end, but the beginning of every new season brings renewed hope. When fall gives way to winter, I'm excited to breathe crisp air. And then there's the coziness of coming inside for warm, comfy clothes and trying a new hot tea. And once again, the cold gets old, and I'm thrilled to see that spring has sprung!

Jesus's plan to refresh us is a good one. Who could've anticipated the quarterly boost that His changing seasons would bring?

But what I'm even more thankful for is the gift of His Spirit inside me to provide refreshment every moment, not just on a quarterly basis. He's fresh air when life gets stale and a cool burst of truth that helps snap me out of a funk. He's a warm blanket of comfort when my heart is hurting and peace like the stillness of swimming underwater in a summer pool.

Although life has its own seasons of ups and downs, heartaches and joys, Jesus is consistent. He is not a changing season, but He is flexible with our weaknesses and needs.

Whatever season you are in, Jesus has something with which to refresh you. —ERIN KEELEY MARSHALL

FAITH STEP: *Take an autumn walk and thank Jesus for His goodness, season by season.*

SATURDAY, SEPTEMBER 29

I know what it is to be in need, and I know what it is to have plenty.
I have learned the secret of being content in any and every situation,
whether well fed or hungry, whether living in plenty or in want.
Philippians 4:12 (NIV)

MY BEES ARE FIGHTING. IT's fall and I've begun feeding them to help them build up their winter honey stores. One hive, though, is stronger than the other and rather than wait in line at their own feeders, they've decided to rob the weaker hive's feeders. As you would expect, those bees are defending themselves. There's enough for everyone but they want more. Like so many of us.

This is a heart problem and Jesus knows our hearts. He warned us to guard against greed saying, "Take care! Protect yourself against the least bit of greed. Life is not defined by what you have, even when you have a lot" (Luke 12:15, MSG).

Greed may be more obvious in the very wealthy. Jesus wore a robe woven without seams, valuable enough that His executioners couldn't ruin it by dividing it. Possessions are neither good nor bad in their essence. It's our attitude toward them that matters.

The rich don't have a monopoly on greed. Discontent and selfishness affect all income levels. When I, the somewhat sheepish owner of more than enough yarn, walk through the aisles of my favorite knitting shop, I have to admit I want even more. When I turn off the television after one too many new car commercials, do I look at my serviceable "old beater" with too critical an eye? *Um*, yes.

We all need to heed Jesus's warning. It's hard to recognize greed in myself. Open my eyes, Jesus. —SUZANNE DAVENPORT TIETJEN

FAITH STEP: *What triggers your discontent? Look at something else, tangible or intangible, that you already have. Pray your thanks for that today.*

SUNDAY, SEPTEMBER 30

When Ahijah heard her walking to the door, he said, "Come in, wife of Jeroboam. Why are you pretending to be someone else?" 1 Kings 14:6 (NCV)

KING JEROBOAM ENCOURAGED IDOL WORSHIP in Israel, but when his son got sick, he wanted help from the Lord's prophet. Jeroboam had his wife take off her royal robes and jewels and visit Ahijah in disguise. Imagine her surprise when the elderly, blind prophet called her out before she stepped into his house, asking why she was pretending to be somebody else.

Have you ever tried to put on a persona other than your natural one? Ever felt pressured to act, dress, or speak in a different way to make a good impression or to fit in with a group of people? Ever tried to imitate the personality or lifestyle of someone you considered superior? Maybe we're not as bad as some politicians, changing like chameleons according to their surroundings and audience so as to make the best impression. We all probably know someone who seems to go through life wearing a disguise that makes him or her hard to get to know. And if we're honest, we might have to admit that there are times when we put up our guard to keep others from seeing "the real me."

Whether because of guilt, poor self-esteem, fear of judgment, or other emotional baggage, it's not always easy being ourselves. But each one of us has been created as a unique individual, with our own custom blend of physical traits, personality bent, and natural gifts and talents. Jesus loves us just the way we are, inside and out. He embraces our unique qualities, so why shouldn't we?
—DIANNE NEAL MATTHEWS

FAITH STEP: *Make a list of things you've always considered imperfections in your appearance or personality. Thank Jesus for loving you just as you are right now. Then look at the list and ask yourself, "Are these things I really need to change?"*

MONDAY, OCTOBER 1

*For everything there is a season, a time for every activity under heaven.
A time to be born and a time to die. A time to plant and a time to harvest.
A time to kill and a time to heal. A time to tear down and a time to build
up. A time to cry and a time to laugh. A time to grieve and a time to dance.*
Ecclesiastes 3:1–4 (NLT)

THIS IS ADDISON'S LAST YEAR in elementary school. There are no
superheroes on his backpack. It's all black with grey trim. Because
life is serious now. He has started slicking his hair over to one side.
He looks like a young executive heading off to class. There are no
lingering drop-offs or goodbye kisses at school. It is all about quick
waves and head nods now.

It is amazing how quickly the seasons of life fly past. It seems like
moments ago that Addie was a baby riding on my hip. And now?
I would throw out my hip if I tried to pick him up. Sometimes I
get a little teary when I think about how fast time goes. But I don't
want to get stuck reminiscing about the past. I want to soak up this
season of Addison growing and changing and slicking back his hair.

Jesus has given each season of our lives its own joys and struggles.
He doesn't want us clinging to seasons past, longing for the way
things used to be. He has grace and peace for the moment we are
living right now. He has new hopes and truth for this day and this
day alone. We don't want to miss out on today's beauty. We need to
soak it up. Revel in it. Sing and dance. And embrace the season we
are living out with gratitude. —SUSANNA FOTH AUGHTMON

FAITH STEP: *What are you thankful for in this season of your life? Pin a
Gratitude List on your fridge as a daily reminder of Jesus's goodness.*

TUESDAY, OCTOBER 2

"And when you are praying, do not use meaningless repetition as the Gentiles do, for they suppose that they will be heard for their many words."
Matthew 6:7 (NASB)

MY SISTER AND I SAT in the loud football stadium, watching my son play his final season in high school. To take my mind off how big his opponents were—and the fact that he was playing offense, defense, and on special teams—we began to talk about funny things from our childhood. I remembered a prayer we were taught that even now, decades later, still has me scratching my head. It's called "The Act of Contrition"—a beautiful prayer about being sorry for our sins. I told my sister I didn't understand why a prayer would start with, "Oh my God, I'm hardly sorry for offending you." She looked at me with a huge smile and yelled, "It says 'heartily,' not 'hardly,' Gari." We laughed our heads off, before realizing I'd probably said that prayer a hundred times when we were young, never understanding what I was saying or why I was saying it!

How often do we pray this way, offering meaningless words, over and over, that we either don't understand or don't mean.

Jesus invites us to be real. I remember hearing a pastor say he quit praying a meal offering for six months because it had become so rote. When he began to pray for his meals months later everything changed. His prayers were rich with meaning and heart. I think Jesus would rather hear a few real words than many words laced with meaningless repetition. —GARI MEACHAM

FAITH STEP: *Take a moment before praying at mealtime or bedtime and pay close attention to what you say. Repeat each word out loud, and if it's meaningless—start over!*

WEDNESDAY, OCTOBER 3

Fixing our eyes on Jesus, the pioneer and perfecter of our faith. . . .
Consider him . . . so that you will not grow weary and lose heart.
Hebrews 12:2–3 *(NIV)*

MY SON, HARPER, AND HIS friends laughed at a joke I thought wasn't funny. Most would probably explain it as he did—just typical teenage stuff. He felt I was making a big deal out of nothing.

The poor kid didn't really have a chance at getting a break, as Granny, my mother, was also present. We tend to fuel each other's fire. Granny asked, "Would Daniel think it's funny?" (Daniel is a friend he respects for his Christian beliefs.)

"I don't know," Harper replied. "Probably."

"Why don't you ask him tomorrow?" Granny suggested.

"Okay, I will."

Granny seemed certain Daniel would vindicate us. Harper hoped to find justification for his actions. If Daniel laughed, my son reasoned, he would be off the hook.

"No," I said. "Go ahead and ask Daniel, but Daniel is not our standard. Jesus is. He's the one you really need to be asking."

Harper looked at me like I was insane. "Who can live up to the standard of Jesus, Mom? I mean, He's the most perfect person who ever lived. Can you?"

"No, I can't. But His power in me can."

I explained that I make mistakes. But Jesus is still my standard. That doesn't mean we're perfect. It means that's what we shoot for, and when we miss, we ask forgiveness and try to do better, always keeping our eyes on Him. —GWEN FORD FAULKENBERRY

FAITH STEP: *Take inventory of your personal standards. Do you define what's okay by what others do, or what Jesus would do?*

THURSDAY, OCTOBER 4

"I am the Lord—I do not change." Malachi 3:6 *(TLB)*

I COULD SPEND HOURS RESEARCHING information about a topic that stirs my curiosity. If I had no other responsibilities in life, I'd easily become a full-time information junkie.

In college I was fascinated with Kennedy's *Camelot* years during the 1960s. Then several years ago I was intrigued by an old pattern of English china my mom used for holiday meals. I'm also always surfing real-estate sites. I've been at it so long, I've gotten familiar with the neighborhoods in my town and nearby ones. Part of what I love about those realty sites is that the information is changing constantly as houses are listed and sold.

I also love to research more about Jesus's Word. But part of what I love is that it is *not* constantly changing. The Lord's plans to share Himself with us, to glorify Himself and to love us, are the same now as they were at Creation. His plan for salvation has not changed either. Jesus is still the only way.

The more I read His Word, the more thankful I feel that He is constant. Even when He's full of surprises, I always know Jesus will be Himself. My Savior will act like Himself, including His responses to me and my weaknesses and sins.

So in that light, I'm finding as I study His Word that the more I learn, the more I realize how magnificent His ways are (Romans 11:33). There is no end to learning about Him—and not just *about* Him but actually getting to *know* Him.

Getting to know Him is worth the countless hours, as we prepare for an eternity to come. —ERIN KEELEY MARSHALL

FAITH STEP: *Think through some of the troubles we'd have if Jesus was ever-changing, like us. Which unchanging qualities of Jesus are you thankful for?*

FRIDAY, OCTOBER 5

Jesus also said, "The Kingdom of God is like a farmer who scatters seed on the ground. Night and day, while he's asleep or awake, the seed sprouts and grows, but he does not understand how it happens. The earth produces the crops on its own. First a leaf blade pushes through, then the heads of wheat are formed, and finally the grain ripens." Mark 4:26–28 (NLT)

LAST WEEK I FELT AS if I accomplished nothing. Interruptions and distractions kept me from my plans. Like a farmer who has scattered seed and keeps peering at the field for a sign of life, I felt disheartened. What difference had I made for God's kingdom?

On the same day that I berated myself on my lack of harvest, a friend shared that she had been encouraged by my e-mail to her. A reader wrote that one of my books had made a difference for her. My husband reminded me how often I make him laugh. It was as if Jesus was telling me that He is at work even when I am not seeing the results. In His parable in Mark, He shows us that the crops are growing even as the farmer sleeps. In fact, even though the farmer participates by planting seeds, the earth "produces the crops on its own."

Our job isn't to see how the crops are doing. Jesus invites us to generously plant our seeds of faith, and trust Him to bring the growth. He seems to accomplish most when we keep our focus on Him, not results. I like to imagine that in Heaven, Jesus will open a scrapbook and show us the marvelous things He was doing behind the scenes when we felt like our lives were barren fields. I still ask Him for glimpses now, because I find it so encouraging, but I'm gradually learning that I can trust that He is producing something of value in my life even when I can't see it. —SHARON HINCK

FAITH STEP: *Think about the most empty field in your life. Tell Jesus that you trust Him to produce a harvest there and thank Him for that.*

SATURDAY, OCTOBER 6

Jacob's well was there; and Jesus, tired from the long walk, sat wearily beside the well about noontime. Soon, a Samaritan woman came to draw water, and Jesus said to her, "Please give me a drink." John 4:6–7 (NLT)

WHEN MY HUSBAND TURNED SIXTY, we decided to celebrate his milestone by doing something extra special. Together with another couple, we rented bicycles and rode along the Danube River from Passau, Germany, to Vienna, Austria. We covered approximately 220 miles in five days. I loved everything about the trip, but I especially enjoyed accomplishing a feat I'd never imagined I could.

The trip demanded every ounce of strength I could muster. When we arrived in Vienna, I collapsed on our hotel bed from exhaustion. I wanted two things: a glass of cold water and a nap.

That's how Jesus surely felt when He arrived in Samaria. He made the sixty-mile journey on foot between Judea and Galilee. Weary and parched, He plopped down next to a well and asked for a drink of water from the first person who came by.

Imagine the Creator of the universe choosing to live with some of the same physical limitations as those He created. Why would He do so? Because He wanted us to know that He understands our weaknesses.

Jesus empathizes with us when we grow tired, because He experienced weariness. He understands when we feel totally spent physically, emotionally, and even mentally. He'll never mock us or tell us to buck up when we come to the end of our resources. Rather, Jesus invites us to come to His throne boldly and promises to extend the mercy and the grace we need to persevere (Hebrews 4:15). —GRACE FOX

FAITH STEP: *Lie down for a few minutes. Close your eyes and relax. Thank Jesus for loving you so much, He chose to live with physical limitations.*

SUNDAY, OCTOBER 7

Be sober-minded; be watchful. Your adversary the devil prowls around like a roaring lion, seeking someone to devour. 1 Peter 5:8 (ESV)

MANY TWENTY-FIRST-CENTURY CHRISTIANS DON'T WANT to linger on the thought of a devil, let alone one who actively prowls for prey; yet, the Bible asserts that he is real and looking to do us harm. Authors like C. S. Lewis and Frank Peretti have written fictional accounts of Satan and his minions conspiring to plant nasty thoughts in our minds. Apparently, he also uses friends and family as instruments to sabotage our good works and good feelings with devious schemes. It was no accident that Jesus Himself was tempted in the desert just as He began His ministry.

C. S. Lewis was chair of Medieval and Renaissance Literature at Cambridge University and an atheist before becoming a Christian. No foolhardy ignoramus, for sure.

I confess that even after becoming a Christian, it took me some time to absorb the idea of the enemy that the Bible describes and Lewis captures so vividly. How might my perspective on the petty annoyances, pesky personal conflicts, and big trials of life be different if I really trusted what the Bible says? Would I be so quick to criticize my husband, magnify the inconvenience of a flat tire, or be wholly derailed by a bigger setback if I thought there was an enemy behind it all?

Jesus spoke the Word of God to Satan and urged the disciples to do the same, assuring them of their true authority over evil. I can believe and claim that truth for myself, even as I navigate the ordinary and extraordinary challenges of life. —ISABELLA YOSUICO

FAITH STEP: *When the next petty annoyance or a major crisis looms, take time to consider a nemesis behind it. Let Jesus take care of it for you.*

MONDAY, OCTOBER 8

"The Lord your God is with you, the Mighty Warrior who saves.
He will take great delight in you; in his love he will no longer rebuke you,
but will rejoice over you with singing." Zephaniah 3:17 (NIV)

I HAVEN'T BEEN SLEEPING WELL lately. My husband, Mike, and I have been going through a lot of changes at a time of life when I expected to be beyond that kind of chaos. We're selling a house, my husband is job-hunting, we're combining households, sorting through possessions, and letting go of what won't fit. We are busy with the added element of suspense as to how it will end. I'm tired when I get in bed. I've lain for hours waiting for peace.

I feel more sympathetic now toward the drug-addicted babies I used to care for in the NICU. They were nearly incapable of relaxing, their hypersensitivity to their surroundings needing to be overcome by other, one hoped, more pleasant sensations. I spent hours cradling infants to my chest, swinging them rhythmically while shushing them with silly songs based on their names. An hour might go by before I felt their tight little muscles relax a bit, even longer before their eyelids began to flutter. Sometimes they couldn't be laid down to sleep before their next feeding time.

I sometimes imagine Jesus shushing me softly and overcoming my anxiety. The wisest man who ever lived said, "It is in vain that you rise up early and go late to rest, eating the bread of anxious toil; for he gives to his beloved sleep" (Psalm 127:2, ESV). I relax a little in Jesus's arms and remember His Father is with me, too. He delights in me, exhausted as I am, and I'm quieted like a baby sung to sleep.
—SUZANNE DAVENPORT TIETJEN

FAITH STEP: *Do you toil anxiously, too? It can be hard to gear down and relax. Imagine Jesus acting lovingly to you in the midst of it all.*

TUESDAY, OCTOBER 9

"The Spirit of God has made me, and the breath of the Almighty gives me life." Job 33:4 (ESV)

HAVE YOU EVER GOTTEN THE wind knocked out of you? Your chest feels like it's carrying a two-ton weight, and you can't get enough air. It's painful and scary, leaving you to wonder whether you're going to breathe again.

It happened to me a few times as a kid. One recess I fell from my school's jungle gym and landed on my back. I lay there as a pathetic groan escaped my mouth because I couldn't get control of my lungs. In the end I was fine, and I went home to my mother's hug.

Sometimes life can knock the wind from us. My family went through a season that's still fairly fresh and still makes breathing difficult just thinking about it. We'd taken several financial hits, life felt very uncertain, and all we'd worked for seemed like it could disappear with a poof. When we thought we were getting ahead, we'd get knocked down again. The hardest months came with unexpected medical bills, higher insurance rates, and surprise house expenses. I struggled hard to breathe.

Do you know how the Bible describes Jesus's Spirit in us? Reread today's verse. Those are the words of Job, a man who got the wind knocked out of him over and over.

That's Jesus's Spirit he was talking about, the One Whose breath gives Job life. Not merely Who *gave* him life, but Who *gives* him life, even now, though He hasn't been on earth for a long time.

We don't have to wonder if we'll be able to breathe again if we place ourselves in Jesus's care. —ERIN KEELEY MARSHALL

FAITH STEP: *Close your eyes and focus on your breathing. Ask Jesus to fill you, and imagine that His Spirit is filling up the pockets of fear and doubt. When you exhale, breathe out the stale stuff that was dislodged from the Spirit's filling.*

WEDNESDAY, OCTOBER 10

And taking the five loaves and the two fish, he looked up to heaven and said a blessing over them. Then he broke the loaves and gave them to the disciples to set before the crowd. Luke 9:16 (ESV)

IT'S ONLY LOGICAL TO BREAK food into pieces before dividing it among people. What's not logical is for an individual lunch to stretch into an all-you-can-eat buffet for a crowd of thousands. Yet in Jesus's hands, a few small loaves of bread and a couple of fish fed five thousand men, plus women and children. What's more, the leftovers filled a to-go basket for each of the twelve disciples.

In this sin-marred world, brokenness is a given. Broken relationships. Broken dreams. Broken hearts. When we get hurt, we have to choose how to respond. Will we walk around wounded, risking resentment and bitterness taking over our spirit? Or will we trust Jesus to take our messed-up situation and turn it into something filled with purpose—and even beauty?

First we have to reach the point where we understand that there are some issues we just can't resolve in our own strength. That's when we're ready to let go and let Jesus go to work. When we bring Him the broken pieces of our life, He performs different types of miracles. Our Savior speaks a blessing over our brokenness, and then He mends us and makes us whole again.

What was once broken probably won't look like it did before. But we can be sure it will have purpose and beauty and will bring Him glory. And who knows how many people will be blessed, all because we were willing to bring Jesus our mess, our brokenness, or our feelings of worthlessness. —DIANNE NEAL MATTHEWS

FAITH STEP: *Think about the broken places in your life. Visualize yourself releasing all your disappointment and hurt into Jesus's loving hands.*

THURSDAY, OCTOBER 11

"I am the way, the truth, and the life. No one can come to the Father except through me." John 14:6 (NLT)

I HAVE THREE FRIENDS FROM college whom I text regularly. We don't live near each other, but we want to stay connected. We want to know what is going on in each other's lives. I love these conversations. The only problem is that my phone does not do well with group texting. Sometimes it sends the same comment to my friends seventeen times in a row! It can be a little annoying, not to mention embarrassing. After this happened multiple times, I quit responding on the text thread.

My friend, Jane, called me out. She said, "Sue, where have you been? We don't care that you keep sending us a bazillion texts. We want to hear from you!" I do love being in on the conversation. It reminds me that if I am not mindful of other conversations because of the busyness of life, I can also easily lose sight of how life-giving my interactions with Him are. He loves me and He wants to hear from me. And I need to hear from Him. Just as I touch base with my friends, I need to touch base with Him in His Word and in prayer.

We all need a moment-by-moment, day-by-day connection to Him. It is life altering when we are disengaged from Him, His guidance, and His truth. Our lives begin to unravel. We need His presence to set the course for our lives. His love cradles us in our moments of doubt and fear. His wisdom sustains us when we are lost and confused. When we connect to Jesus, we find abundant life. —SUSANNA FOTH AUGHTMON

FAITH STEP: *Spend time listening to your favorite worship song. Connect with Him through prayer and praise. Let Jesus know you are thankful for your daily conversations with Him.*

FRIDAY, OCTOBER 12

---

*And we know that in all things God works for the good of those
who love Him, who have been called according to his purpose.
For those God foreknew He also predestined to be conformed to the
image of His Son. Romans 8:28–29 (NIV)*

I'M FORTY-FOUR YEARS OLD, OKAY? Old enough to know that a junior
high football game won't have much significance in the scope of a
lifetime. I *know* this. And yet, yesterday I was sick to my stomach
all day before the game, developed a migraine during the game, and
bawled my eyes out after the game along with my teenage son, who
happens to be the quarterback.

It was the first football game he lost, ever. He and his buddies
have been playing together since third grade, and in six years, until
last night, they had never lost a single game. They're that good. But
last night, the Dardanelle Sand Lizards played better. And Harper
experienced the pain of defeat.

In the huddle after the game the coach said, "This one game does
not define us. It's called adversity. And how you respond to adversity
shows your true character." I liked that. And I liked what Harper said
later, which was that he and his buddies have never cried together
before now, and he noticed it creates a deeper kind of bond.

There are things to be learned in pain and loss that we cannot get
any other way. We'd rather not go through it, that's for sure, but it's
not optional. The best thing is that Jesus walks through adversity
with us. And in all things—joy and grief—He works for our good.
God uses everything, even Sand Lizards, to make us more like Jesus.
—GWEN FORD FAULKENBERRY

FAITH STEP: *Make a list of all of the things you're going through right now.
Then, after each one, draw an arrow and write the name Jesus.*

SATURDAY, OCTOBER 13

GOD holds the hands of his people. Psalm 135:14 (MSG)

I'LL NEVER FORGET THE PANIC I felt as a young child when I was separated from my mother in a large department store. After winding my way through the maze of clothes in the women's section, I discovered I was alone. At that time, not much daylight showed between the racks, and they seemed to stretch for miles in my little girl eyes. When I finally reached the end of the clothing rack, I looked around. Mother was nowhere in sight.

I backtracked through the clothes until daylight appeared again. Still no Mom. I started running through the aisles whimpering, "Mama, Mama!" It seemed like an eternity before Mother's worried face appeared. Eager arms scooped me up and she clasped my small hand in hers. For the rest of the trip, I stayed close by my mother's side.

In the same way, even as a young child, I recognized the feeling. Being separated from Jesus made me feel lost. The moment I understood how my sin had alienated me from God and how much I needed Jesus in my heart, I cried out as the Psalmist did in Psalm 63:8 (VOICE): "Your right hand reaches down and holds me up."

Throughout my years as a child of God and as a follower of Christ, I've been so grateful that even when I would temporarily lose my way in a maze of confusion, Jesus would always be there, holding my hand. I can never be lost to His Spirit, and His right hand will always guide me (Psalm 139:7, 10, TLB). Nothing can ever separate me from His love (Romans 8:38–39).

With a love like that, why would I ever want to wander away?
—REBECCA BARLOW JORDAN

FAITH TEST: *Remember a time when you felt "lost." Thank Jesus today that He will never turn your hand loose from His.*

SUNDAY, OCTOBER 14

At that time Jesus prayed this prayer: "O Father, Lord of heaven and earth, thank you for hiding these things from those who think themselves wise and clever, and for revealing them to the childlike." Matthew 11:25 (NLT)

MY SON IS IN SEMINARY, and I love discussing theological issues or difficult biblical chapters with him. The last time we visited, we chatted at the supper table about various denominational differences and the Scriptural basis for their views. Later I glanced around and realized that my daughter-in-law had cleared the table, everyone else had left, and hours had passed while we talked. I also noticed that my brain cells hurt. No matter how much intelligence we bring to bear on understanding Jesus, we ultimately comprehend that we are children catching only glimmers of the truth that is so far beyond us.

Going deeper into an intellectual understanding of Scripture is a fine pursuit, but it can leave me thinking that I'll never get it right—that my little mind can't figure out the nuances. When people I respect have huge disagreements about a spiritual issue, I can feel overwhelmed and confused. There are times I fear that my understanding is so poor, it must frustrate Jesus in the same way the disciples' questions and doubts sometimes frustrated Him. That's why I'm grateful that Jesus made it clear that His truth is revealed to the childlike. His central call is both profound and simple. We are loved by our Maker, and in Christ we are redeemed. Not through our effort, not through our goodness, not through our intelligence, but through Jesus.

We don't have to be the sharpest crayon in the box. The gift of salvation doesn't have to be fully understood, just accepted. —SHARON HINCK

FAITH STEP: *Choose an activity you engaged in as a child that helps you remember wonder. Thank Jesus that He treasures our childlike trust.*

MONDAY, OCTOBER 15

For I am confident of this very thing; that He who began a good work in you will perfect it until the day of Christ Jesus. Philippians 1:6 (NASB)

THE MINUTE THE SPEAKER FINISHED her talk I bolted to find my place in the line of women who wanted to speak to her. She spoke on knowing our purpose and being assured we're doing what Jesus has called us to do. When it was my turn to whisper my confusion, I could barely get the words out. "I want to serve God in so many ways. I want to write books and speak to women like you. But I'm stuck in a job I don't love—and need the income to help support my family. Am I missing God's call?" She looked at me with love and gently told me that God was perfecting my skills for opportunities He would one day open up. She said He would finish the good work He started in me. I believed her, but it wasn't always easy. I was in that job for sixteen years before my first book was published, but I often thought about the words she spoke to me and the way Jesus was perfecting me in the process.

Now, years later, I see that every skill I learned as a teacher and consultant prepared me for writing, speaking, and leading a nonprofit ministry. There's no way I'd be effective in what I do had I not had those years of learning and perfecting.

If you feel stuck in a job or situation that seems to be leading you away from your call rather than toward it, rest assured—Jesus is perfecting you for the very things you long to do. Keep your eyes and heart locked on Him and the future will unfold in ways you never imagined. —GARI MEACHAM

FAITH STEP: *Make a chart in your journal with two columns labeled "Where I am" and "Where I want to be." Over the course of a year continue to write under each column. Watch how God is perfecting you.*

TUESDAY, OCTOBER 16

Before daybreak next morning, Jesus got up and went out to an isolated place to pray. Later Simon and the others went out to find him. When they found him they said, "Everyone is looking for you." But Jesus replied, "We must go on to other towns as well, and I will preach to them, too. That is why I came." Mark 1:35–38 (NLT)

RETIRED FRIENDS TELL ME THEY'RE busier now than ever before. Based on what my life looks like, it's hard to imagine picking up the pace when I reach that life stage.

I begin every morning with a to-do list. Inevitably, e-mails and phone calls bring other requests for my time. The trouble is, every request represents a genuine need, and I'm tempted to say yes because I want to help. In order to not overcommit, I ask the person to pray about this need or opportunity. Then my husband and I look at our schedule to see whether or not saying yes would allow us to be faithful to existing commitments and still breathe.

To describe Jesus as a man in demand is an understatement. He mentored His disciples, cast out demons, taught in synagogues, and visited His followers' homes. Imagine His to-do list!

Everyone wanted Jesus's time and attention, but He knew when to say no. He knew where to focus and He stayed on task. What enabled Him to do so? He spent time in His Father's presence alone, praying. We don't know what He said, but perhaps He asked the Father to direct Him.

Jesus had twenty-four hours in each day, just like we do, and He completed His life's purpose in three years. Obviously He did something right and we can learn from Him. —GRACE FOX

FAITH STEP: *Write today's tasks on a piece of paper. At the end of the list, add a short prayer. Commit your day to Jesus and ask Him to direct every part of it.*

WEDNESDAY, OCTOBER 17

"You're blessed when you're content with just who you are—no more, no less. That's the moment you find yourselves proud owners of everything that can't be bought." Matthew 5:5 (MSG)

SOMETIMES I LIVE AS IF God needs me to uphold His reputation. If I'm cranky getting to church, you can bet I'll fix my expression into some semblance of pleasantness before I walk through the doors. Am I really trying to protect God by pasting on a smile? If I'm honest, I'm more concerned with myself and what people might think than with how my behavior reflects my heavenly Father. Our actions can make someone curious about our faith, but following Jesus doesn't require us to pretend or be dishonest.

Jesus never did that. He was always truthful and loving, even though He ruffled some feathers with His honesty. Eugene Peterson, writing *The Message*, explains the word "meek" as "content with just who you are." Jesus claimed to be meek and lowly in heart (Matthew 11:29). His brand of meekness requires self-awareness, humility, and gentleness—never hollow pretense.

When Jesus told the crowd, "Blessed are the meek, for they shall inherit the earth," He was preaching from Psalm 37, one of David's songs, as His text. Its message was to trust and rest in the Lord, Who is our Savior and stronghold. To do good and to wait patiently for Him without worrying about how anyone else is doing. The Lord guards our steps when we take joy in Him, and if we fall, He catches us. *He* helps, saves, and delivers us. The Lord is our safe place and the One Who does the saving.

So we don't need to. —SUZANNE DAVENPORT TIETJEN

FAITH STEP: *Read Psalm 37. There is a wealth of promises. Relax into the thought of Jesus close beside you. He'll never forsake you. Delight in His ways.*

THURSDAY, OCTOBER 18

*But the other criminal rebuked him. "Don't you fear God,"
he said, "since you are under the same sentence? We are punished
justly, for we are getting what our deeds deserve. But this man has done
nothing wrong." Then he said, "Jesus, remember me when you come
into your kingdom." Jesus answered him, "Truly I tell you, today
you will be with me in paradise." Luke 23:40—43 (NIV)*

MY GRANDSON, ROMAN, HAD A hard time paying attention in kindergarten, until testing revealed that he read beyond fifth-grade level and scored exceptionally high on other skills. Once the school put Roman in more challenging settings, his behavior improved. At the start of the next year, he again had trouble adjusting before similar arrangements were made. One morning Roman didn't want to go to school after getting in trouble the day before. My daughter tried to reassure him. But Roman explained, "The other kids probably think I'm just a lost cause."

We might be quick to label someone as a lost cause, but Jesus never is. He gave us proof of that as He hung dying on the Cross. Jesus pardoned a man who had been labeled a lost cause. One of the thieves crucified beside Jesus acknowledged Him as the Messiah and asked to be remembered when Jesus came into His kingdom. Jesus said that he would be with Him in paradise.

Jesus can redeem any life. If we remember His transforming power, we will never label someone as a lost cause; we will never think of ourselves or our circumstances that way. In Jesus's hands, any "lost cause" has good reason to hope for great and wonderful things. —DIANNE NEAL MATTHEWS

FAITH STEP: *Is there a person, relationship, or situation that you're tempted to give up on? Ask Jesus to breathe life into what looks like a lost cause.*

FRIDAY, OCTOBER 19

"And when you pray, do not heap up empty phrases as the Gentiles do, for they think that they will be heard for their many words. Do not be like them, for your Father knows what you need before you ask him."
Matthew 6:7–8 (ESV)

WHEN MY SON, ISAAC, WAS born with Down syndrome six years ago, I was devastated. Even though we'd been warned of the possibility early in my pregnancy, I had frankly prayed it wouldn't be so. When Isaac arrived and the diagnosis proved accurate, I confess I was shocked and crushed with disappointment and dread. How could God do this to me after all I'd been through? Was I being punished for something?

Those first few months after Isaac was born, I struggled. Ashamed and fearing what others might think, I felt like I could only turn to God. I prayed desperately, read my Bible, and searched for something that would change my feelings. Meanwhile, I did daily tasks. I cared for Isaac and cooked dinner.

At some point, my feelings miraculously shifted. I discovered God had *blessed us* with Isaac. We are *lucky* to have him!

Isaac has changed us all in remarkable ways, bringing out the best in each of us and blessing others. I realize that such a statement may sound like some kind of platitude, the consolation prize when you don't win. But it's abundantly and amazingly true.

And because our Jesus is truly personal and I'm a bit of a diva, I feel like Isaac is a gift, custom-designed for me. Isaac is God's instrument for helping me to become the woman He intended.

Thank God I haven't always gotten what I wanted. And thank God I have a Savior Who knows just what we *need.* —ISABELLA YOSUICO

FAITH STEP: *Think of a time when God didn't give you what you wanted. Can you recognize how He gave you what you needed? How?*

SATURDAY, OCTOBER 20

What shall we say about such wonderful things as these? If God is for us, who can ever be against us? Romans 8:31 (NLT)

I GREW UP IN A small town in Northern California. As in many small towns there was a local rivalry. Our rivalry team was the Mt. Shasta Bears, and we were the Weed Cougars. Yes, the town I grew up in was named Weed, and as you can imagine the Bears came up with all types of slogans. "We're going to smoke Weed," or "We're going to weed-eat Weed," their cheerleaders would chant. My favorite was, "We're going to tumble Weed!" At every football or basketball game there was the Home section and the Away section, and it was clear who you were for and who you were against. Small-town rivalries are like that.

As Christians, the line between *for* and *against* gets fuzzier. There are many people in the world who are against Christian beliefs, yet our role as believers is still to share the love of Jesus with them. More than that, until we were *for* Jesus, we were *against* Him. Romans 5:10 says, "For since our friendship with God was restored by the death of his Son while we were still his enemies, we will certainly be saved through the life of his Son" (NLT). Once we are saved through the life of Jesus, we are no longer enemies. He will always be for us.

High school rivalries come and go, but it's important to remember that Jesus is on our side. It's easy to get discouraged. It's easy to let the taunts of the enemy get under our skin, but when Jesus is for us we will always be on the winning side…even if we come from a place called Weed. —TRICIA GOYER

FAITH STEP: *What challenges are you facing today? Make a list. Then, next to each challenge, write, "Jesus is for me." Let Jesus's joy fill you as you're reminded you're on the winning side.*

SUNDAY, OCTOBER 21

"How did this man get such learning without having been taught?" John 7:15 (NIV)

ONE OF THE STRENGTHS I'VE long admired about homeschooling is a principle our family adopted even though we opted to send our children to a small public school—"lifestyle learning."

Making homemade applesauce taught skills like coordination, following directions, cooperation, fractions, the science of seeds-to-fruit-to-freezer, and others. Apprenticing simple home repairs developed problem-solving skills our children use now as adults. Involving them in the dailiness of life helped equip them for decision making, budgeting, and spiritual health.

We're told very little about how Jesus was schooled as a boy. He was no doubt instructed in reading, writing, science, math, and other subjects, and was schooled in the Old Testament. In biblical times, responsibility for education rested with the father of the household. The Bible makes little mention of Joseph after Jesus's ministry began. Many assume the stepfather died early, leaving Mary to school her Son in lifestyle learning.

All young men of the time were educated in the Law of Moses. And yet, Jesus's ministry (while He was in His early thirties) included teaching in the temple. The Jewish leaders said, "How did this man get such learning without having been taught?" John 7:1 (NIV). He spoke with authority.

Oh, He had been taught. By His stepfather, Joseph, while Jesus apprenticed as a carpenter. At His mother's knee. And at the right hand of His Father, who literally taught Him everything.

Will you and I say: "Jesus, faithful student. Jesus, faithful Teacher. Here I am, at Your knee, ready to learn more"? —CYNTHIA RUCHTI

FAITH STEP: *Today, sit before Jesus ready instead to receive instruction.*

MONDAY, OCTOBER 22

"I'll show up and take care of you as I promised and bring you back home. I know what I'm doing. I have it all planned out—plans to take care of you, not abandon you." Jeremiah 29:10–11 (MSG)

ONE MORNING I WENT FOR a walk with our family puppy, Bea. It's one of her favorite adventures. Part of my joy comes from her excitement. Some days she senses the end of school. She'll stand by the door, wagging to say it's time to walk to meet the kids' bus. She's the cutest, with her apricot-colored ears flopping and her little legs prancing between stops to sniff grass, signposts, bugs.

She hasn't been deterred by a couple of scary run-ins with bigger dogs. The first time involved two retrievers that bounded out of their door before their owner could stop them. It turned out okay, but it has me on high alert now.

The second time was scarier. Two houses down from ours, the garage door opened as we passed. A big black Labrador charged out, straining against the leash his owner struggled to hold on to. One look at little Bea sent the dog into attack mode. Baring his teeth, he lunged across the yard, then spun Bea and me in circles as we tried to escape. He ended up trampling his owner.

Life is not entirely safe.

But I'm learning from Bea to trust that Someone bigger is looking out for me. She trusts that the potential for hurt won't outweigh the joy of the journey. She knows that I am there for her.

How much more does Jesus know of how to get us through life until we're safely home with Him? —ERIN KEELEY MARSHALL

FAITH STEP: *What experiences have shown you Jesus's faithfulness to guide you? How have you felt His protection? Trust Him with whatever your journey brings.*

TUESDAY, OCTOBER 23

Be hospitable to one another without complaint. 1 Peter 4:9 *(NASB)*

MY SENIOR YEAR OF COLLEGE should have been a breeze. Each of my roommates had assignments during the summer so we'd be ready to launch a smooth new year when we arrived at San Diego State University for the fall semester. Within a day or two of arrival I knew the transition was going to be anything but smooth. The roommate who was supposed to secure our apartment failed to fill out the proper forms, so we got there to face an angry landlord who'd already rented the place to someone else. Feeling sorry for us, he let us sleep in an unrented apartment filled with storage items for almost two weeks.

Two of our roommates couldn't stand the stress so they packed up and left, leaving me and one other roommate virtually homeless. The dreaded day came when the landlord set our things out on the curb and said, "Figure it out!" I remember walking to a phone booth and dialing the number of a girl I barely knew. I'd only been a follower of Jesus for a few short months, but she was a loving Christian that God planted in my life at just the right time. With shaking fingers I dialed her number, embarrassed to ask if my roommate and I could stay at her place until we could find a place of our own. It took her four seconds to say, "Stay at that curb, I'll be right there to get you!"

We slept on her floor for three weeks, and never once did she complain. Her hospitality taught me more than a thousand church services could have about serving with a Christian heart. —GARI MEACHAM

FAITH STEP: *Hospitality is more than opening our homes; it's opening our lives. Is there someone or something you can open your life to today?*

WEDNESDAY, OCTOBER 24

But when he saw the strong wind and the waves, he was terrified and began to sink. "Save me, Lord!" he shouted. Jesus immediately reached out and grabbed him. "You have so little faith," Jesus said. "Why did you doubt me?"
Matthew 14:30–31 (NLT)

THREE YEARS AGO MY HUSBAND and I rented the basement of a large empty house as our ministry office. It later seemed logical to rent the upstairs for ourselves, but we needed to find renters for our townhouse first to make it financially feasible.

We hired a property manager and explained that we had a very narrow window for a move.

My stress level soared as the date grew close with no renter in sight. I began doubting our wisdom, but in the midst of packing boxes, I sensed Jesus saying, "Trust Me."

In the end, we missed the window, but Jesus had everything under control. Friends sold their house during that week for thirty thousand dollars more than their asking price, and they chose to bless a number of missionaries, including us. They hired a professional mover for us and their gift made our scheduling concerns a nonissue.

As I unpacked our belongings in our new space, I thanked Jesus for His sovereignty and provision. That's when I heard Him gently whisper, "Why did you doubt Me?"

That's a good question. Jesus's power to do what seems impossible is undeniable. Why, then, do we doubt Him?

The issue is more than turning our focus from Him like Peter. We doubt because we don't really know Who He is.

Let's do as the disciples in the boat did. Worship Him and declare, "You really are the Son of God!" —GRACE FOX

FAITH STEP: *Write "Jesus walks on water. I can trust Him and have no fear."*

THURSDAY, OCTOBER 25

But those who wait for the Lord [who expect, look for, and hope in Him]
will gain new strength and renew their power. Isaiah 40:31 (AMP)

ONE THING I APPRECIATE ABOUT my husband, John, is that he's a
man of his word. If we have a broken sink and he says he's going to
fix it, he does. If he promises to take me out on a date, he will. If
he offers to take the kids to the park so I can have some quiet time,
it's as good as done. After years of following through on his words,
I know what I can expect from him. I know I can look for help
when I need it and this takes the burden off my shoulders, knowing
that what I hope for will happen.

But John is human. There are times I really needed him and he
was on a work trip halfway around the world. There have been
things he couldn't fix and there have been many moments when
the help he offered fell short. No human person can meet all of our
expectations, but Jesus can. Only Jesus can strengthen us and renew
us from within. He can fill us with such hope inside that all our
outward troubles fade.

I used to think that waiting on the Lord was physically being still
and expecting Jesus to show up and do that work for us. While it's
important to make time and space for Jesus, waiting has more to
do with looking for Jesus to show up with hope than anything else.

For all the problems I face, do I expect that Jesus will show up?
Do I look for Him, hope in Him? This type of waiting makes all
the difference. It strengthens me internally when I feel like giving
up. —TRICIA GOYER

FAITH STEP: *Think of an issue that's troubling you. Take a moment and picture
Jesus seeing that issue and walking up to it as He rolls up His sleeves to do His
good work. Thank Him for always being Someone you can count on.*

FRIDAY, OCTOBER 26

"It is the Lord who goes before you. He will be with you; he will not leave you or forsake you. Do not fear or be dismayed." Deuteronomy 31:8 (ESV)

ONCE A MONTH A NUMBER of local novelists gather at my home. All morning we write in silence, but for the tapping of our laptop keys. Being with other authors fuels our motivation to keep going in our stories. After lunch we discuss chapters and offer feedback. Our gathering always inspires me.

A few months ago a pastor in our group, whose creative input delighted us all, accepted a call to serve a church in another state. This month a dear friend in the group is also moving out of state. I'm happy for the new directions in their lives, but I will miss their presence. Yes, we'll stay in touch via e-mails, but it's not the same.

Do you ever feel forlorn or forsaken when friends have to move away? Life on this planet is so transient. Even our closest family members may move away. Ultimately, those we love move on to Heaven. No matter how tightly we hold on, we can't keep relationships from changing. Except for one. Jesus has promised to never leave or forsake us and to be with us always. We can move to the ends of the earth and He will be with us. We can stay put and mourn as others move away, yet He will still be with us.

When friendships change or friends move away, I have a secret fear that I'll never make new friends—that my life will become more and more empty. Yet Deuteronomy reminds us not to live in fear. Because of Jesus, we will never be forsaken. —SHARON HINCK

FAITH STEP: *Reach out to a friend who has moved away. Thank Jesus for being the Friend Who will never leave.*

SATURDAY, OCTOBER 27

Make allowance for each other's faults, and forgive anyone who offends you. Remember, the Lord forgave you, so you must forgive others.
Colossians 3:13 (NLT)

THIS MORNING I WOKE UP with an unpleasant memory stuck in my brain. Over and over my mind replayed the scene: I walked into a room just as someone was telling a lie about me, obviously trying to cast me in a negative light with several people. The liar was someone who pretended to care about me. Someone I trusted. Since the incident was never acknowledged by any of the parties involved, the feelings of hurt and betrayal still cut sharply, even though almost four decades had passed.

Later, I took a break from work and turned on the news. The anchor introduced a man who had finally gained his freedom after spending twenty years in prison for a crime he didn't commit. The man smiled as he explained why he felt no bitterness: "With all that the Lord has forgiven me for, who am I to refuse to forgive someone else?" This man had been set free in more ways than one. He had chosen to leave behind resentment and embrace the new life granted to him.

Nursing a grudge for a past wrong is like allowing the perpetrator to hold us hostage. We only continue to hurt ourselves. Jesus wants us to live in freedom from anger, bitterness, and resentment. Even if the person who hurts us never apologizes or admits the offense, we can learn to forgive and free our souls by seeking help from the One Who has forgiven us. Once we let go of old grievances, then we can fully embrace the new life that Christ wants us to have. —DIANNE NEAL MATTHEWS

FAITH STEP: *Examine your heart for any traces of bitterness from past wounds. Tell Jesus that with His help you forgive the person who hurt you. Whenever the memory resurfaces, list the sins and shortcomings that Jesus has forgiven you for.*

SUNDAY, OCTOBER 28

The seventh time the servant reported, "A cloud as small
as a man's hand is rising from the sea." 1 Kings 18:44 (NIV)

BECAUSE OF KING AHAB'S REFUSAL to honor God, for almost three years rain had not drenched the earth in Israel. But after demonstrating His power repeatedly, including the massacre of 450 Baal prophets, God once again used Elijah, His prophet, to announce the ending of the drought.

Elijah told his young servant to look out toward the sea, but the young man saw nothing. The prophet told him to keep looking, and on the seventh trip the servant reported seeing only a tiny cloud. But that was all it took for Elijah. He sent the servant to tell Ahab that rain was coming.

In times of drought, I've often looked to the heavens for answers. Haven't you? Healing, the return of a prodigal son or daughter, or a solution to a financial crisis. We watch; we hope; we pray. Time passes. But we see nothing. Jesus remains silent. Then one day we notice a small cloud: a slight change in symptoms, a phone call, a small check in the mail. It's only a tiny speck of hope, but we cling to His promise and hang on to hope.

And then—the miraculous happens. That tiny speck turns into a downpour of blessings. The clouds burst; Jesus answers. Does He always answer the way we ask? No, but it's always in His way and in His timing.

As we continue to hold on, Jesus will never disappoint. Whether the change comes in us or in our circumstances, we can trust the One Who knows us best. —REBECCA BARLOW JORDAN

FAITH TEST: *Find a promise in God's Word that speaks to a "drought" in your life right now. Hold on, and keep believing until Jesus brings the rain.*

MONDAY, OCTOBER 29

Jesus said to them, "I am the bread of life; whoever comes to me shall not hunger, and whoever believes in me shall never thirst." John 6:35 (ESV)

I LIKE SHOES. EVEN THOUGH as a mom of small kids who works from home I have few chances to get dolled up, I still have *a lot* of shoes. I just appreciate any good-looking shoe.

My ten-year-old son suffers from the same affliction, though for basketball shoes. Aside from the moral question of such extravagance for mere shoes, it seems crazy to buy expensive high-tops for a kid who seems to grow an inch a month. We have a sensible spending limit and he spends his allowance within reason. Regardless, no matter what shoes we get, there's always another pair, a new pair, a cooler, cuter pair. Where does it end?

Today I recognize that our shoe fetish is insatiable. An itch that can never be satisfied. And like any bad itch, the more you scratch, the worse it gets. Better to apply medicine and resist the temptation to scratch from the very start.

The remedy is filling up on the Bread of Life, Jesus. For me, this means immersing myself in God's Word, prayer, meditation, worship, fellowship, and service. When I feast on Jesus I'm more content. My priorities and desires align more closely with His. The urge to buy another pair of shoes is quelled.

I'm not demonizing the buying of a few pairs of shoes. But I just know one more pair will never fully satisfy.

Jesus, Who Himself faced temptation, knows that He alone can satisfy our deepest longings, whether it be the need for love, meaning, or, yes, shoes. —ISABELLA YOSUICO

FAITH STEP: *Before your next shopping trip, ask yourself what underlies the craving. Consider investing your time and treasure in the One who fully satisfies.*

Tuesday, October 30

I want to know Christ and experience the mighty power that raised him from the dead. I want to suffer with him, sharing in his death, so that one way or another I will experience the resurrection from the dead!
Philippians 3:10–11 (NLT)

I CAN BARELY TURN ON my computer without being confronted by the suffering in the world. Headlines and social media can plunge me into a day's worth of depression. I am empathetic. The thought of refugee families ripped from their homes and left destitute leaves me wondering what my family would do if we were in that same situation. I can't fathom it. *What if one of my boys was kidnapped by a trafficking ring? How could we even stand it? Or what if some rare strain of virus made its way to our corner of the world? What then?*

It is easy to be overwhelmed by the world's suffering. It is easy to want to turn away from it so that we don't have to think or feel too much about it. But the plight of the suffering is right where Jesus's heart is found. He has always had compassion for those who were hurting, even shattered. He gets it. He lived and died...suffering.

When we let our hearts be broken for those who suffer, we are walking in the footsteps of Jesus. He loves us. When we hurt, so does He. When we cry, so does He. And then, in the midst of our suffering, His healing begins. It's hard to ignore those suffering around us but we all have a choice to share their burdens and pray on their behalf. When we share in their pain, hearts flung open, it is an invitation for Jesus to come rushing in with His presence and healing. And that is what hope looks like. —SUSANNA FOTH AUGHTMON

FAITH STEP: *Pray a prayer of hope for someone you know who is suffering. Remember that Jesus's heart is for each one of us who suffers and He longs to bring healing.*

WEDNESDAY, OCTOBER 31

"Yes, come," Jesus said. So Peter went over the side of the boat and walked on the water toward Jesus. But when he saw the strong wind and the waves, he was terrified and began to sink. "Save me, Lord!" he shouted.
Matthew 14:29–30 (NLT)

MY DOG, RUE, IS A good little swimmer but, like me, she has a problem with focus. She swam the length of a football field into frigid Lake Superior to check out a couple of floating seagulls. Tuned in to the birds, she seemed not to hear me calling her back to safety. She finally got close enough that the birds took flight and the spell was broken. Her big ears twitched at the sound of my voice and she turned around, wide-eyed at the distance to shore.

I'm more like Peter. I start well but I get distracted easily by the obstacles, the chaos around me, even other options I could choose. Peter may have spoken impulsively when he asked Jesus to confirm His identity by telling Peter to walk to Him on the water, but Peter didn't hesitate to obey. I imagine Peter, his eyes on Jesus, as he vaulted onto the surging surface of the Sea of Galilee.

He walked on water. Until he lost his focus.

Instead of the face of his Master, he looked away at the spray of the wind-whipped waves. Trying to look two ways at once doesn't work, as Peter found out when he began to sink. Once again, he looked to Jesus, his focus single and true. "Save me!" he yelled to the One Who could. And did.

Jesus can be trusted. He is always there. Look to Him, as determined as Rue swimming for the seagulls, and redirect the target of your devotion. —SUZANNE DAVENPORT TIETJEN

FAITH STEP: *Is there something Jesus wants you to do? Not sure it's Jesus? Ask, like Peter. If it is, do it, looking to Him.*

THURSDAY, NOVEMBER 1

Now we learn that some of you just loaf around and won't do any work, except the work of a busybody. So, for the sake of our Lord Jesus Christ, we ask and beg these people to settle down and start working. Dear friends, you must never become tired of doing right. 2 Thessalonians 3:11–13 (CEV)

DURING THE 2016 PRESIDENTIAL ELECTION, a friend wrote that she found the campaigns so discouraging she just wanted it to be over. Another said he didn't know what to do, that he couldn't vote for either candidate in good conscience, but he also felt he had to vote. I could relate. I often felt like checking out of all media as one controversy swirled after another. There seemed to be no truly good options. It was paralyzing.

And yet, I found, there was still plenty of work to do. Plenty of opportunities to be kind, to speak truth, to love. Maybe not on any grand scale. Maybe not even in a way that allowed me to see I was making much of a difference. But as Paul wrote, for the sake of Jesus, we must not grow weary in doing good.

One of my favorite poets, Rita Dove, said, "Our situation is intolerable, but what's worse is to sit here and do nothing." I think that applies to situations like that election as well as it applies to any place we find ourselves feeling powerless, or short of options. We always have the option of doing the next right thing. Even if the work is something small, or something unseen like prayer. We do it for the sake of Christ, so settle down and start working.
—GWEN FORD FAULKENBERRY

FAITH STEP: *Write out a prayer asking God to show you ways you can work within your situation to reflect His grace.*

FRIDAY, NOVEMBER 2

Therefore we do not lose heart, but though our outer man is decaying, yet our inner man is being renewed day by day. 2 Corinthians 4:16 (NASB)

AS I GRABBED MY TOOTHBRUSH from a drawer near my sink, four bottles of beauty products tumbled to the ground. On the floor lay a jar of cream for radiant eyes, a serum for flawless skin, a pore minimizer, and a lotion promising to shrink any baggage I carry under my eyes. *Seriously?* I sighed. None of this stuff has stopped my crow's feet from increasing to duck's feet, and I don't think one pore has minimized—heaven knows I've tried!

Imagine the headline of *Glamour* or *InStyle* magazines saying "You're decaying...but don't worry...serum's here to save the day!" There's nothing pretty about decay, but that's precisely why the apostle Paul used that word. We spend countless hours and bundles of money trying to cover up decay—while God invites us to something deeper and more intimate—a daily renewal of His love.

Like most beauty routines, His promises need to be applied every morning. We get out of bed and immediately wash ourselves with Jesus's grace and compassion. Next, we apply dabs of peace and patience to the corners of our eyes—eyes that will see various shades of joy, challenge, and surprise as the hours pass. The final touch is hope. We slather that over our entire body to protect us from the dull, dry effect of life's harsh elements. This beauty routine won't make you look years younger, but it will make you feel years wiser.
—GARI MEACHAM

FAITH STEP: *While washing your face or putting on your makeup, thank God that your insides are being renewed each day, even if your outside is wrinkling.*

SATURDAY, NOVEMBER 3

... Now you also must complete the doing of it; that as there was a readiness to desire it, so there also may be a completion out of what you have. For if there is first a willing mind, it is accepted according to what one has, and not according to what he does not have. 2 Corinthians 8:11–12 (NKJV)

WE'VE COMPLETED A PROJECT I'VE dreamed of for over thirty years: an in-ground greenhouse. We hope to grow vegetables that need more time than our short season allows, eat fresh salads through winter, then start seeds inside while the snow melts away. We kept a large garden for years on my husband's family farm but never got around to building the greenhouse.

We finally dug into the hill beside our cabin and poured the footings after we moved to the North Woods. We really needed the little greenhouse, but we got busy again and didn't finish. Until this summer. My garden this year consisted of late-season orphans rescued from parking lot clearance sales. The winter squash and eggplant containers will move in before the first frost and I'm sowing salad seeds.

We're eating pretty well from that ragged little garden we planted in July. It didn't look like much, but it produced plenty. I think too often that I haven't done what I could, because the garden I was able to have wasn't the one in my mind. Perfect was the enemy of possible and I ended up with nothing.

Pinterest with its perfection paralyzes us. Jesus didn't care about appearances; He cared about accomplishing what He was sent to do. His food was to do the will of His Father (John 4:34).

Finish what you can with what you have. You'll be blessed.
—SUZANNE DAVENPORT TIETJEN

FAITH STEP: *Do you have a dream you've neglected? Dust it off and prayerfully consider completing it. Ask Jesus how. Start with what you already have.*

SUNDAY, NOVEMBER 4

"I came that they may have life and have it abundantly." John 10:10 (ESV)

AFTER CHURCH ONE SUNDAY, WE found ourselves surrounded by other church members who had chosen the same small but charming restaurant. Three young adult couples sat at the table behind us. A high-top table of high school boys was beside us. An elderly couple several tables away.

My husband and I had greeted each group on our way to our table, common courtesy undergirded with genuine love for each person.

Midway through our meal, the high school boys seemed to pay special attention to us, smiling broadly every time we looked their way. We smiled back, grateful for their exuberance and young faith. I'd worked with several of them in a recent fine arts competition, so I assumed the extra connection might have fueled their interest.

When the young men engaged in deeper conversation with one another, a man from the table behind us came near. He whispered, "Those young men think you paid for their meals. Let's let them think that. I don't want them to know *I* did. Just keep smiling. Okay?"

What a kind gesture on his part. He wanted to bless the boys but not take any credit. Double blessing—he deepened the connection between those high schoolers and us. When the time is right, we'll tell them the truth so they can thank the giver and develop their own habits of invisible generosity.

If they or their parents are reading this, maybe I just did.

It's that kind of selfless, overt generosity Jesus shows us. Offering us not just a survivable life but an abundant one. Kindness is part of what makes life abundant! —CYNTHIA RUCHTI

FAITH STEP: *Drive-by, anonymous kindness. Does that give you any ideas for what you can do today to boost someone's understanding of the way Jesus cares?*

MONDAY, NOVEMBER 5

Don't worry about anything; instead, pray about everything.
Tell God what you need, and thank him for all he has done.
Then you will experience God's peace, which "exceeds anything"
"we" can understand. His peace will guard your hearts and
minds as you live in Christ Jesus. Philippians 4:6–7 (NLT)

I HAVE KNOWN AND LOVED today's key verse for years. I've written it on recipe cards and posted it on my fridge. I've even memorized it. But truth be told, I haven't fully understood it until recently.

I've spent a great deal of time telling God about my needs but too little thanking Him for all that He's done. The result? Focusing on my concerns caused me to worry more. But things have changed since studying Jesus's life.

The story of Lazarus's death and resurrection resonated with me. Jesus knew He would call forth a man from the tomb who'd been dead for four days. He could have focused on the enormity of the task. Instead, He said, "Father, thank you for hearing me," and then He performed the miraculous (John 11:41–44).

Rather than fixating on the problem of how to feed thousands of hungry people, Jesus thanked God and then fed the masses with just five loaves and two fish (Luke 9:14–17).

God invites us to tell Him about our needs but doing so is only half of the equation. Giving thanks for all that He's done is the other half. As Jesus demonstrated, gratitude turns our focus from our concerns to the One Who's greater than those concerns.

Prayer and thanksgiving—two parts of the equation. Together they add up to bring us the peace we all desire. —GRACE FOX

FAITH STEP: *Give thanks to God for one thing that He's already done for you.*

TUESDAY, NOVEMBER 6

So flee youthful passions and pursue righteousness, faith, love, and peace, along with those who call on the Lord from a pure heart. Have nothing to do with foolish, ignorant controversies; you know that they breed quarrels.
2 *Timothy 2:22–23* (ESV)

DURING THE EXTRAORDINARY 2016 ELECTION season, I found myself unusually tempted to engage in debates about the defects or merits of the various candidates. Normally I'm not big on confrontation, but the remarkable political climate was ripe for controversies, providing plenty of fodder for fine, and not-so-fine, quarrels. As we saw played out on national media, these quarrels seldom if ever produced changed hearts or minds.

I think Miss Manners is credited with the advice not to talk politics, sex, or religion in polite company, but Timothy made the point nearly two thousand years ago. Young Tim was no doubt inspired by the example of Jesus, who rarely argued with those who tried so very hard to engage Him in useless and deceptive debates.

Only submission to Christ's Spirit in me prevents me from taking the bait. Whether it's arguing "why" with one of my small children or debating the strengths of a presidential candidate, I can save myself from "foolish, ignorant controversies" and let Jesus take over. When I pause and connect with that Spirit, I realize it is sometimes the only way I can resist controversy, recalling Jesus's own powerful example of silence in the face of the foolish. —ISABELLA YOSUICO

FAITH STEP: *Whether it's a young child fishing for endless explanations or a colleague or a fellow church member voicing conflicting views on a matter, try using the powerful silence that Jesus employed.*

WEDNESDAY, NOVEMBER 7

And we all, who with unveiled faces contemplate the Lord's glory, are being transformed into his image with ever–increasing glory, which comes from the Lord, who is the Spirit. 2 Corinthians 3:18 *(NIV)*

IT'S SOMETHING A PARENT PRAYS for. My husband, John, and I dropped off our daughter, Leslie, at camp when she was fourteen years old, and when we picked her up she was different. The messages and worship times at camp truly made a difference deep inside her. She'd always been someone who loved Jesus, but on the drive home she bubbled over as she talked about Him. She told us how she felt transformed inside and declared that she'd given herself completely to Him.

Even though Leslie had accepted Christ when she was six-years-old, through her camp experience she realized her relationship with Jesus could be more real, present, and relevant than before. Leslie decided that following Jesus wasn't something that only her parents did but something she wanted to commit her life to also.

Leslie was not perfect after that, but she was changed. Her dad and I have continued to see her being transformed into His image, and at twenty-four years old she is a missionary in Europe. We still pray that she will continue to be transformed into His image with ever-increasing glory. It's something we want for all our kids.

It may seem prideful to ask for more of His glory, but that's exactly what Jesus wants. John 17:22 says, "I have given them the glory you gave me, so they may be one as we are one," (NLT). The more room we give Jesus in our lives, the more others will see Him. The change that Jesus made in Leslie's life still affects others today, as they see Jesus in and through her. —TRICIA GOYER

FAITH STEP: *Who has reflected the glory of Jesus to you? Let that person know in a short note. Let him or her know that the difference shows!*

THURSDAY, NOVEMBER 8

Finally, all of you, have . . . a tender heart. . . . 1 Peter 3:8 (ESV)

I DUMPED THE DISH OF venison into the trash and sighed. I'd had such hope for that recipe. My husband is a hunter, and while I like having wild game in our freezer, sometimes it's hard to get the gamier meats tender.

It's sobering to think that even though meat can be difficult to tenderize, a human heart can be even more so. Life toughens us up.

Do you know many tenderhearted people? They're not common. They not only show compassion but feel it. When someone hurts, the tenderhearted hurt, too. Tenderhearted people are who you'd want at the side of your sickbed, the people you'd go to with a problem, and the first you'd consider trusting your children with. They bring comfort wherever they go.

But having a tender heart makes a person more prone to emotional injury. A tender heart feels hurts more strongly, its own and others'. So why would Jesus's Word tell us to have a tender heart if it's a surefire path to pain and suffering?

Because a tender heart is a unifier, bringing compassion into a world that tries to pull us apart. A tender heart is powerful.

Jesus showed His tender heart many times. When He heard that Lazarus died, He wept (John 11:35). He showed compassion for individuals and entire groups (Matthew 9:36). He healed people because He cared, often touching them with His own hands, guarding hearts from hardening beneath life's load.

Let's check our own hearts to see how tender they are, to Jesus and to others. There's power in tenderness. —ERIN KEELEY MARSHALL

FAITH STEP: *Cook one of your favorite meals today. While its comfort fills you, ask Jesus to show His tenderness through you.*

FRIDAY, NOVEMBER 9

*Since you have been raised to new life with Christ, set your sights
on the realities of heaven, where Christ sits in the place of honor at
God's right hand. Think about the things of heaven, not the things of earth.*
Colossians 3:1–2 (NLT)

As a writer, I look at screens. All. The. Time. And when I stop
looking at the big screen in front of me, somehow I end up reaching
for the cell phone in my purse to look at. It is crazy how so much
of my day can get sucked up checking on friends on Facebook or
watching funny videos. In this tech age, the pull of the screen is
always present. I can't seem to stop myself from surrendering to its
siren song of "I'm so important...don't ever stop looking at me."
But I also realize that staring at a screen for days on end makes my
back seize up and my calves hurt. It is a poor substitute for engaging
with the real world. And it distracts me from important things like
real people, my purpose in this life, and Jesus.

It is hard for me to hear what someone is saying to me when I am
reading a headline or listening to a song or answering an e-mail. It
is even harder to hear Jesus. It takes strength and discipline to peel
ourselves away from the distractions of life. Jesus wants us to focus
on Him and the things of heaven, not just of this earth.

What we focus on here on earth determines our destiny. We get to
make the conscious choice of what we concentrate on. Jesus would
like it to be Him, so that we can devotedly know Him and His life-
changing power. So that we can understand the depths of forgiveness that He has for us and what life in His presence looks like. The
life He has for us is truly glorious. —SUSANNA FOTH AUGHTMON

FAITH STEP: *Take some screen–free time and journal your thoughts as you focus
completely on Jesus and His goodness.*

SATURDAY, NOVEMBER 10

After dismissing the crowds, He went up on the mountain by Himself to pray. When evening came, He was there alone. Matthew 14:23 (HCSB)

WHEN I GO OUT TO eat with friends or family, they know what I'll be doing while we wait for our order. Collecting the paper that came off the straws and the slips of paper wrapped around the napkins holding the utensils. I like to twist it, fold it, and maybe shape it into something. Yep, I'm one of those people who have to keep their hands busy. Years ago I learned cross-stitching, needlepoint, and knitting so I could be doing something while visiting family or watching television with my husband. As the sticker on my thread box says, "Busy hands, happy heart."

I often meditate on all that Jesus accomplished with His hands. I visualize Him methodically breaking apart the small loaves and fish to feed the famished crowd of thousands. Mixing mud to spread on blind eyes and restore sight. And mercifully taking the hand of a dead child to bring her back to life. How many lives were transformed by those strong carpenter's hands?

Just as important are the times those hands were still. Several Scriptures show that despite His busy schedule, Jesus often went to a private place to pray. These extended times of talking with His Heavenly Father sustained Him during periods of testing, reenergized Him, and strengthened Him for the suffering to come.

Using our hands to serve others is important, but we can't afford to neglect quiet times of stillness and prayer. Busy hands may make for a happy heart, but hands folded in prayer guarantee the most joyful heart and spirit. —DIANNE NEAL MATTHEWS

FAITH STEP: *Read the story of the famous painting called Praying Hands (Albrecht Dürer). Let this image remind you that prayer is important work.*

SUNDAY, NOVEMBER 11

God is our refuge and strength, a very present help in trouble....
The Lord of hosts is with us; the God of Jacob is our fortress.
Psalm 46: 1, 7 (ESV)

MY FATHER CAME TO THIS country as a refugee. After spending five of his teenage years in a displaced person's camp following World War II, his family was sponsored by a church in Minnesota and they began to make a new home here. From the stories I heard as a girl, I got a sense of the relief they felt when they finally found refuge. Their experiences help me appreciate the blessings of freedom and putting down roots.

The children of Israel were also refugees. They fled Egypt and wandered for years. The story of how God led them to their promised land foreshadows the way Jesus is leading us home.

There are days that remind me I'm a traveler in need of refuge. Yesterday was a rough day: irritating e-mails, frustrating computer problems, a tangled up scene in the novel that I'm writing. Anxiety and discouragement built up as the day went on. Then I learned that a friend's husband is facing cancer. Everywhere I looked, I saw reminders that this world is no longer the home we were given in Eden. Every task feels harder than it should be. Loss and failure lurk around each corner. We are refugees.

But Jesus doesn't leave us wandering in the wilderness of sin. He has secured a new home for us in eternity. And even while we long for that day, He is also our daily refuge here on earth.

As followers of Jesus, we can appreciate His very present help in troubling situations. Refugees appreciate the blessing of a refuge. —SHARON HINCK

FAITH STEP: *Find time today to reach out to someone who's just moved into your community, remembering that we are all refugees.*

MONDAY, NOVEMBER 12

"But seek first His Kingdom and His righteousness, and all these things will be added to you." Matthew 6: 33 (NASB)

As I TYPED THE SCRIPTURE above, two more urgent e-mails landed in my in-box, and one voice mail with an explanation point popped up on my phone. It seems that everyone I talk to is saying the same thing, "Why is my life so hectic and my schedule so full?" From young moms, to business colleagues, to Bible study friends, to students and parents everywhere...the assault on our time and sanity is on—and most of us are losing the battle!

When I was young, I was good at making lists and checking items off as I completed them. But now the lists are more sophisticated (day-timers, google calendars, reminders on my phone) and the tasks are endless. It seems the onslaught of communication never stops. We used to be able to get away from tasks by simply not answering the phone. Now, multiple layers of communication are making us an overstressed, overactive society. I get work messages by text, e-mail, Facebook, Twitter, Whats App, voice mail, and the occasional letter. It's virtually impossible to escape, and truthfully, I don't want to fully escape...I just want to be peaceful in the midst of it all.

One day I asked Jesus how He handled stress while on earth. Certainly the business of healing, teaching, and saving humankind had its share of stress! I was reminded of the words He spoke when offering a cure for anxiety. He said two simple things: seek first God's kingdom, and seek His righteousness—everything else will fall into place. I'm going to trust that it will. —GARI MEACHAM

FAITH STEP: *At the top of your calendar or list of things to do, write: seek God's kingdom and His righteousness, and think about it throughout your day.*

TUESDAY, NOVEMBER 13

And the peace of God, which transcends all understanding, will guard your hearts and your minds in Christ Jesus. Philippians 4:7 (NIV)

MY HUSBAND IS A COLLEGE tight end turned high school football coach. My son is a quarterback in middle school. Practices, games, films, weights, and strategy consume the summer and fall of every year. Needless to say, even with three girls plus me in the family, around our house we process a lot of things in terms of football.

I can't remember where I first heard this, but it's a description that sticks with me. Someone said to imagine the peace of God like an offensive line, guarding your heart and mind in Christ Jesus like the line guards the quarterback.

The most important people to me on the team are the offensive line, because they are the ones who guard my boy. When they block strong and tough, nobody gets to him. He has time to think and look and make a perfect pass. He can also tuck that ball and run right through the hole they create, gaining yards without being touched by a defender. It's beautiful. The most stressful times for me during games are when opponents blast through the line and come after Harper to tackle him. It seems everyone is always out for the quarterback. The peace of God really is our offensive line. In Jesus, it guards my heart and mind.

Committed to my well-being, guarding me from harm, and providing me time and space to think and make good decisions without rushing in or feeling panicked. And in Jesus, that peace never fails. It never encounters an enemy too great to hold off. It is always brave and strong. —GWEN FORD FAULKENBERRY

FAITH STEP: *Claim the peace of God as your shield and protector today. It is yours in the name of Jesus.*

WEDNESDAY, NOVEMBER 14

Give thanks in all circumstances, for this is God's will for you in Christ Jesus. 1 Thessalonians 5:18 (NIV)

I'VE ALWAYS STRUGGLED WITH THIS verse, whether I encountered it in my Bible reading or sang it as a chorus in church. Really? In everything, give thanks? Everything?

I've always been a "glass half empty" kind of gal and have always been able to think of plenty of things for which I wasn't the least bit thankful. I secretly thought it was kind of unreasonable for God to expect this of me or others whose lives were much more difficult than mine.

Through the years the verse niggled at me. I still offered thanks out of obedience, wishing I was better at it.

It's been gradual, but I've changed. I read the Bible and saw how Jesus lived. His gratitude was so natural as to be almost invisible to me. Jesus was often heard thanking His Father and I couldn't imagine Him doing it half-heartedly. Jesus loved God and was sure of His love in return. He never lost sight of it.

I *don't* always like my circumstances, but I now recognize that I'm unqualified to judge them. Jesus has shown me the Father. I've finally seen His uninterrupted, never-ending love for me.

And now I can't keep quiet or thank Him enough!

—SUZANNE DAVENPORT TIETJEN

FAITH STEP: *Consider reading Psalm 136 aloud in a modern translation like The Message before your Thanksgiving meal. (If you're eating with children, they love to say the "His Love never quits" refrain.) Let the repetition drum the truth of God's love into your heart today.*

THURSDAY, NOVEMBER 15

*"Blessed is the one who trusts in the Lord, whose confidence is in him.
They will be like a tree planted by the water that sends out its roots by the
stream. It does not fear when heat comes; its leaves are always green.
It has no worries in a year of drought and never fails to bear fruit."*
Jeremiah 17:7–8 (NIV)

RECENTLY, MY FAMILY AND I went through a season of financial reduction that has launched me back to some basics of faith and following Christ, including whether blessings and money are linked at all.

Here are some key questions in my thoughts: Is having money a sign of worth, spiritual maturity, or Jesus's approval?

Is not having money a sign of spiritual discipline from Jesus?

Could not having money make room for other blessings?

Did that last question catch your heart like it caught mine?

Bountiful finances are not how Jesus blesses most of the time. They could be a test. I need to be careful, though, because there's pride in thinking I'm special if Jesus is blessing us with greater growth and dependence on Him through reducing us, or in judging others who have more. Those are no-good patterns of thinking, too.

But aside from that, it's biblical truth that loving money can be a huge distractor from trusting wholly in Jesus (Ecclesiastes 5:10; Matthew 6:24; 19:21, 24; Hebrews 13:5). Not just as we collect fancy toys in our oversized garages but as we grow prideful in *our* good works, the dollars *we* give, the importance of *our* names, and the good feeling we mistake for joy because of *our* possessions.

Most of the time, Jesus blesses us *for* trusting Him and *through* more of Himself. Not money. —ERIN KEELEY MARSHALL

FAITH STEP: *Rest in knowing "minimalist" finances often draw us closer to Jesus than great riches.*

FRIDAY, NOVEMBER 16

Devote yourselves to prayer, being watchful and thankful.
Colossians 4:2 (NIV)

WHEN I WAS IN MY early twenties, a friend at work asked to borrow ten dollars. She said she'd repay it by the end of the day. A few hours before the conclusion of the workday, she'd made no mention of the loan. Ten dollars might sound like too minor an issue to worry if it was *ever* repaid, but this was during a time when my husband and I—newlyweds—had to think hard before purchasing a pack of gum.

I reminded her. Then I reminded her again an hour later. The third time I mentioned it, her face darkened. "I told you I'd pay it back before the day's over. And I will."

My pestering showed lack of trust in her word. And it revealed my regret that I hadn't been in a financial position to lend to anyone if my heart wasn't prepared to risk not getting it back. She made a point of returning the ten dollars before we clocked out for the day. But my impatience had driven a small wedge in our work relationship, one that never fully disappeared.

When does prayer become pestering? When does our repeating a familiar request show lack of trust in Jesus? The answer is less about timing than it is attitude. The Bible records instances when our persistence in prayer is applauded, and other times when we're reminded that He knows what we need before we even ask.

Where does that leave us? In need of a heart check. Does my pleading reveal an honorable persistence? Or does it show a lack of faith in Jesus—the ever faithful One? —CYNTHIA RUCHTI

FAITH STEP: *Note the second half of Colossians 4:2—"... and guard your prayers with thanksgiving." Memorize this as a reminder that our gratitude for answers on their way guards our prayers from turning into nagging.*

SATURDAY, NOVEMBER 17

"This is my command—be strong and courageous! Do not be afraid or discouraged. For the Lord your God is with you wherever you go."
Joshua 1:9 (NLT)

BOTH MY HUSBAND, SCOTT, AND I have dealt with some fear issues when it comes to public speaking. In high school, Scott would have rather died than give an oral report. His hands would shake. His voice would crack. It wasn't pretty. But, miraculously, the first time Scott spoke in front of his church college group, Jesus transformed Scott's fear into articulate, powerful words. Scott never looked back. That talk launched his dream of becoming a pastor.

When my first book came out, I never thought that I would be asked to speak at events. The first time I was invited to speak, I answered the e-mail with an excited yes. Then I put my head down on the table and sobbed. I didn't want to miss out on the adventure that Jesus had for me...but I was terrified. I spoke four times in one weekend. It was a fear breakthrough. Not because I spoke perfectly but because Jesus met me in the middle of my fear and used me anyway.

There are still moments when I am scared. Any step outside of my comfort zone is scary. But Jesus isn't looking to use people with no fears; He is looking to use people who are willing to trust Him in spite of their fears, their inadequacies, and their struggles. He doesn't open the door to a new opportunity and say, "Good luck working this out on your own!" He surrounds us with His powerful presence and says, "Don't be afraid. Don't be discouraged. I am with you!"
—SUSANNA FOTH AUGHTMON

FAITH STEP: *Is Jesus asking you to do something that scares you? Give your fear to Him, knowing that He is with you and will empower you every step of the way.*

SUNDAY, NOVEMBER 18

"How do you know me?" Nathanael asked. Jesus answered, "I saw you while you were still under the fig tree before Philip called you." Then Nathanael declared, "Rabbi, you are the Son of God; you are the king of Israel." Jesus said, "You believe because I told you I saw you under the fig tree. You will see greater things than that." John 1:48–50 (NIV)

JESUS AMAZED NATHANAEL BY PROVING that even before He met him, He could see him standing under a fig tree—what's more, Jesus also knew Nathanael's character. This revelation prompted Nathanael to proclaim his belief in Jesus as the Messiah. Jesus assured him that he would see far greater things than that.

Those who followed Jesus saw many miracles. A crowd of thousands fed with a single meager lunch. Sight restored to people born blind. Those with paralyzed legs miraculously running, and the mute shouting praises. Bodies ravaged by leprosy healed instantly. The demon-possessed and seriously ill restored to wholeness and health. Many followers conversed with Jesus after He rose from the dead. Some watched Him ascend to heaven.

Each of us has a unique story about the amazing way Jesus has worked in our lives. Testimonies of answered prayers and unexpected blessings. Times that He empowered us to do something we considered impossible. But with the pressures and busyness of daily life, it's easy to forget what He's done. We get stuck in a rut. Or we may start feeling as though our best days are behind us.

How would life be different if we woke up every day anticipating the great things that Jesus would do, in our personal lives and in the world around us? Because Jesus is still ready to amaze those who trust and believe in Him. —DIANNE NEAL MATTHEWS

FAITH STEP: *For one week, begin each day by asking Jesus to show you great things that He's doing around you. Record your thoughts each evening.*

MONDAY, NOVEMBER 19

Jesus was sleeping at the back of the boat with his head on a cushion. The disciples woke him up, shouting, "Teacher, don't you even care that we're going to drown?" Mark 4:38 (NLT)

SEVERAL YEARS AGO I LEARNED about Asperger's syndrome, a form of high-functioning autism. Articles explained that people with Asperger's often demonstrate a lack of empathy toward others in distress. Based on personal experience, I'd found this to be true. But then I read a recent study that said this trait was misunderstood.

It's not that those with Asperger's don't care about others' feelings. In reality, it's that they feel others' pain so keenly that they have to erect a self-protective wall. This insight helped me better understand individuals with Asperger's within my circle of family and friends.

Jesus knew what it felt like to be misunderstood. When He slept during a storm, the disciples assumed He didn't care if they might drown.

When Martha bustled around the house trying to prepare a meal for Jesus and the disciples, she assumed that He didn't care about her workload: "She came to him and asked, 'Lord, don't you care that my sister has left me to do the work by myself?'" (Luke 10:40 NIV). She may have felt the same way when Jesus didn't come immediately upon hearing that her brother, Lazarus, was dying (John 11:4–7).

Sometimes we might feel Jesus doesn't care about us. This is especially true when we pray without finding the answer we want. The truth is that Jesus cares deeply. Certainly His willingness to die for us demonstrates this. So do His promises. —GRACE FOX

FAITH STEP: *Write out 1 Peter 5:7—"Give all your worries and cares to God, for he cares about what happens to you." Thank Him for caring deeply about those things that trouble you.*

TUESDAY, NOVEMBER 20

Enter with the password: "Thank you!" Make yourselves at home, talking praise. Thank him. Worship him. Psalm 100:4 (MSG)

ENJOYING ALL THE BENEFITS OF many Internet sites requires that we enter a password. I often forget that password and may even fail to write it down. So I begin again, either searching my brain for the right combination or entering a new password.

Forgetfulness affects us all, regardless of our age or computer savvy. And nowhere does it happen more often than in our relationship with Jesus. But unlike the Web, Jesus creates a simple password that pushes us into His presence: "Thank You." An attitude of gratitude will open up new areas of fellowship. Jesus loves for us to enter His presence with thanksgiving.

Spending moments praising and thanking Jesus on most mornings has topped my day's to-do list for a long time. But sometimes, I need to do more. That's what happened the other day. My husband and I were reminiscing about the past: places we'd been, trials we'd encountered, lessons we'd learned. In doing so, Jesus opened up an entire room of thanksgiving. We recalled blessings we'd forgotten and people who had touched our lives. Tears flowed as we reached deep into the mercies Jesus had given, and laughter rose as we acknowledged His sense of humor in the course of life lessons that taught us more about Him.

The list of memories continued, until we realized that the morning was half spent. But we felt full, and perfectly "at home" with Jesus. That simple password of "Thank You," had not only sweetened our fellowship with each other but with the One Who deserves our praise. —REBECCA BARLOW JORDAN

FAITH STEP: *Use the password of "Thank You!" often to enter Jesus's presence. Today take time to identify as many blessings and mercies as you can remember.*

WEDNESDAY, NOVEMBER 21

Do not be anxious about anything, but in everything by prayer and supplication with thanksgiving let your requests be made known to God.
Philippians 4:6 (ESV)

OLD TESTAMENT AND NEW BOTH reinforce the notion that gratitude is an important part of faith. Several times in the Bible there appears to be a link between thankfulness and prayer and admonitions against fretting. Why is that?

One explanation I hear orbits around first thanking God for what we have before asking for something else. If we're not grateful for what God has already provided, how can we be grateful for His provision for what we now say we want or need?

Some argue that it's more about affirming our grateful confidence that God is hearing and will answer our prayers than merely saying "thanks" for anything. Because, after all, it's about trust. And while trusting God is a good thing, in its extreme form, this belief can be a "name it, claim it" gimmick that makes God a genie rather than Sovereign of the Universe.

Personally, I've found the power of gratitude lies in changing my behavior. I can't manufacture the *feeling* of gratitude myself, but simply choosing to honor God by recognizing all that I have serves to frame my experience of His provision. Thanking God for everything also frees me from the fear that is so often about an unknown future; things I'm worried will or won't happen, things I will or won't get. When I approach His throne with an attitude of gratitude, I don't have to be anxious about anything. —ISABELLA YOSUICO

FAITH STEP: *Identify a sister in Christ with whom you can share a daily Gratitude List via e-mail or text. Start with three items, and work your way up.*

THURSDAY, NOVEMBER 22

Then he took the seven loaves and the fish, and when he had given thanks,
he broke them and gave them to the disciples, and they in turn to the people.
Matthew 15:36 (NIV)

ALL THE BURNERS ON MY stove were busy with potatoes, gravy, and green beans. The oven wafted scents of roasting turkey. As we prepared for family to arrive for Thanksgiving dinner, music played from my iPod. I hummed along as I stirred the gravy. "I love my Thanksgiving mix," I said to my husband. "All of my favorite hymns and great praise music. I always look forward to listening to it on the holiday."

My husband checked the turkey. "You know, you could play it on other days."

I laughed. "I know, but I never think of it."

It struck me then; his reminder applied to more than music. I whispered a prayer, "Lord, help me turn on a thanksgiving mix in my heart each and every day."

Jesus gave a consistent example of gratitude during His time on earth. Scripture records several instances where He gives thanks. In Matthew's account, He demonstrates a thankful heart for the miracle God was about to supply—before it even unfolded.

We don't have to wait until prayers are answered the way we wish before we express gratitude. We don't have to wait for special occasions and holidays. Like Jesus, we can give thanks during our everyday living and during the anticipation of blessings to come. Let's set the music of our soul on a selection of appreciation, contentment, and joy and hear it play all day long. —SHARON HINCK

FAITH STEP: *Play a favorite Thanksgiving hymn. Watch for opportunities to give thanks at various moments throughout your day.*

FRIDAY, NOVEMBER 23

And I am certain that God, who began the good work within you, will continue his work until it is finally finished on the day when Christ Jesus returns. Philippians 1:6 (NLT)

THERE ARE DAYS I THINK back wistfully as I contemplate the size jeans I wore in high school, but the older I get the less I want to go back to those days. I don't want to return to the immature, self-centered, self-indulgent person that I was. Even when I gave my heart and life to Jesus at age seventeen I had a long way to go. And Jesus was patient with me. Over the years I've faced joy and suffering, gain and loss. I've had success and failure, and embraced new life in my family. Through it all, I've learned more about myself and more about Jesus. I can see the good work that He started when I prayed my first honest prayer of submission. I can see the journey He's taken me on. It's a journey that hasn't been easy, but I wouldn't trade it for the relationship I have with Jesus now.

Looking back also causes me to look forward. In my middle-age years it's possible that I still have half my life to go. Thankfully God will continue his work in me until "the day when Christ Jesus returns." As Peter says, "May God give you more and more grace and peace as you grow in your knowledge of God and Jesus our Lord" (2 Peter 1:2 NLT). I used to think this grace and peace focused on dealing with others, but now I understand it also means acceptance myself. We all need to know how to give ourselves grace—and have peace deep inside—knowing that Jesus is still working and He won't give up on us...ever. —TRICIA GOYER

FAITH STEP: *Think of one or two areas where you need to give yourself grace and peace. Pray and ask Jesus to help you to be gracious to yourself as you travel on your journey to maturity.*

SATURDAY, NOVEMBER 24

"Have the people sit down." John 6:10 (NASB)

JESUS AND HIS DISCIPLES HAD been among a crowd of thousands for some time while He shared His teachings. After hours of teaching thousands of people, panic set in as Jesus asked His disciples "How are we going to feed all these people?" He didn't ask because He was unsure. He knew he could feed those people—after all; He is the bread of life. Jesus asked because He wanted to see what they would say. Phillip clarified the money situation...no way could they afford to feed the thousands that were there. Then Andrew explained that they only brought a sack lunch, barely enough for Jesus and His disciples. Instead of Jesus saying something rich with spiritual insight or meaning, He simply instructs His disciples to have people sit down. This was no easy task. Imagine crowds of thousands standing around, mulling, complaining, and hungry. "Just sit down!" probably sounded like the dumbest thing they could do. Yet, that's precisely what Jesus instructs.

Perhaps it's what He's telling *us* to do, too. Sometimes in our pursuit to be godly; work hard; raise a good family; be a good spouse, friend, and church member...we forget to sit down. We forget it's not about what we do; it's about who we become. To sit down means we relax our posture. We forgo all temptation to "help" Jesus perform His miracles of provision in our lives and the lives of others. We simply sit and wait to be filled by the miraculous hands of our Savior. When we sit down we allow God to work on our behalf, filling us with the nourishment we need in order to go back to our lives and flourish. —GARI MEACHAM

FAITH STEP: *Go to a quiet spot in your home or the outdoors and sit down. Plan to sit for ten minutes, asking God to fill you with the nourishment you need for today.*

SUNDAY, NOVEMBER 25

Bless—that's your job, to bless. You'll be a blessing and also get a blessing.
1 Peter 3:9 (MSG)

WE LIKE THE IDEA OF blessings. We're sure we need blessings, and we do. But do we really understand what Jesus means by *bless*?

We say "bless you" when someone sneezes. In Arkansas, women say "Bless your heart." And we ask for blessings when we pray.

I can't help but think that Jesus's teachings are summed up in this simple, all-encompassing verse about blessings. Namely, being a blessing. All of the Bible can be tied back to this truth.

The Old Testament spoke of the blessing to come through the Savior, Jesus. Then the New Testament told of Jesus's life and the costly blessing of the Cross, followed by the early church and living to bless others with salvation's good news.

Jesus came as the Greatest Blessing. Because of Him we are blessed and can be a blessing back to Him and others.

But what does it mean to bless someone, from Jesus's point of view? Jesus's blessings go to the heart. They meet needs. Blessings can be simple or profound. They can come in backward ways, even painful ones. Growth and healing through distressing times can bring wonderful blessings we couldn't experience without the pain.

Since our primary need is for redemption, talking about blessings in general is good, but it isn't complete if we don't use our lives to point others toward the greatest blessing—the core of all the rest—Jesus's death for us on the Cross.

When we live to bless Jesus and others, we're living the whole Scripture (Matthew 22:36–40). —ERIN KEELEY MARSHALL

FAITH STEP: *Make a list of the best blessings Jesus has given you that can't be touched—love, grace, peace, salvation, etc. Think of specific examples.*

MONDAY, NOVEMBER 26

He who calls you is faithful; he will surely do it. 1 Thessalonians 5:24 (ESV)

IT'S HUMBLING TO ADMIT THAT sometimes I've taken Scripture out of context. I'll latch onto a verse that supports my side in a disagreement with my husband, for instance. Or I'll lean on my own interpretation of a tiny portion of a verse to justify my decision to purchase new sheets on sale.

I suspect some reading this right now have done the same. Jesus is both faithful and forgiving. His Word is true and always applicable... when used as He intended.

I'm seeing a favorite verse of Scripture in a new light these days.

"He who calls you is faithful," reads 1 Thessalonians 5:24 (ESV), and "he will surely do it." Do what? I used to answer that question with "whatever I set my mind to." But that promise, that divine encouragement is tied to the previous verses. It doesn't wave a "Go for it!" flag over wild ideas. Although Jesus sometimes does call us to ideas we consider wild and unnerving, in this context, the "it" that He promises to do for us is the benediction at the end of these glorious words. This is the "it."

"Now may the God of peace himself sanctify you completely, and may your whole spirit and soul and body be kept blameless at the coming of our Lord Jesus Christ. He who calls you is faithful; he will surely do it," 1 Thessalonians 5:23–24 (ESV).

Jesus promised that He will move within us to cause us to be dedicated to Him and to be found blameless when He returns.

What a wide umbrella of spiritual protection and confidence for us to stand under! —CYNTHIA RUCHTI

FAITH STEP: *If you own an umbrella, consider attaching a tag to the handle with the verse 1 Thessalonians 5:23–24. He is faithful. He will do it.*

TUESDAY, NOVEMBER 27

I have so many things to say that concern you, judgments to make that affect you, but if you don't accept the trustworthiness of the One who commanded my words and acts, none of it matters. John 8:26 (MSG)

MY DAUGHTER, GRACE, AND HER friend, Ethan, have been friends since they were born. Ethan's mom, Sheila, and I have been friends almost that long. Now we're raising our families in our small hometown where we all go to the same church.

Yesterday after Praise Team practice, Sheila and I compared notes on the first semester of high school in terms of grades, driving privileges, peer pressure, dating, and such. As usual our conversation turned back to the good old days when we were dressing them up in matching outfits for Halloween and taking them on playdates to Disney movies. It all seemed so simple then.

Now we must navigate the world of letting go while still holding on, giving them space while staying in their business, allowing increased independence complemented by strict accountability. It's easy to be critical of other parents who are either too strict or too lenient but getting the right balance is tough.

Sheila and I observed that it's hard when they don't understand why we have certain rules, why we say *yes* to certain things and *no* to others. I find myself explaining ad nauseum. Sheila had a helpful observation. She said "I told Ethan he doesn't always have to understand. But he does have to trust me."

This turns out to be a useful skill for adult followers of Jesus. Like He said in John 8:26, if we don't trust Him, nothing else He has to offer really matters. —GWEN FORD FAULKENBERRY

FAITH STEP: *Quit demanding an explanation for everything and learn to live with some unanswered questions in your faith. Make this your mantra: Jesus, I trust You.*

WEDNESDAY, NOVEMBER 28

"We are taking every thought captive to the obedience of Christ."
2 Corinthians 10:5 (NASB)

A POWERFUL IMAGE CAME TO mind as I stood over the kitchen sink draining murky water through a strainer filled with delicate pasta. "This is just like taking our thoughts captive!" I blurted to my husband as I smiled. "We need to leave the good thoughts in the strainer, and let the murky ones flow down the drain." If only it was as easy as pasta and water.

Murky thoughts can take the form of fear, worry, negativity, criticism, anger, blame, and self-hatred. If left unchecked, they can water down the flavor of our lives. I used to think I had to filter every thought that ran through my mind and put it in a category. These are the good thoughts, these are the selfish thoughts, and these are the worrisome thoughts. It was exhausting. With practice, I learned it's much easier than that. Jesus's character reflects four strong words—*peace, hope, freedom, purpose*—and if my thoughts aren't aligned with one of these "Jesus traits," I let them run through the strainer of my mind into the drain. When thoughts of worry threaten to choke my faith, into the strainer they go.

When I feel hopeless and see no resolution, I remember Jesus's hope, and wash the despair away. If I feel trapped or imprisoned by habits—I swirl them in the strainer. And when my life is dull or void of purpose I remember that Jesus has a recipe He's using to make me the person He wants me to be. My job is to keep the healthy, true, appealing thoughts in my "mind-strainer" while letting the negative thoughts drain. —GARI MEACHAM

FAITH STEP: *Write the words peace, hope, freedom, and purpose on an index card and set it in your strainer.*

THURSDAY, NOVEMBER 29

With all my heart I will praise you, O Lord my God. I will give glory to your name forever, for your love for me is very great. You have rescued me from the depths of death. Psalm 86:12–13 (NLT)

LAST WEEK I WAS STRUGGLING to meet a writing deadline, dealing with sore back issues, and trying to pick up around the house. I was failing on all fronts. Life had me on the mat. My husband, Scott, hugged me and encouraged me saying, "Sue, you know everything is going to be okay. It will all work out. It always does." I answered him, "Can you believe I am supposed to be writing a book about hope when I feel hopeless?" One of my sons piped up from the kitchen, "Mom! You need to read your own book!" Scott and I started laughing.

Sometimes a particularly rough week can leave you feeling like you got the wind knocked out of you. A tough job situation can work on your last nerve. And a frayed relationship can strip you down to your most vulnerable. It can feel hard to cope with day-to-day living when life has you on the mat. But we are not hopeless. We have great hope.

In every situation and circumstance, no matter how dire, Jesus brings hope. We know this because He has done it in the past...in us. He is our Savior. He saves us with His overwhelming love and His show-stopping grace. There is no relationship that He cannot heal, no problem that He cannot solve, and no project that He cannot navigate. Jesus has hope for you today. And it doesn't get better than that! —SUSANNA FOTH AUGHTMON

FAITH STEP: *What are some of the ways that Jesus has shown up and saved you in the past? Take a moment to praise Him for what He has done and will do in your life.*

FRIDAY, NOVEMBER 30

And when the Lord saw her, he had compassion on her, and said unto her,
Weep not. Luke 7:13 (KJV)

MY FRIEND, STEVE, WAS TELLING me about a trip he recently took with his ninety-year-old mother. I'm always impressed by the honor he shows her in her old age, because I know he had a difficult upbringing. His mother was not affectionate, nor kind.

Steve's mother wanted to go see her sister who lived in another state. So Steve, who is a retired physician, drove her there. He stayed with her at his aunt's house and reconnected with family.

He said something extraordinary happened as he listened to his mother and her sister's conversation. They told stories of their own upbringing, which was so hard. His grandfather, their dad, was an abusive alcoholic. Steve got tears in his eyes when he said, "You know, for the first time I realized maybe my mother wasn't trying to neglect me. Maybe she was just doing the best she could."

To me this was such a precious picture of compassion that I cried, too. I wondered if his mother has any idea how lucky she is to have a son who sees her—and forgives her.

Weep not. This is what Jesus says, in Luke 7:13, to the widow who has lost her only son. Jesus is just passing through the city gate, but He takes the time to see her. And when He sees her, he has compassion. Then He alleviates her suffering. *Weep not.*

I wonder sometimes if I really take the time to see others. And when I truly see them—what is my response? It seems that if we look with Jesus's eyes we'll have compassion for everyone—just like He has for us. —GWEN FORD FAULKENBERRY

FAITH STEP: *Put on the spectacles of Jesus before you encounter others today. Note how that changes your understanding of them, and act accordingly.*

SATURDAY, DECEMBER 1

The angel went to her and said, "Greetings, you who are highly favored! The Lord is with you." Luke 1:28 (NIV)

IT'S NO WONDER GABRIEL'S WORDS startled Mary. Various translations of this passage describe her as confused, troubled, even deeply disturbed. Here stood a young woman from a poor family in a small village that was looked down upon by many Jewish people in other areas. Then one day an angel shows up and tells her she is highly favored by God. Mary could not understand why she would be addressed in this way—until Gabriel shared the news that God had chosen her for the role of giving birth to the Messiah.

The exact form of the word Gabriel used to describe Mary is found in only one other place in all of Scripture. In Ephesians 1:6 Paul praises God for the "glorious grace, which he has freely given us" (NIV). This special favor or grace lavished on those who accept Jesus includes redemption and forgiveness of sins; we stand before God holy and blameless on the basis of Christ's sacrifice. We are God's children endowed with an inheritance of spiritual riches. He has assigned each one of us a special role and purpose to fulfill, just as he did Mary.

Does it startle you to think that the same words Gabriel applied to Mary also describe you? Maybe recent bad choices or moral failures make it hard for you to believe that God sees you as redeemed and blameless. Perhaps you feel so ordinary that the thought of being singled out for special honor boggles your mind. Or your life seems so mundane that you can't imagine being assigned a special role to fill. But that doesn't change the truth that, thanks to Jesus, you are highly favored and the Lord is with you. —DIANNE NEAL MATTHEWS

FAITH STEP: *Read Luke 1:5–38. Contrast Zechariah's doubt-filled response (verse 18) with Mary's acceptance and obedience (verses 34 and 38).*

SUNDAY, DECEMBER 2

---

*"This very day in King David's hometown a Savior was born for you.
He is Christ the Lord. You will know who he is, because you will find him
dressed in baby clothes and lying on a bed of hay." Luke 2:11–12 (CEV)*

GROWING UP, MY FAMILY ALWAYS opened gifts on Christmas Eve. We
kids would go into a back bedroom and wait...and wait. Finally,
we'd hear the *ding-a-ling* of bells, followed by Dad's hearty voice:
"Santa has come!" We could always tell the "Santa" gifts. No tags
were needed. Under the tree sat our fulfilled hopes: a shiny bicycle,
a new baby doll, or a fun bake-oven. The anticipation was over. We
felt happy and satisfied.

The world awaited another time of expectancy as prophecy
after prophecy foretold the coming of One Who would bring
love and peace. Centuries of oppression had led to confusion and
disappointment. Would the promised One ever come?

And then one starry night as shepherds waited on a hillside, the
heavens opened up and an angelic chorus announced that the time
of waiting had ended: "Jesus has come!" The hopes and dreams
of all the years were fulfilled in the birth of a baby named Jesus.
Messiah, Son of God, Redeemer, Christ the Lord.

And as the shepherds followed the angels' instructions and drew
near to the babe lying on the bed of hay, they had no doubt that this
shining gift was from God. Those who heard the good news and
received the gift felt joy and satisfaction.

Over two thousand years have passed, but we who know
the Gift and the Giver can share the joyful message: "Jesus has
come...and He's coming back again!" —REBECCA BARLOW JORDAN

FAITH STEP: *Think about when you first understood Jesus, God's gift, had
come—for you. Ask Him to prepare your heart for the celebration of Christmas.*

MONDAY, DECEMBER 3

"Don't assume that I came to bring peace on the earth. I did not come to bring peace, but a sword. For I came to turn a man against his father, a daughter against her mother, a daughter-in-law against her mother-in-law; and a man's enemies will be the members of his household. The person who loves father or mother more than Me is not worthy of Me; the person who loves son or daughter more than Me is not worthy of Me. And whoever doesn't take up his cross and follow Me is not worthy of Me." Matthew 10:34–38 (HCSB)

ACKNOWLEDGING THAT MY FAITH CONTAINS endless paradoxes that I may never understand helps me in my study of the Bible. So does the reality of my life experience.

Although none of my family members have raised a sword against me, there has been an undeniable change in those relationships since I gave my life to Christ. When my beliefs were mostly subtle, we were fine. But since my faith has deepened and, consequently, I've shown more openly the depth of my faith commitment, I've dealt with divisions between me and them. Division isn't Jesus's only message here. He wants us to prioritize.

If pleasing my family stands in the way of Jesus's path for me, I have to reject that. Otherwise I am choosing something else over Him. Ask yourself: Am I willing to turn from them and risk their rejection to follow His leading?

If your shoulders have just slumped in sadness because you're devoted to your family, don't despair! Because Jesus took up the Cross, we are forgiven for the times we struggle to take up ours. Trust that when we fix our eyes on Jesus, He will grant us the peace to deal with whatever comes. —ISABELLA YOSUICO

FAITH STEP: *Consider a small step you can take to prioritize Jesus over your family. Ask Jesus for guidance and the courage to choose Him.*

TUESDAY, DECEMBER 4

You will show me the way of life, granting me the joy of your presence and the pleasures of living with you forever. Psalm 16:11 (NLT)

OUR FAMILY CHRISTMAS IN COLORADO last year was a full week of joy, sledding, shopping, "big rounds" (Grandma's special crepe-like pancakes), presents, and cousin time. The first day back in the school saddle was rough. Will calmly announced that he was quitting school when I picked him up in the afternoon. Reentry is always difficult. "I have a better idea for school," he suggested. "What would that be?" "Let's get all the cousins to go back to Colorado and Grandpa and Grandma can teach us." "I am not sure Grandma and Grandpa would be down with homeschooling." Will got a dreamy look on his face. "No, it would be fun! Math would be like…a bowl of ice cream…divided by a can of soda…plus whipped cream equals…." "Equals what?" He grinned, "Equals happiness." He sat back contentedly. "It would be the best school ever."

I agree with Will. Happiness is being in the presence of so much love. To be known and wanted and given presents? Who wouldn't want that? That same spirit of happiness is what overtakes us in the presence of Jesus. We are so loved. So wanted. He gave His last breath on our behalf. The gift of salvation and eternal life is offered to each of us because of it. When we come into His presence and the knowledge of His deep affection for us, we are overwhelmed with joy. Our greatest moments are with Him. And the best part is knowing that, because of His great love, we get to live with Him forever. —SUSANNA FOTH AUGHTMON

FAITH STEP: *Think back to the moment when you found yourself cradled in the deepness of Jesus's love. How did it make you feel? What was it about that experience that brought you the most joy?*

WEDNESDAY, DECEMBER 5

But I am like an olive tree flourishing in the house of God; I trust in God's unfailing love for ever and ever. Psalm 52:8 (NIV)

I'VE BEEN MARRIED TO MY husband, John, for twenty-six years, but for many years I didn't think that would be the case. My doubt was due to the fears and mistrust I carried into my marriage. I didn't know my biological dad, and my stepfather was uninvolved in my life. With a love-hungry heart I started dating at age thirteen and found myself hurt time and again. John loved Jesus, and he loved me well, but I put up walls to protect myself. I couldn't flourish in our marriage because I was so busy guarding my heart.

Looking back I see that I did the same thing with Jesus. I wanted to love and to be loved, but I was also afraid. What if I gave my whole heart to Him and was disappointed? What if I sinned too badly? Deep down I questioned if Jesus would really show up as He said He would, and so I built walls around my heart to protect myself from disappointment.

Thankfully, over time the walls crumbled. The steadfastness of my husband and my Lord showed me they could be trusted. As the walls came down, the energy I put into protection became avenues of growth—in my marriage and in my spiritual walk.

Even though not everyone has a marriage that can be counted on, when we trust in Jesus's unfailing love, we will never be disappointed. When we take the energy we had been using to protect ourselves and open ourselves up to Jesus, we flourish in ways never previously imagined. —TRICIA GOYER

FAITH STEP: *Draw a picture of a brick wall and in each brick write down something you do to protect your heart from Jesus. Then pray over each brick. Ask Jesus to show you the truth of His unfailing love.*

THURSDAY, DECEMBER 6

"For in Christ Jesus you are all sons of God, through faith.
For as many of you as were baptized into Christ have put on Christ. . . .
And if you are Christ's, then you are Abraham's offspring,
heirs according to promise." Galatians 3:26–27, 29 (ESV)

YEARS AGO I WENT WITH my husband to his office Christmas party. He introduced me to various coworkers, and they all began each conversation the same way: "What do you do?"

Facing the question over and over left me stammering for a response. "Um, I'm a mom. Four young ones at home right now." Sometimes I mentioned that I used to be a choreographer, or that I did a bit of writing, but since those activities weren't bringing in any income, it didn't seem to answer the question they were asking.

That wasn't the only time I grappled with my vocation. I've gone through a variety of careers, and I've often had a hard time answering the "What do you do?" question.

Have you ever had an identity crisis? Perhaps you've left the vocation you once loved. Or perhaps your role as spouse, or parent, or friend has changed. When we face those shifts, it's wonderful to lean on the unchanging love of Jesus. Because of Him, we are not defined solely by a temporary vocation or interpersonal role. We gain an identity as a beloved child of our Father, allowing us to be fully who we were meant to be. Jesus restores our ability to live in freedom, to serve Him, and to have a purpose that transcends a title or a paycheck. When we're asked, "What do you do?" we can answer, "I ask Jesus to love others through me in any role where I'm placed." —SHARON HINCK

FAITH STEP: *List all the jobs you've held and all the roles you fill. Thank Jesus that no matter how much those may shift or change, you are constantly God's child through Him.*

Friday, December 7

When Jesus spoke again to the people, he said, "I am the light of the world. Whoever follows me will never walk in darkness, but will have the light of life." John 8:12 (NIV)

THINKING OF JESUS AS LIGHT is an image I can appreciate. I live way out in the country where I find myself in the dark a lot. There are no other houses around—my parents and brother live on either side of me but through the woods—and we are far from the road. No streetlights. No lights from businesses or cars. We're pretty isolated.

Don't get me wrong, I like it. I like to go outside at night and look up in the sky and see total blackness dotted by diamonds. I like to call my mom and tell her to turn on her porch light because I'm on the way down the path. I like to see the sun rise out of the darkness, competing with no other light. I like to watch fireflies sparkle on an otherwise dark landscape.

The thing about darkness is that it amplifies the light. Stars aren't nearly as bright when you're in a city surrounded by lights. And porch lights in a neighborhood, while friendly, don't serve a serious purpose. Even the sunrise is anticlimactic in a place of artificial light.

American novelist Edith Wharton said, "There are two ways of spreading light: to be the candle or the mirror that reflects it." In our relationship with Jesus, He's the candle. We are the mirror that reflects His light to the world. The deeper the darkness, the brighter we shine. —GWEN FORD FAULKENBERRY

FAITH STEP: *Remember that song you learned as a child, "This Little Light of Mine"? Sing it. Go ahead, you know you want to. Sing it like you mean it.*

SATURDAY, DECEMBER 8

Jesus entered Jericho and made his way through the town. Luke 19:1 (NLT)

I WONDER HOW OFTEN I'VE said to an approaching salesperson, "Just looking."

"Can I interest you in a sample of our new—?"

"No, thank you. I'm just passing through."

Usually, that phrase—*passing through*—is a casual expression. When Jesus is involved, that's never what it means. His "just passing through" may *look* casual, but every time those words are used regarding His journeys, something big happens.

So, when I began my Scripture reading one day with Luke 19 and read, "Jesus entered Jericho and was passing through town," I leaned forward in my chair and grabbed my highlighter. So much history here. Joshua's famous battle where the walls came tumbling down. Jesus healed Bartimaeus who was blind before his encounter with the Messiah.

And now, while passing through Jericho, Jesus intentionally stops at a place where a crowd has gathered. He looks up. So many times when Jesus looked up, He was catching the eye of His Father. Maybe He did the same on this day, too. He saw Zacchaeus, and beyond Zacchaeus, the watchful eye of the One Who sent Him. Can you picture God nodding in agreement as Jesus ignored all others clamoring for His attention and singled out Zacchaeus, one of the least lovable?

Jesus intended to get through town. Continue His journey. How many "big things" do I miss when my intention is to simply pass through? Next time, I'll lean forward. Look up. And uncap my highlighter. —CYNTHIA RUCHTI

FAITH STEP: *If you carry a highlighter, write on it: Look Up. No matter how casual the task, Jesus may be asking you to be part of something bigger.*

SUNDAY, DECEMBER 9

At the very time Simeon was praying, she showed up, broke into an anthem of praise to God, and talked about the child to all who were waiting expectantly for the freeing of Jerusalem. Luke 2:38 (MSG)

THE PROPHETESS ANNA PROBABLY MARRIED young, as did most Jewish girls of her time. But after seven years, Anna lost her husband. Instead of remarrying, she lived as a widow, denying herself the joys of marriage for eighty-four years. There's no indication she was unhappy. So I've often wondered why she *chose* to remain single when most of her young friends in similar situations probably remarried.

Anna had grown into an old woman, likely over a hundred years old. Why would she choose to forgo a companion with whom she could laugh and cry? Why would she deny herself the joys of physical intimacy with one who loved her? I found the answer to those questions between the lines of Scripture. Perhaps Anna had found a deeper Love.

Devoted in prayer, fasting and worshipping daily, never leaving the temple—the meeting place for God's presence—she lived for the day when she would see the promised Messiah.

Through our decades of marriage, God has faithfully brought my husband and me through the fire—flames that could have devastated us. But as deep as our love has become, it doesn't hold a candle to a Love that's only grown deeper—that of Jesus.

When Mary and Joseph entered the temple carrying the promised Christmas Babe, Anna broke out in spontaneous praise. She had finally seen the greatest Love of her life.

Not even death can separate us from that Love. —REBECCA BARLOW JORDAN

FAITH STEP: *Ask Jesus to be the greatest Love of your life.*

MONDAY, DECEMBER 10

Thy word is a lamp unto my feet, and a light unto my path.
Psalm 119:105 (KJV)

IT'S DARK IN THE WOODS, but we have a plethora of flashlights—at least two in each car and each building on the property, on keychains and in purses. My favorite is an orange oval-shaped flashlight that was my dad's. It's lightweight and ergonomic. Push the button once and the beam falls on the path in front of me. A second push adds another beam directed at my feet so I can avoid hazards. A third turns on a "tail-light," blinking red to alert others to my presence. It is "a lamp unto my feet and a light unto my path," helping me see where I'm headed.

Always looking for an analogy, I wondered if and where the third option—the one that lets people know where I am—fits in. I may have found it.

Jesus told His followers, "Ye are the light of the world" (Matthew 5:14). And, "If you are filled with light, with no dark corners, then your whole life will be radiant, as though a floodlight were filling you with light" (Luke 11:36, NLT).

We can't help but stand out, like bright lights in a dark world (Philippians 2:15).

I probably strained that analogy, but Jesus intended something like that. It *is* a dark world and many can't see the light of the Good News. We follow Jesus. Christians may not look like much, but we are carrying a treasure around in our oh-so-ordinary selves. And somehow, it shows through.

People will be drawn to that light. When they are, we can introduce them to Jesus. —SUZANNE DAVENPORT TIETJEN

FAITH STEP: *Do you feel awkward letting your light shine? I do. Jesus wants our lights to shine for the benefit of others. Think of a way and do it today.*

TUESDAY, DECEMBER 11

This means that anyone who belongs to Christ has become a new person. The old life is gone; a new life has begun! 2 Corinthians 5:17 (NLT)

MY FRIEND, TATUM, IS PREGNANT with her third baby. I could barely contain my joy when I found out. There is something so utterly delightful about a new baby. I love babies. Their smell. Their tiny hands and feet. Their amazingly sweet faces and the way they curl into your arms when they are sleeping. Tatum is excited, too. And nervous. Because babies tend to rock your world. Each time you welcome a new little one into your family, it changes everything. You can't continue on with the same routine you had in the past. You have to adjust to a new way of living.

Even though it can be scary, it is entirely worth it. Because new life is so beautiful. So joyful. So hopeful. Each new little person that graces this planet is a reminder of Jesus and the new life He offers us. When we are born again, we are asking Jesus to take over our lives completely. He begins to transform us into the person He created us to be.

As Jesus infuses our lives with His presence, everything changes. He invites us to leave our old way of life and begin to embrace a life of trusting Him for everything. His life in us begins to transform us from the inside out. The result of that transformation is new life in Him. Love abounds. Grace surrounds us on all sides. And His forgiveness enables us to live a life of freedom. New beginnings. New ways of thinking. Belonging to Him will change us forever…and that is exactly what we really long for! —SUSANNA FOTH AUGHTMON

FAITH STEP: *What are some of the ways that Jesus has changed you since you gave your life to Him? Write out this verse from 2 Corinthians and carry it with you today as a reminder that you are a new creation.*

WEDNESDAY, DECEMBER 12

But the Lord answered her, "Martha, Martha, you are anxious and troubled about many things, but one thing is necessary. Mary has chosen the good portion, which will not be taken away from her." Luke 10:41–42 (ESV)

TYPE A FOLKS LIKE MARTHA and me easily lapse into fretting and frantic control, certain that without our diligent attention, the planets would stop orbiting around the sun. Or, at the very least, our dinner party would flop. This mind-set is usually accompanied by some self-righteous finger-pointing at others who aren't fussing like I am.

In Matthew 6:31–33 Jesus teaches us to not worry over the things of this world and instead seek first the Kingdom. I can see the results of trusting that advice in my own life. When I risk putting Him before anything, mundane or monumental, I often see Him miraculously provide—the time, the money, the skill, the solution, or the wisdom not to worry. Everything is "added unto me."

My past has informed my present and so today, when I find myself motivated by that "anxious and troubled" feeling, whether because there's a lot of laundry to fold or some genuine catastrophe seems imminent, I'm able to pause long enough to linger at Jesus's feet and wait for His counsel. When I'm attentive to what He has to tell me, I know I'll gain perspective, find my priorities reordered, and feel greater peace. —ISABELLA YOSUICO

FAITH STEP: *Try it! Take an index card and write out Matthew 11:27–30. Next time you feel "anxious and troubled," make the choice to pause, breathe, and read this verse quietly a few times. Receive His rest.*

THURSDAY, DECEMBER 13

Listen and hear my voice; pay attention and hear what I say. Isaiah 28:23 (NIV)

ONE OF MY FAVORITE TIMES of the day is reading aloud to my younger kids. I've read books like *Little House in the Big Woods, Charlotte's Web, Betsy-Tacy,* and many more wonderful classics. I love sharing some of my most cherished stories with my kids, and I love exploring new books together. When we adopted our older girls, one of the first things I incorporated into our routine was reading aloud to them every day. I missed so many years with them, and I wanted this time to bond us together. I wanted them to become familiar with my voice, to feel the emotions, to know the cadence as I read. I wanted them to have that to carry into their adult lives even though they were still teens.

Just like I want my kids to know my voice, Jesus wants us to know His. During our time on this earth we may not hear an audible voice speaking to us, but we can "hear" Him just the same. Jesus communicates to us through His Word. Over the years the more I've read the Bible the more I understand His voice, feel the emotion, and know the cadence as I read. Even though the Bible is written by dozens of men in different styles, the heart of Jesus comes through. More than that, God's Word contains power. The Holy Spirit uses His words to connect with our hearts.

As Hebrews 4:12 says, "For the word of God is alive and powerful. It is sharper than the sharpest two-edged sword, cutting between soul and spirit, between joint and marrow. It exposes our innermost thoughts and desires" (NLT). Want to connect with Jesus today? Sit down and read His Word, listening to His tender voice as you do. —TRICIA GOYER

FAITH STEP: *Create a Bible reading plan. Read God's Word daily even if it's just a few minutes a day. Ask Jesus to help you connect with His heart as you read.*

FRIDAY, DECEMBER 14

The first time I was brought before the judge, no one was with me.
Everyone had abandoned me. May it not be counted against them.
But the Lord stood with me and gave me strength so that I might preach the
Good News in its entirety for all the Gentiles to hear.
And he rescued me from certain death. 2 Timothy 4:16–17 (NLT)

TODAY I RECEIVED AN E-MAIL from a woman I knew as a teenager many years ago. She told me how Jesus has been identifying the hurt places in her heart and then healing them one by one.

She described her journey, beginning with her childhood. Abandoned by her biological parents, she spent years in foster homes where she endured many kinds of abuse. She sought help but no one believed her. "You have a wild imagination," people said, and so she learned to keep quiet. When she entered her teen years, she survived by praying to Jesus at night. He became her confidant and best friend. As He did with Paul, Jesus stood with her and gave her strength when everyone else turned their backs on her. And as He did with Paul, He saved her from certain death.

Several years ago, Jesus brought a godly mentor into her life. This relationship has contributed to her restoration, and she's moving forward trusting that Jesus will someday use her story for His glory.

One of my favorite worship songs declares Jesus as the hope of the nations. Indeed He is. But He's more than that—He's the hope for individuals like you and me. Circumstances overwhelm us, and people disappoint or hurt us. But Jesus never fails us. He stands with us and strengthens us to become the men and women He's called us to be, empowered to tackle the work He's called us to do. —GRACE FOX

FAITH STEP: *Read Matthew 12:18–21. Thank Jesus for promising not to crush the weak. Ask Him to bring hope to those people who desperately need it today.*

SATURDAY, DECEMBER 15

"And blessed is she who believed that there would be a fulfillment of what had been spoken to her by the Lord." Luke 1: 45 (NASB)

IT'S AMAZING HOW A COMPLIMENT or word of encouragement can nourish our spirit. A simple string of words, delivered at just the right time, assures us we can *do* or *believe* anything God sets before us. I wonder if that's why after hearing the words of the angel Gabriel, Mary hightailed it to Elizabeth's house.

Elizabeth was a faith builder. Mary hadn't even made it through her front door and Elizabeth was blessing her with words of power and faith. In her final blast of encouragement Elizabeth says to Mary, "Blessed is she who believed that there would be a fulfillment of what had been spoken to her." Essentially she complimented the gutsy faith Mary showed by believing that what God said He will do, He will do. This statement was a turning point for Mary as she awaited the arrival of baby Jesus. She needed Elizabeth's words to affirm the mighty miracle taking place in her life. Truthfully, we're all giving birth to something: new ideas, new hope, new direction, and new challenges. Without an encourager we'll feel like the load is too heavy and our faith is too light.

Yesterday a boy came to my home selling greenery for his scout troop. His tan-and-red shirt was decorated with the emblems of hard work and commitment. I listened respectfully as he nervously went through his speech. When he was done, I wanted to hug him because I was so proud of him. I spoke words of life over him as I told him he was a great salesman and an impressive young man. His anxious frown lifted to a wide-toothed smile as he replied, "Thanks so much. This is scary." We *all* need encouragement. It's a powerful balm to a weary soul. —GARI MEACHAM

FAITH STEP: *Offer encouraging words to at least two people today.*

SUNDAY, DECEMBER 16

They were terrified, but the angel reassured them. "Don't be afraid!"
he said. "I bring you good news that will bring great joy to all people."
Luke 2:9–10 (NLT)

LIFE HAS ITS UNPLEASANT MOMENTS, but when I think of happy occasions, I remember celebrations from the past: the day I graduated from high school, the day I married, the birth of our children and grandchildren, special birthdays, anniversaries, vacations—and more. The memories bring joy to my heart.

When Luke describes some happy occasions involving both the birth of John the Baptist—the forerunner of Jesus—(Luke 1:14) and the announcement of Jesus's birth, he records the angels using the qualifier, *great* joy. I've always thought of joy as, well, joy. I found the same words in other passages as well. And most of them referred to a degree of emotion involving the Deity.

Jesus Himself prayed before His death that His disciples would experience the full measure of His joy (John 17:13, NIV). And speaking to His disciples in John 15:11, Jesus told them He wanted His joy to remain in them, that it would be *full*. Other translations use the words *complete joy* or joy that *overflows*. Is it any wonder then that the angels would describe Jesus's birth at Christmas as bringing *great* joy, *complete* joy, *overflowing* joy?

We still experience pain and heartache in this world. But the *great* joy that Jesus brings remains embedded in our hearts, ready to explode in celebration when we see Him face-to-Face.

At that moment, every believer who has ever known Jesus, will experience a complete and lasting joy. —REBECCA BARLOW JORDAN

FAITH STEP: *Thank Jesus for happy moments and celebrations in your life that have brought you a measure of joy. Then write "Great Joy!" beside Luke 2.*

MONDAY, DECEMBER 17

And Christ lives within you, so even though your body will die because of sin, the Spirit gives you life because you have been made right with God. Romans 8:10 (NLT)

THIS MORNING I'M HAVING DEVOTIONS near a window that looks out over a peaceful pond. Birds sing and the sky is dusted with soft shades of blue and white. It's easy to be aware of Jesus's presence.

But I've dwelt in other places. Sometimes my view has been less serene with a littered alley in a crime-ridden neighborhood as a backdrop. Or I've been distracted by the ventilation fans on the roof of a noisy hotel, or a swarm of mosquitoes outside my tent. When our geography isn't idyllic, can we still find Jesus?

Skimming through the Gospels, I looked for the many locations where Jesus was found: a stable, an Egyptian desert, a noisy temple, a mountaintop, Herod's palace, a cross, a tomb.

As Jesus walked this earth, He shared His love in all sorts of places. It comforts me to know that wherever my path leads, He will be there. He isn't limited to places that remind us of the Garden of Eden, or to tranquil church pews.

More than that, we know that Jesus will be with us everywhere we go, because Scripture tells us He lives within us. There is nowhere we can go—no hospital room, no graveside, no corporate office, no traffic jam, no empty apartment, no luxury suite, no cramped basement or classroom—where we are apart from Him.

In a world full of changing places, changing views, and changing circumstances, Jesus is a constant, joining us in each place we journey and living in and through us. —SHARON HINCK

FAITH STEP: *List some of the places you've lived or visited. Thank Jesus for being with you there and with you today.*

TUESDAY, DECEMBER 18

Whatever is good and perfect is a gift coming down to us from God our Father, who created all the lights in the heavens. He never changes or casts a shifting shadow. James 1:17 (NLT)

FOR MOST OF MY LIFE I've struggled with feelings of falling short. If most of my house was clean, I'd fret about the room that wasn't. If I exercised, I'd feel guilty about a poor food choice I made. If my child had trouble with a school subject, I'd worry I wasn't doing enough as a homeschooling mom. And when adopting children to our family, the feelings intensified. Instead of focusing on all I was doing right, I'd feel burdened by things left undone like chores.

One day a wise friend pointed out, "You feel as if you're failing, and throughout the day you confirm it by what's left undone. Instead, try focusing on what you're doing well and confirm all the things you're getting right." This advice was life-changing. My attitude improved and things became easier. I started seeing more clearly the good things that Jesus had brought into my life.

Our lives are filled with so many good and perfect gifts, but often we fail to see them because our minds are tuned into all of our shortcomings. The good news: We can control our minds! Once I started focusing on the goodness in my life, my heart was ready to release the frustration. Now when those feelings rise up inside of me, I look to find something to thank Jesus for. Instead of thinking, "I'm failing," I try to look around and think, "Thank you, Jesus, for all I am and all that I have." Jesus is faithful. He provides so many good and perfect things in our lives, but it takes shifting our minds to remember that! —TRICIA GOYER

FAITH STEP: *Today whenever you're thinking "I'm failing," transform your thoughts. Thank Jesus for all He's done in you and through you.*

WEDNESDAY, DECEMBER 19

"The work of God is this: to believe in the one he has sent." John 6:29 (NIV)

YEARS AGO IF YOU HAD asked me to name my favorite kitchen/cooking task, I'd have answered, "Baking bread." A friend's hearty wholewheat bread recipe made a heavy loaf—filling, satisfying, and a good Christmas gift for neighbors who didn't bake their own bread.

Arepa. Brioche. Chapati. Foccacia. Injera. Matzo. Naan. Obi Non (not to be confused with Obi-Wan). Pita. Rieska. Tortillas. Wonder. Zopf.

Every culture, every region, every era's culinary history includes some version of bread. Many of them look and taste similar, especially the flat varieties.

It's no wonder (pardon the pun) that Jesus used a common—cross-cultural, multigenerational, multiethnic, timeless item like bread for many of His illustrations. In John 6:26–35 (NIV), shortly after the feeding of the five thousand, He makes references to Himself as the bread of life. "You are looking for me," He said, "not because you saw the signs I performed but because you ate the loaves and had your fill. Do not work for food that spoils, but for food that endures to eternal life, which the Son of Man will give you. For on him God the Father has placed his seal of approval." (vs. 26–27).

Still confused, the crowd asked, "What must we do to do the works God requires?" (v. 28). Jesus gave a clear and direct response: "believe in the one he has sent" (v. 29).

A gift of bread. The bread of life. The enemy of our souls is allergic to that kind of bread. —CYNTHIA RUCHTI

FAITH STEP: *Try a bread from another country the next time you're at the grocery store. As you eat it, pray for the people of that country or region.*

THURSDAY, DECEMBER 20

God saved you by his grace when you believed. And you can't take credit for this; it is a gift from God. Ephesians 2:8 (NLT)

OUR YOUTH PASTOR RECALLS THE months as a newlywed when he and his bride owned no living room furniture. Lacking both a sofa and the money to buy one, they sat on the floor. They hesitated to invite guests because they felt uncomfortable asking others to do the same.

One day a man phoned and asked if they still needed a couch. "Yes, we do," said the pastor.

"Well, I have one. It's free—my gift to you. I'll bring it today."

That free gift changed the way the pastor and his wife lived life. No longer was sitting on the floor a necessity. And no longer did they hesitate to practice hospitality.

Our eternal salvation is a free gift, too. We can neither buy it nor earn it. Jesus paid for it with His blood, and He offers it to us. We simply need to accept it. When we do, that free gift ought to change the way we approach life.

We begin to treat people with greater respect and kindness. We see ourselves and our purpose in a new light. We view money differently—as a resource to share rather than to hoard. We rethink our priorities, and we even look at the environment through a new lens.

The free gift of salvation provides more than a ticket to heaven. It shapes our identity and defines the way we relate to God, our family and friends, coworkers and neighbors, and our career or calling. It brings hope and empowers us to live victoriously. —GRACE FOX

FAITH STEP: *Salvation is the best gift we could ever receive. List three ways it has changed the way that you live.*

Friday, December 21

"I have come as a light to shine in this dark world, so that all who put their trust in me will no longer remain in the dark." John 12:46 (NLT)

I HAVE NEVER BEEN A fan of the dark. Everything is unknown. Noises sound worse at night. The shapes I can see look menacing. Making it through the hallway without tripping on a wayward shoe or knocking a picture off the wall is almost impossible. The dark can be scary. This is why I am a great fan of electricity. I flip a switch and everything becomes crystal clear. There is no risk of injury once you can see the shoe in the middle of the hallway. The weird, whirring sound in the night is revealed to be a fan that has been left on in the corner. Light brings clarity, safety, and understanding. All good things.

Jesus knew that we would need the truth to light our way on this journey through life. Life can be scary. There are so many unknowns. Do we go left or right? Do we rush in or hold back? His Word brings light to our journey. His truth and promises are what make known the pitfalls of this world. The path of life is fraught with hard decisions and Jesus's Word casts a beam of clarity. Then a trail of light follows into the murkiness of real living. He makes a way for us, hemming us in on every side with His hope and faithfulness. We can trust His Word to guide us and lead us to eternity with Him. —SUSANNA FOTH AUGHTMON

FAITH STEP: *Sit in the dark with the lights out and try to identify what is surrounding you. Now turn the lights on. Read Mark 8:12, knowing that Jesus will never leave you in the dark.*

SATURDAY, DECEMBER 22

"This is what my Father wants: that anyone who sees the Son and trusts who he is and what he does and then aligns with him will enter real life, eternal life. My part is to put them on their feet alive and whole at the completion of time." John 6:40 (MSG)

WE LIVE NEAR THE SOUTH shore of Lake Superior—also known as the shipwreck coast. Its sandy floor is littered with wrecks. You can drift over them in a glass-bottomed boat or walk beside the beached wreck of the *Mary Jarecki*, or even see the ship's bell recovered from the ill-fated *Edmund Fitzgerald*. My great-great-grandfather captained a ship that had the misfortune of running aground on the ice of Munising Bay, fifteen miles north of where I sit typing.

That was before the range lights. Two paired sets of lighthouses straddle Grand Island between two approaches to the city. The channels are deep but narrow. Hazards like sandbars and whirlpools abound and natural landmarks are few. The first of the Munising Range Lights stands on shore, and the second behind it up the hill behind town. Approaching vessels line up the red lights to stay safely in the West Channel. The Christmas Range Lights provide the same service for the East Channel. Aligning the lights ensures the craft will be in deep water all the way into the harbor.

Wise sailors look to and trust the lights showing them the way.

The Greek word *pisteuo*, translated *believe*, carries the meaning of "commit to." We need to let go of our way and follow His. When we align ourselves with Jesus, we place ourselves in His keeping instead of relying on our own efforts. We can trust Him to bring us home safely. —SUZANNE DAVENPORT TIETJEN

FAITH STEP: *Turn anywhere in the Gospels and look for something Jesus said. Visualize Him saying those words and imagine yourself aligning with Him.*

SUNDAY, DECEMBER 23

For a child is born to us, a son is given to us. The government will rest on his shoulders. And he will be called: Wonderful Counselor, Mighty God, Everlasting Father, Prince of Peace. His government and its peace will never end. Isaiah 9:6–7 (NLT)

THE JEWISH PEOPLE OF JESUS'S day who lived under the tyranny of Rome longed for when real peace—true cessation of enemy control—would come. And that's what they thought when they heard Isaiah's prophecy of a soon arriving Prince of Peace.

Naturally when Jesus was born, they thought He would usher in that peace. Hadn't the angelic message heard by some shepherds included the words, "Peace on earth, and good will toward men?" But the events that followed didn't measure up for many people. Only those who understood the real peace that Jesus came to bring experienced it. But they did so in their hearts, and it wasn't necessarily reflected in their government.

Is it really any different today? I long for wars to cease around the world and for confused and burdened lives to grasp the only kind of peace that lasts. It won't come from our government or from world leaders. "It" already came over two thousand years ago. "It" was—and is—Jesus (Ephesians 2:14). This Prince of Peace is the One Who made it possible for us to know true peace—not a temporary cease fire—but a permanent truce with God. Only through Jesus can we find both peace with God—a joyful, loving relationship with Him—and the peace of God, the kind of reassurance that puts complete trust in Jesus (Philippians 4:7). Christmas is a great place to begin to understand that kind of lasting peace. —REBECCA BARLOW JORDAN

FAITH STEP: *Has Jesus's peace found a place in your heart? If so, write a letter expressing how much that peace means to you. Leave it under the tree for Jesus.*

CHRISTMAS EVE MONDAY, DECEMBER 24

We know that the whole creation has been groaning together in the pains of childbirth . . . as we wait eagerly for . . . the redemption of our bodies. For in this hope we were saved. Romans 8:22–24 (ESV)

I LOVE CHRISTMAS DAY. JESUS's birthday, time with family and friends, planning the perfect gifts, the anticipation of receiving gifts.

But I might love Christmas Eve even more. It's the pinnacle before the Gift, the height of knowing, trusting, hanging on because something wonderful is coming. Christmas Eve is a great faith anchor for anyone waiting for Jesus to show Himself to us in a real way.

Some two thousand years ago Christmas Eve was an unassuming twenty-four hours. Quiet hovered over hills dotted with sheep and shepherds, the stillness outside town broken by occasional bleats.

The town of Bethlehem bustled with travelers claiming the last rooms at the inns, oblivious to the tiny King and His family arriving soon. Those ancients weren't preparing for Christmas Day. No family feasts, no wrapped gifts or stuffed stockings.

Imagine if they knew what we know! The whole tone of that day before would've been elevated as heaven prepared to gift earth with Jesus.

The scene must have sparkled in heaven's throne room that first Christmas Eve. Imagine it! Heaven counting down earth's final hours until the Savior Baby would cross the line between the generations spent waiting and the endless era of redemption.

Those who know Jesus will witness a similar scene someday when He returns and brings us back to glory with Him.

Tomorrow holds promise, but today is pregnant with faith that elevates today to heavenly heights. —ERIN KEELEY MARSHALL

FAITH STEP: *Today, Christmas Eve, enjoy the wait until the Big Day tomorrow.*

CHRISTMAS, TUESDAY, DECEMBER 25

But the angel said to them, "Do not be afraid; for behold, I bring you good news of a great joy which will be for all the people; for today in the city of David there has been born for you a Savior, who is Christ the Lord."
Luke 2:10–11 (NASB)

IT'S AMAZING THAT GOD USED lowly shepherds to be His first evangelists. It must have been quite a sight when the angel came telling them not to be afraid. There they were, watching in wonder as the heavens opened and the angels sang, "Glory to God in the highest, and peace to men in whom he is pleased."

After hearing this message, the shepherds didn't fall back into the lull of the night. They left everything they owned—their sheep—and journeyed down the hill to find the Savior. What they didn't know was a girl named Mary needed them to show up.

I can't help but think she may have been wondering if she missed God's best. After all, she just gave birth and her son lay in a manger. But in come these shepherds, out of breath and anxious to share their news. Mary's heart must have soared when she heard the angels were singing about her son…THE SON…Savior of the world wrapped in scraps of cloth; asleep in a food trough meant for livestock. "But Mary treasured all these things, pondering them in her heart" (Luke 2:19). Today, I'm pondering a few things, too. Like the shepherds, can I leave everything I hold dear to behold my Savior? And am I watchful like Mary? Although circumstances didn't unfold the way she'd wished or planned, she bowed her life to God for His remarkable purposes. —GARI MEACHAM

FAITH STEP: *All day thank God for the brave shepherds, and pray to be a brave shepherd, too.*

WEDNESDAY, DECEMBER 26

*At this point many of his disciples turned away and deserted him.
Then Jesus turned to the Twelve and asked, "Are you also going to leave?"
Simon Peter replied, "Lord, to whom would we go? You have
the words that give eternal life." John 6:66–68 (NLT)*

I ONCE MET A COUPLE celebrating seventy years of marriage. Naturally, they were often asked the secret of their successful relationship. They emphasized that their marriage had not been a fairy tale. Both recalled tough times when they felt like giving up, but each time they reminded themselves of their commitment.

Some of Jesus's followers may have expected a fairy-tale ending. Many of them were only interested in seeing Him perform miracles. But when His teachings became difficult to understand or accept, they deserted Him. Jesus turned to His twelve disciples and asked if they also wanted to leave.

Have you ever felt like walking away from the Christian life when it seemed too demanding? Let's face it, obedience is tough, especially when we don't like a specific command in the Bible or the direction in which Jesus is leading us. Sometimes we may wish we could just briefly step away when we find ourselves in a group of people who scoff at "the Jesus thing."

Jesus warned that the narrow road of following Him would not always be smooth. We'll face difficult patches, steep climbs, and occasional obstacles. But any time we step off that path, we miss out on the joy, peace, and sense of purpose that Jesus gives. And as Peter said, "Where else would we go?" No one offers what Jesus does: words that give eternal life. —DIANNE NEAL MATTHEWS

FAITH STEP: *Can you think of a time when you felt tempted to give up on the Christian life? Renew your commitment to follow Jesus wholeheartedly.*

THUSDAY, DECEMBER 27

Make it your ambition to lead a quiet life and attend to your own business and work with your hands.... 1 Thessalonians 4:11 (NASB)

AFTER MANY YEARS OF WORKING odd hours in chaotic Neonatal Intensive Care Units in four different states, I'm following the apostle Paul's recommendation. Retired and living deep in the woods, I again have chickens, keep bees, and garden.

I have even more to do, but now it's of my own choosing. We've created a little ecosystem. With the help of thousands of red wigglers, we've gone as long as three weeks between garbage pickups. My husband and I are learning to use an in-ground greenhouse for fresh salads all winter and we've started plants for next spring.

I write (pretty much) daily, but fail at marketing, building a platform, or making myself known beyond my doorstep. I do some public speaking. I read my Bible. I'm active in church and a monthly book club. I spin, knit, and weave when I'm indoors and I hunt agates, fly-fish, and cross country ski when I'm outside.

It's a quiet but active life and I love it. Still, I wonder if it has meaning in the spiritual scheme of things.

Jesus said, "Live out your God-created identity. Live generously and graciously toward others, the way God lives toward you" (Matthew 5:48, MSG). Some of the most life-changing Christians I've met are unknown outside their communities. They lead youth groups, shovel neighbors' driveways, and share what they have. They work Jesus's words into the fabric of their lives, and it shows. It can't help but show. The Light of the World shines through our ordinary lives. —SUZANNE DAVENPORT TIETJEN

FAITH STEP: *Drop self-evaluation for today and let your life unfold around you. Stay grounded where you are. Do your work unto the Lord.*

FRIDAY, DECEMBER 28

"Because of his grace he made us right in his sight and gave us confidence that we will inherit eternal life." Titus 3:7 (NLT)

TWENTY-FIVE YEARS AGO FRIENDS OF ours wanted to do something with their grandchildren's inheritance that would set them up for the future. My friends didn't just want to put money into a bank account. Instead, they sought to provide job opportunities and a steady income for their grandchildren. They bought a series of video rental stores. This couple figured that even as teenagers their grandchildren could learn to run a business. But not too many years later those stores have become obsolete. With Red Box and Netflix there's no longer a need for customers for store rentals and this investment amounted to nothing.

As parents and grandparents we know how challenging this world is, and anything we can do to provide a hand up to our children or grandchildren is worth it. Yet no inheritance on earth can compare to sharing the knowledge of Jesus Christ. Our words about Jesus will make a lasting impact, and an eternal one.

One day our children and grandchildren will stand before Jesus. In that moment, will they have confidence about their eternal life? As Matthew 25:34 (NLT) says, "Then the King will say to those on his right, 'Come, you who are blessed by my Father, inherit the Kingdom prepared for you from the creation of the world.'" The best inheritance we can provide has nothing to do with physical opportunities. Guiding our offspring to the knowledge of what Jesus has for them is what they need most. —TRICIA GOYER

FAITH STEP: *Take a moment to pray for your children, grandchildren, or other young people you know and love. Also pray for boldness to share with them the inheritance that Jesus has waiting for those who believe in Him.*

SATURDAY, DECEMBER 29

*Do you want to be counted wise, to build a reputation for wisdom?
Here's what you do: Live well, live wisely, live humbly. It's the way you live,
not the way you talk, that counts. . . . Boasting that you are wise isn't
wisdom. James 3:13 (MSG)*

WHAT DOES WISDOM LOOK LIKE? Is it the absence of confusion?
Knowing the answers? I'd love to have wisdom at my fingertips.

According to James 3:13, having true wisdom affects how we live
and talk. That makes sense, because I'd like to have wisdom so I
know how to answer someone, guide my children, support my husband, and respond well to irritating things (and people).

Wisdom doesn't just involve the head or the heart although it
may begin there. Sure, it can remain still and wait, but not in futile
inactivity. Wisdom never toots its own horn and knows when to
keep its opinion to itself.

Wisdom refrains from talking a lot. It's hard to get away from
chatter that isn't true wisdom. We turn on the TV and check our
social media outlets. We go to lunch and hear opinions of our
friends. We're invaded by opinions. But are they wise ones?

Just this morning I saw a news story about a guy who said it's okay
for parents to curse in front of their kids. The fact that some man's
opinion made the news doesn't shout "wisdom" to me!

Our hearts are bent toward advancing ourselves, whether it is promoting our opinions or skills and accomplishments. Luke 21:15
says the Lord gives wisdom, but life and human nature can make it
difficult to want Jesus's wisdom more than our own.

True wisdom seeks its Source. —ERIN KEELEY MARSHALL

FAITH STEP: *Spend time praying over part of Luke 21:15 (ESV), "I will give
you . . . wisdom."*

SUNDAY, DECEMBER 30

Be not conformed to this world: but be ye transformed. . . . Romans 12:2 (KJV)

FOR THE FIRST LESSON IN my daughter Adelaide and her cousin Sophia's Bible study for kids at our church, they chose Saul's conversion on the road to Damascus. Sophia read the story aloud and then they fielded questions from their audience. While Maddox, three, chewed on a crayon, Stella and McKinley, four and five, both raised their hands.

"Why did Saul get blinded?" Stella asked.

McKinley followed up. "Why did Jesus change his name to Paul?"

The teachers tried their best to explain Saul's transformation. "Jesus wanted to give him new eyes. He was changing him into someone different. Someone *new*."

Adelaide poured heavy whipping cream into a Mason jar and secured the lid. "See how this looks? We're going to shake it up. That transforms the cream into something new."

Everyone took turns shaking the jar. The girls returned to the lesson, and while they drew pictures of Paul and Jesus, my sister-in-law and I shook the jar till our muscles ached. Finally, the cream became butter.

Adelaide and Sophia put the butter in a dish and showed the kids, who were all amazed. Then we sprinkled it with salt, spread it on crackers, and we got a chance to taste it. Yummy.

—GWEN FORD FAULKENBERRY

FAITH STEP: *Are you all shook up? Sometimes transformation can be painful. Decide to trust Jesus in the process—taste and see that He is good.*

MONDAY, DECEMBER 31

The faithful love of the Lord never ends!
His mercies never cease. Great is his faithfulness; his mercies
begin afresh each morning. Lamentations 3:22–23 (NLT)

HOW DOES ONE BEST DESCRIBE New Year's Eve? I equate it with the word *celebrate*.

When I was a teenager, my parents invited our church's youth group to celebrate New Year's Eve at our home. My sister and I decorated the basement with streamers and balloons, and we prepared enough snacks to feed a small army. The troops arrived early in the evening, and we played music and games until after midnight.

Several decades later, New Year's Eve looks different to me. But I still equate it with the word *celebrate*.

When I reflect on the past year, I celebrate Jesus's faithfulness through thick and thin. I thank Him for guiding me away from regrettable choices, comforting me in sorrow, encouraging me amid disappointment, strengthening me in weakness, forgiving me, and inspiring me to pursue the dreams He's planted in my heart. He's lavished His love on me, and that's cause to rejoice!

When I ponder the incoming year, I celebrate Jesus's faithfulness again. What will 2019 hold? We can't know the answer now, but we know one thing for certain: Jesus holds us. Just as He demonstrated His goodness to us daily during this last year, so He promises to express it throughout the coming year.

Happy New Year, my friend! Celebrate Jesus tonight and welcome the dawn with joy, knowing that His mercies will greet you every morning in the year ahead. —GRACE FOX

FAITH STEP: *List three ways in which Jesus proved His faithfulness to you this year. Then list three situations for which you trust Him to be faithful in 2019.*

ABOUT THE AUTHORS

 SUSANNA FOTH AUGHTMON is the author of several books that use humor, Scripture, and personal stories to explore how God's grace and truth intersect with our daily lives. Her daily life is devoted to her children: sixteen-year-old Jack, fourteen-year-old Will, and eleven-year-old Addison. Susanna is the wife of Scott Aughtmon, lead pastor of Pathway Church in Redwood City, California. She loves connecting with her fellow readers through her blog, newsletter, and speaking engagements. You can read about Susanna's "good, crazy life" at tiredsupergirl.com and on Facebook.

 GWEN FORD FAULKENBERRY is the author of five novels and four devotional books and she loves to connect with her readers. She has a sincere passion for Jesus and the devoted family that He has given her. She enjoys traveling the world with sixteen-year-old Grace, riding the range with fourteen-year-old Harper, baking with nine-year-old Adelaide, and discovering wondrous books with four-year-old Stella. Gwen holds a master's degree in liberal arts, and enjoys teaching literature, writing, and playing the piano at her church. She lives and writes in the mountains of Ozark, Arkansas. Check out her personal blog at gwenfordfaulkenberry.com.

 GRACE FOX and her husband are codirectors of International Messengers Canada—a mission organization serving in twenty-five countries. She loves to begin each day with a visit to the gym and then return home to spend time in God's Word. She also enjoys spending time with her kids and six grandchildren. She's written more than a thousand magazine articles and eight books including *Moving from Fear to Freedom: A Woman's Guide to Peace in Every Situation.* Grace resides in Abbotsford, British Columbia, and would love to hear from her readers everywhere via gracefox.com and fb.com/gracefox.author.

TRICIA GOYER has been married to John for twenty-seven years and is a homeschooling mom and writer. When their two children graduated and their third was only a few years away from graduation—God called them to adoption. Since then, they have adopted seven children. Tricia is a bestselling, award-winning author of sixty-five books, including *Prayers That Changed History* and *Balanced: Finding Center as a Work-at-Home Mom*. She lives with her family in Little Rock, Arkansas. You can find Tricia on her Web site at TriciaGoyer.com, Facebook, Pinterest, Instagram, and Twitter @TriciaGoyer.

SHARON HINCK writes stories about ordinary people experiencing the extraordinary grace of God in unexpected ways. Her novels have won three Carol awards and a Christy finalist medal, and all of her books explore the challenges and joys of following God's call. Sharon and her husband enjoy spending time with their children and energetic grandchildren. She also spends her time gardening, remodeling, and having laughter-filled conversations with friends. Sharon loves spending mornings—and all day—with Jesus. And she likes interacting with readers on her blog and Web site and would love to have you visit her at sharonhinck.com.

REBECCA BARLOW JORDAN is a best-selling author and contributing author of over twenty books, including the *Daily in Your Presence* series and the *Day-votions®* three-book series for women—and more than two thousand greeting cards, articles, and devotions. She is a "day-voted" follower of Jesus who remains passionate about home, family, and helping others to foster a relationship with God. Rebecca and her minister-husband have two children and four grandchildren and live in northeast Texas. Visit her at rebeccabarlowjordan.com.

 ERIN KEELEY MARSHALL has enjoyed contributing to *Mornings with Jesus* since its beginning in 2011. She is the author of several books, including *Tea Rose* (the second book in Guideposts's Tearoom Mysteries. She is also a collaborating writer for *365 Pocket Prayers for Mothers; The Hope of Heaven: God's Eight Messages of Assurance to a Grieving Father;* and the *Revolve Devotional Bible.* Erin lives in Arkansas with her husband, Steve, and their kids, Paxton and Calianne. She calls www.erinkeeleymarshall.com her home on the Web and she can also be found on Facebook and Twitter @EKMarshall.

 DIANNE NEAL MATTHEWS is the author of four daily devotional books including the Selah Award-winner, *Designed for Devotion: A 365-Day Journey from Genesis to Revelation.* She also writes for Web sites, blogs, and a number of periodicals. Dianne and her husband, Richard, have been married for forty-three years and live in southwest Louisiana, which she considers to be too much of a distance from their three children and three (adorable) grandchildren. Dianne loves to connect with readers through her Web site DianneNealMatthews.com, Facebook, and Twitter @DianneNMatthews.

 GARI MEACHAM is a popular speaker, writer, and author of the acclaimed series *Spirit Hunger, Watershed Moments,* and *Truly Fed,* which are read in book groups and churches across the country. Gari is president and founder of *The Vine*—a ministry to orphans and widows in Uganda, and *SHINE*—a trendy YouTube show she hosts with her daughter, Ally. She is married to former New York Yankee Bobby Meacham, and they have three children. The Meachams call Houston their home.

CYNTHIA RUCHTI is the award-winning author of fiction and nonfiction stories as well as devotionals that are, as she puts it, "hemmed in hope." Her books have been recognized with industry honors including Christian Retailing's BEST awards, the Selah awards, and *Publishers Weekly* starred reviews. She and her husband are nestled in the heart of Wisconsin, close to their three children and five grandchildren. Cynthia serves as the professional relations liaison for American Christian Fiction Writers. Her prayer is to encourage readers or attendees at her speaking events to say, "I can't unravel. I'm hemmed in hope." Visit her at cynthiaruchti.com or hemmedinhope.com.

SUZANNE DAVENPORT TIETJEN is in her fourth year of writing for *Mornings with Jesus*. Other titles she's written include *The Sheep of His Hand* and *40 Days to Your Best Life for Nurses*. She and her husband, Mike, live in a cabin deep in the Hiawatha National Forest of Michigan where they enjoy breathtaking beauty and an outdoor way of life. A former shepherd, neonatal nurse practitioner, and transport nurse, Suzanne misses that work, along with her beloved sheep, but now she gardens and keeps bees. You can find out more at suzannetietjen.com or follow her on Twitter @suzishepherd.

ISABELLA YOSUICO is a longtime health, wellness, and inspirational writer whose work has been included in various publications. Her *Embracing Life: Letting God Determine Your Destiny* Bible study, radio series, and upcoming book are aimed at helping people through major life challenges with renewed hope, purpose, and faith in God's ultimate good. Holding a master's degree in public relations management, Isabella is also founding president of *MightyTykes*, a company inspired by her youngest son, who has Down syndrome. Isabella and her family live a fun-filled life on Florida's Suncoast. Connect with her at mightytykes.com, or on Facebook.

SCRIPTURE REFERENCE INDEX

Topical Index